POVERTY, INEQUALITY, AND DEVELOPMENT

POVERTY, INEQUALITY, AND DEVELOPMENT

Gary S. Fields

Cornell University

CAMBRIDGE UNIVERSITY PRESS
Cambridge
London   New York   New Rochelle
Melbourne   Sydney

Published by the Press Syndicate of the University of Cambridge
The Pitt Building, Trumpington Street, Cambridge CB2 1RP
32 East 57th Street, New York, NY 10022, USA
296 Beaconsfield Parade, Middle Park, Melbourne 3206, Australia

First published 1980

Printed in the United States of America
Typeset by Graphic Technique, Inc., Lancaster, Pa.
Printed and bound by Hamilton Printing Co., Rensselaer, N.Y.

Library of Congress Cataloging in Publication Data
Fields, Gary S
Poverty, inequality, and development.
Bibliography: p.
Includes index.
1. Economic development.
2. Income distribution.
3. Equality. I. Title.
HD82.F456   330.9   79-21017
ISBN 0 521 22572 8 hard covers
ISBN 0 521 29852 0 paperback

Chapter 3 is reprinted from the author's article titled "A Welfare Economic Analysis of Growth and Distribution in the Dual Economy," originally published in the August 1979 *Quarterly Journal of Economics*. Copyright © 1979 by the President and Fellows of Harvard College. Reprinted by permission of John Wiley & Sons, Inc.

The last section of Chapter 4 originally appeared as "Decomposing LDC Inequality," published in the 1979 *Oxford Economic Papers*.

For Vivian

Contents

Preface   ix

1   Introduction: a new approach to poverty,
    inequality, and development   1

2   Approaches to income distribution and development   13
    Concepts of income distribution   14
    Measuring income distribution changes: an
       illustrative example   18
    Distribution and development: four classes of
       measures   21
    Comparing the classes of measures   29
    Conclusion   32

3   Growth and distribution: a welfare economic
    analysis   33
    Basic welfare judgments on distribution and
       development   33
    A general welfare approach for assessing dualistic
       development   36
    Welfare economic analysis of dualistic development:
       the general case   40
    Welfare economic analysis of dualistic development:
       special cases   46
    Empirical significance   56
    Conclusion   58

4   Inequality and development   59
    Inequality at different stages of development:
       cross-sectional evidence   59
    Relative inequality trends in less-developed
       countries   77

Decomposing LDC inequality   98
Conclusion   122

5   **Absolute income, absolute poverty, and
    development**   **125**
    Absolute incomes and earnings functions   125
    On labor market segmentation   129
    Absolute poverty: definitions, numbers, and
    profiles   137
    Economic growth, absolute income, and absolute
    poverty   162
    Conclusion   178

6   **Development progress and growth strategies:
    case studies**   **181**
    Costa Rica   185
    Sri Lanka   195
    India   204
    Brazil   210
    The Philippines   218
    Taiwan   228

7   **Development progress and growth strategies:
    conclusions**   **239**

    Notes   245
    Bibliography   258
    Index   273

Preface

Until very recently, the agreed-upon goal of economic development was thought to be aggregate economic growth. Now it is recognized that GNP measures are incomplete. To assess a country's economic performance and its progress toward economic development, we must supplement if not supplant the growth rate of GNP by other, more microeconomic measures.

How are we to do that? At least two research strategies suggest themselves. One approach, which the profession followed in the 1970s, is to emphasize growth but to weigh the growth performance by the distributional record. Another approach, more novel than the first, is to emphasize changing poverty and inequality as the principal indicators of development. Rather than asking whether the type of distributional pattern in a country promotes or hinders growth, the alternative approach asks instead if the rate and type of growth promote or hinder distributional goals. This book utilizes the second of these approaches.

In 1973, I began a series of studies that led ultimately to this book. I started with a belief in the usefulness of a microeconomic approach to the study of economic development. After several years of research, that conviction is renewed and reinforced.

The microeconomic framework I have adopted has far-reaching implications for the field of economic development. It requires that development economists look at labor markets, earnings structures, the distribution of productive activities and opportunities, and other less aggregative phenomena. It calls for new models and new analytical approaches to explain why countries fared as they did in their development efforts. It highlights the need for new data–

micro as well as macro – to trace countries' growth histories. And it calls for new planning procedures for future development. These concerns will dominate the attention of the development community in the 1980s. This book informs planners, scholars, and students of some of the lessons of the 1970s.

A long-term project like this would have been impossible without the support of many research organizations, donor agencies, and individuals. For congenial and stimulating research environments, I thank the Economic Growth Center at Yale University, the Center for the Study of Economic Development at the University of the Andes (Centro de Estudios sobre Desarrollo Económico, Universidad de Los Andes) in Bogotá, and the Departments of Labor Economics (School of Industrial and Labor Relations) and Economics (College of Arts and Sciences) at Cornell University. Financial assistance came from the World Bank, which financed my early work on development and distribution in Colombia; the U.S. Department of Health, Education and Welfare, which provided a grant to the Council on Latin American Studies at Yale to support my teaching of a graduate course on income distribution and economic development in Latin America; the Concilium on International and Area Studies at Yale, which supplied a research assistant at a critical stage of the work; the U.S. Agency for International Development, which commissioned several papers on poverty, inequality, and development, parts of which constitute some sections of this book; and the host institutions themselves, which expended many of their core funds on my behalf. Research assistants who have helped with some of the more tedious tasks include Farrukh Iqbal, Helena Jaramillo Ribe, Douglas Marcouiller, Fred McKinney, and Se-Il Park. A sequence of secretaries did the typing; I acknowledge the professionalism and good cheer of Diane Rocklen, Lois Van de Velde, and Nancy Notar.

My debts to professional colleagues are several. Special thanks are due to Gustav Ranis and John Fei for their steady encouragement in the early stages of the research; without their help, this book would probably never have come into being. I thank them, along with Martin Baily, John Eriksson,

Robert Evenson, James McCabe, and T. Paul Schultz, for many interesting discussions and helpful comments on various chapters. In addition, Olivia Mitchell and Sherman Robinson should be singled out as the only friends brave enough to wade through the entire manuscript; their comments were many and instructive.

The chapters of this book have evolved from lectures in my graduate courses on economic development. In fact, the impetus for the book originated from students' suggestions that the lessons from the course might profitably be shared with a larger audience. Several classes of graduate students served as guinea pigs for earlier formulations; in so doing, they gave me many ideas and helped sharpen the exposition at various junctures. I have always believed in the symbiotic relationship between graduate teaching and scholarly research; the synergistic effects have been particularly positive in the preparation of this book.

Finally, my greatest thanks go to my wife, Vivian. She has broadened my horizons to include other lands and other peoples, deepened my concerns for the less fortunate, and reminded me of the human dimensions of poverty, inequality, and development when I have wavered. For those contributions, and for her loving backing of my professional pursuits, I am pleased to dedicate this book to her.

G.S.F.

1

Introduction: a new approach to poverty, inequality, and development

The extent of poverty and inequality in the world is staggering. Recently compiled data on absolute poverty and relative inequality in a large number of countries may be found in Tables 1.1 and 1.2 respectively. Just in the countries assisted by the U.S. Agency for International Development (AID), nearly 800 *million* persons receive annual incomes below $150 (as of about 1970, in 1969 prices).

The president of the World Bank has voiced the human dimensions of these data well:

Among our century's most urgent problems is the wholly unacceptable poverty that blights the lives of some 2,000 million people in the more than 100 countries of the developing world. Of these 2,000 million, nearly 800 million are caught up in what can only be termed absolute poverty–a condition of life so limited as to prevent realization of the potential of the genes with which they were born; a condition of life so degrading as to be an insult to human dignity. [McNamara in World Bank, 1975:v].

In terms of inequality, the richest 5% of income recipients in less-developed countries receive income shares that on the average are five or six times higher than the income shares of the poorest 20% (which means that the income ratios of richest to poorest are more than twenty to one). If the poor in poor countries were compared with the rich in rich countries, the gap between rich and poor would be many times higher.

Until very recently, the agreed-upon goal of economic development was thought to be aggregate economic growth. This goal was reflected in the concern among development economists with macroeconomic phenomena: Industrialization strategy, the process of capital formation, the workings of financial institutions, and the impact of trade policies are

Table 1.1. *Poor majority populations in AID-assisted countries*

Country/date	Total population (millions)	% of population receiving less than $150 per capita	"Poor majority" population (millions)
Near East and South Asia			
India (1964–5)	537.0	91	488.7
Pakistan (including Bangladesh) (1966–7)	111.8	72	80.5
Egypt (1964–5)	33.3	50	16.6
Turkey (1963)	35.2	45	15.9
Sri Lanka (1963)	12.5	68	8.5
Tunisia (1970)	4.9	52	2.5
Regional subtotal	734.7	83	612.7
East Asia			
Thailand (1962)	34.7	65	22.6
Korea, South (1970)	32.0	45	14.4
Philippines (1971)	37.1	32	11.9
Vietnam, South (1964)	17.9	44	7.9
Regional subtotal	121.7	47	56.8
Africa			
Sudan (1963)	15.2	81	12.3
Tanzania (1967)	13.2	91	12.0
Kenya (1968–9)	10.8	86	9.3
Madagascar (1960)	6.5	88	5.7
Malawi (1969)	4.5	96	4.3
Chad (1958)	3.2	96	3.1

Senegal (1960)	3.8	69	2.6
Dahomey (1959)	2.5	94	2.3
Ivory Coast (1970)	4.2	45	1.9
Sierra Leone (1968–9)	2.5	70	1.8
Zambia (1959)	4.2	20	.8
Botswana (1971–2)	.6	84	.5
Gabon (1968)	.5	22	.1
Regional subtotal	71.7	79	56.7
Latin America			
Brazil (1970)	93.6	45	42.1
Colombia (1970)	21.1	42	8.9
Peru (1970–1)	13.6	35	4.8
Ecuador (1970)	6.1	70	4.3
Dominican Republic (1969)	4.3	38	1.6
Chile (1968)	9.8	16	1.6
El Salvador (1969)	3.5	43	1.5
Honduras (1967–8)	2.6	58	1.5
Guatemala (1966)	5.2	22	1.1
Uruguay (1967)	2.9	23	.7
Jamaica (1958)	2.0	27	.5
Costa Rica (1971)	1.7	14	.2
Panama (1969)	1.5	16	.2
Guyana (1955–6)	.8	28	.2
Regional subtotal	168.7	41	69.2
All regions (37 countries)	1,096.8	72.5	795.4

Note: Countries included are the thirty-seven AID-assisted countries for which income-distribution data are reported in Shail Jain, "Size Distribution of Income: Compilation of Data," International Bank for Reconstruction and Development, Bank Staff Working Paper No. 190, November 1974. Twenty-seven AID-assisted countries are not included for lack of income-distribution data. These are Afghanistan, Bolivia, Burundi, Cameroon, Central African Republic, Ethiopia, Gambia, Ghana, Guinea, Haiti, Indonesia, Khmer Republic, Laos, Lesotho, Liberia, Mali, Morocco, Nepal, Nicaragua, Niger, Paraguay, Rwanda, Swaziland, Togo, Upper Volta, Yemen Arab Republic, and Zaire. But the total 1970 population of these countries was only 242 million, compared to 1,097 million for the countries included in the table. The method and sources for the table are as follows. Population and GDP data are for 1970 (converted to 1969 prices in all cases), except for Pakistan, Sierra Leone, Tanzania, Thailand, India, Senegal, Sudan, South Vietnam, Egypt, and Zambia (1969 data); Botswana (1968 data); Chad (1963 data); and Dahomey (1967 data). Dates for the income-distribution data are shown in parentheses next to the country name. Income-distribution data in the IBRD source just cited were presented in the form of income shares accruing to twenty equal subgroups of the population. To calculate the percentage of the population receiving an annual per capita GDP below $150 the income share of a subgroup was multiplied by the total GDP figure for that country. This product was then divided by the number of individuals in that subgroup or the total population divided by 20. GDP and population refer to the most recent year for which data are available. With $150 as a guide, the closest 5% interval was located and, assuming equal distribution within this interval, the approximate percentage determined. The order in which countries are presented within regions was determined by the magnitude of the poor majority of the population (col. 3).

Sources: AID (1975). The sources for the population and GDP figures were the *U.N. Statistical Yearbook, 1969* and the *U.N. Yearbook of National Accounts Statistics, 1971,* V, III, respectively. GNP deflator indexes found in "Gross National Product," AID, F M SRD, May 1974, were used to convert all GDP figures to 1969 prices. (Exceptions: Botswana, Jamaica, Sri Lanka, Chad, Dahomey, and Guyana GNP deflators were taken from an appropriate regional table of Africa or Latin America in the *U.N. Statistical Yearbook, 1973.*)

4

Table 1.2. *Size distribution of personal income before tax in fifty-six countries*

Country and level of GDP per head	Below 20%	21%–40%	41%–60%	Percentiles of recipients 61%–80%	81%–95%	96%–100%
Under $100						
Chad (1958)	8.0	11.6	15.4	22.0	20.0	23.0
Dahomey (1959)	8.0	10.0	12.0	20.0	18.0	32.0
Niger (1960)	7.8	11.6	15.6	23.0	19.0	23.0
Nigeria (1959)	7.0	7.0	9.0	16.1	22.5	38.4
Sudan (1969)	5.6	9.4	14.3	22.6	31.0	17.1
Tanzania (1964)	4.8	7.8	11.0	15.4	18.1	42.9
Burma (1958)	10.0	13.0	13.0	15.5	20.3	28.2
India (1956–7)	8.0	12.0	16.0	22.0	22.0	20.0
Madagascar (1960)	3.9	7.8	11.3	18.0	22.0	37.0
Group average	7.0	10.0	13.1	19.4	21.4	29.1
$101–$200						
Morocco (1965)	7.1	7.4	7.7	12.4	44.5	20.6
Senegal (1960)	3.0	7.0	10.0	16.0	28.0	36.0
Sierra Leone (1968)	3.8	6.3	9.1	16.7	30.3	33.8
Tunisia (1971)	5.0	5.7	10.0	14.4	42.6	22.4
Bolivia (1968)	3.5	8.0	12.0	15.5	25.3	35.7
Ceylon (Sri Lanka) (1963)	4.5	9.2	13.8	20.2	33.9	18.4
Pakistan (1963–4)	6.5	11.0	15.5	22.0	25.0	20.0
South Korea (1966)	9.0	14.0	18.0	23.0	23.5	12.5
Group average	5.3	8.6	12.0	17.5	31.6	24.9

Table 1.2. *Continued*

Country and level of GDP per head	Below 20%	21%–40%	41%–60%	Percentiles of recipients 61%–80%	81%–95%	96%–100%
$201–$300						
Malaya (1957–8)	6.5	11.2	15.7	22.6	26.2	17.8
Fiji (1968)	4.0	8.0	13.3	22.4	30.9	21.4
Ivory Coast (1959)	8.0	10.0	12.0	15.0	26.0	29.0
Zambia (1959)	6.3	9.6	11.1	15.9	19.6	37.5
Brazil (1960)	3.5	9.0	10.2	15.8	23.1	38.4
Ecuador (1968)	6.3	10.1	16.1	23.2	19.6	24.6
El Salvador (1965)	5.5	6.5	8.8	17.8	28.4	33.0
Peru (1961)	4.0	4.3	8.3	15.2	19.3	48.3
Iraq (1956)	2.0	6.0	8.0	16.0	34.0	34.0
Philippines (1961)	4.3	8.4	12.0	19.5	28.3	27.5
Colombia (1964)	2.2	4.7	9.0	16.1	27.7	40.4
Group average	4.8	8.0	11.3	18.1	25.7	32.0
$301–$500						
Gabon (1960)	2.0	6.0	7.0	14.0	24.0	47.0
Costa Rica (1969)	5.5	8.1	11.2	15.2	25.0	35.0
Jamaica (1958)	2.2	6.0	10.8	19.5	31.3	30.2
Surinam (1962)	10.7	11.6	14.7	20.6	27.0	15.4
Lebanon (1955–60)	3.0	4.2	15.8	16.0	27.0	34.0
Barbados (1951–2)	3.6	9.3	14.2	21.3	29.3	22.3
Chile (1968)	5.4	9.6	12.0	20.7	29.7	22.6
Mexico (1963)	3.5	6.6	11.1	19.3	30.7	28.8
Panama (1969)	4.9	9.4	13.8	15.2	22.2	34.5

	4.5	7.9	12.3	18.0	27.4	30.0
Group average	4.5	7.9	12.3	18.0	27.4	30.0
$501–$1,000						
Republic of South Africa (1965)	1.9	4.2	10.2	26.4	18.0	39.4
Argentina (1961)	7.0	10.4	13.2	17.9	22.2	29.3
Trinidad and Tobago (1957–8)	3.4	9.1	14.6	24.3	26.1	22.5
Venezuela (1962)	4.4	9.0	16.0	22.9	23.9	23.2
Greece (1957)	9.0	10.3	13.3	17.9	26.5	23.0
Japan (1962)	4.7	10.6	15.8	22.9	31.2	14.8
Group average	5.1	8.9	13.9	22.1	24.7	25.4
$1,001–$2,000						
Israel (1957)	6.8	13.4	18.6	21.8	28.2	11.2
United Kingdom (1964)	5.1	10.2	16.6	23.9	25.0	19.0
Netherlands (1962)	4.0	10.0	16.0	21.6	24.8	23.6
Federal Republic of Germany (1964)	5.3	10.1	13.7	18.0	19.2	33.7
France (1962)	1.9	7.6	14.0	22.8	28.7	25.0
Finland (1962)	2.4	8.7	15.4	24.2	28.3	21.0
Italy (1948)	6.1	10.5	14.6	20.4	24.3	24.1
Puerto Rico (1963)	4.5	9.2	14.2	21.5	28.6	22.0
Norway (1963)	4.5	12.1	18.5	24.4	25.1	15.4
Australia (1966–7)	6.6	13.4	17.8	23.4	24.4	14.4
Group average	4.7	10.5	15.9	22.2	25.7	20.9
$2,001 and above						
Denmark (1963)	5.0	10.8	18.8	24.2	26.3	16.9
Sweden (1963)	4.4	9.6	17.4	24.6	26.4	17.6
United States (1969)	5.6	12.3	17.6	23.4	26.3	14.8
Group average	5.0	10.9	17.9	24.1	26.3	16.4

Source: Paukert (1973: tab. 6).

examples. We economists know, or think we know, a great deal about the determinants of economic growth, at least at the macroeconomic level.

The limitations of gross national product (GNP) and its rate of growth as indicators of economic well-being are now well appreciated.[1] GNP does not tell us how the benefits of economic activity are distributed. Two countries may have the same GNP, yet the lower income groups may have a larger share in one than in the other. Likewise, although two countries may grow at the same rate, the poor may share widely in the benefits of growth in one country and be excluded from participation in the other. Analysts and planners now recognize that to assess a country's economic performance and its progress toward economic development, the level of GNP and its growth rate must be supplemented if not replaced by other, more microeconomic measures.

The consequent refocusing of attention on microeconomic aspects of development with specific concern for the poverty population is little less than revolutionary. Academicians, aid agencies, and policy makers in less-developed countries (LDCs) alike have become aware of the severity of poverty and inequality and are now trying to deal with them. The international development community has awakened to the income-distribution problem with calls for "Redistribution with Growth" (World Bank), "Meeting Basic Needs" (United Nations International Labour Office), and "New Directions in Development Assistance" (United States Agency for International Development). Governments' development plans now include specific antipoverty policies. Even students of economic development now receive the message in at least one popular text: "As reflected in this new edition, the 'leading issues' now coalesce in a central theme: policies which are designed to eradicate poverty, reduce inequality, and deal with the problems of employment."[2]

The tasks confronting the development economics profession at present are to synthesize the lessons of the past and to chart for the future how to ameliorate poverty to the greatest extent possible in the least time. How are we to do that? At least two research strategies suggest themselves.

One approach is to keep the conventional focus on growth

but to weigh the growth performance by the distributional record. This clearly was the course followed by the profession in the 1970s. There seems to be an unspoken consensus that countries' development experiences may be ranked as follows (ordered from best to worst):

1. Rapid growth, good distributional performance
2. Rapid growth, poor distributional performance
3. Slow growth, good distributional performance
4. Slow growth, poor distributional performance
5. Nongrowth

Typically, when distributional aspects of development have been taken into consideration, they have been entered secondarily, only after analysis of the rate of aggregate economic growth.

Another approach is possible. Rather than regarding GNP growth as the principal *outcome* of a country's development performance, what if we were to look upon the growth rate of GNP as a principal *determinant* of changing poverty and inequality? Suppose we set aside for now the traditional question, Does the type of distributional pattern found in a country promote or hinder growth? Suppose we ask instead, Do the rate and type of growth promote or hinder distributional goals?

This second approach has far-reaching implications for the study of economic growth. It makes growth much more a microeconomic phenomenon than has hitherto been recognized. It calls for new data to trace countries' growth histories. It calls for new models to understand why countries fared as they did. And it calls for new planning approaches for future development. *Can be adapted to here,*

An Here I adopt this alternative approach. I start with poverty and inequality as the phenomena to be explained and then see how the rate of growth and type of development help explain them. This method is reflected in the ordering of the words in the title: *Poverty, inequality, and development.* To my mind, poverty and inequality are the most pressing problems and merit the greatest prominence.

I should make clear that I am not rejecting the first approach. Much can be learned by beginning with the macro-

It has been mentioned by Fields that

economics of growth and then proceeding to the micro-economics of distribution. Others in the profession are trying to do just that. Several new lines of inquiry offer great promise. Among them are large-scale models such as those of Blitzer, Clark, and Taylor (1975) and Adelman and Robinson (1978); the Social Accounting Matrices of Pyatt and Thorbecke (1976) and their collaborators; and the neoclassical modeling of Fei, Ranis, and Kuo (1979) linking growth and distribution via theories of the functional and size distributions of income. These various approaches should help us unify the causal linkages from growth to distribution and from distribution to growth, both simultaneously and recursively. That challenge confronts the profession in the 1980s.

Meanwhile it is important to fill the gap in knowledge of distributional aspects of growth. This book appears now in the hope of informing planners, scholars, and students both of the lessons of the past and of the questions that remain to be answered.

The central question addressed here is, Who benefits how much from economic development and why? Among the subsidiary questions to be examined are these: What is known about the distributions of income and poverty in the poor countries of the world? What are the correlates of the observed patterns? What are the main sources of inequality? What indexes should be used to measure the participation of the poor in economic development? What is the welfare economic basis for this choice? To what extent have individual countries alleviated their poverty and reduced their inequality in the course of economic growth? What accounts for the differences among countries? If the agenda for the book is ambitious, so too is the job of developing the world's poorest economies.

This book is addressed to the broad community of scholars and students. For many, it will be the first serious exposure to the microeconomics of development. Mathematical statements and formal theoretical developments are used where rigor is needed, but where included, these formal procedures are explained heuristically. The result, I hope, is a volume comprehensible to all those who seek to lessen poverty and inequality through economic development.

The plan of the remainder of the book is as follows. Chapter 2 sets out the various approaches to income distribution that are found in the literature. At issue is how to gauge who receives how much of the benefits of economic development; and absolute and relative measures are distinguished. The validity of different approaches depends largely on the observer's value judgment, which is the subject of Chapter 3.

Chapter 3 offers a welfare economic analysis of growth and distribution in the dual economy. We confront fundamental ethical judgments on the question, When is one income distribution better than another? Some basic axiomatic judgments are set forth and scrutinized in the context of social welfare functions, and different patterns of dualistic development are analyzed in general and in stylized models. The relative inequality and absolute income and poverty approaches are not always in agreement and, more disturbingly, the most notable discrepancy is found in the most relevant stylized model – growth via the transfer of population from a backward to an enlarging advanced sector. Given these discrepancies, each of us must decide how to measure changing income distribution in a manner consistent with the welfare judgments we wish to make. At that point, my personal preference for the absolute poverty approach in poor countries receives further elaboration.

The next two chapters summarize the available empirical evidence on the relationship between income distribution and development in as many countries as reliable data are available for. Chapter 4 deals with relative inequality, Chapter 5 with absolute incomes and poverty.

Chapter 4 addresses three major aspects of relative inequality, beginning with a review of cross-sectional evidence on inequality at different stages of development and the correlates of the observed patterns. Working from data on relative inequality changes that have taken place in LDCs, I then look for relationships between changes in inequality and such economic factors as the stage of economic development and the rate of growth. The final section of Chapter 4 introduces decomposition analysis and uses it to examine the structure of inequality within each of a number of LDCs.

Chapter 5 investigates distributional aspects of development in absolute terms. The technique of earnings-function analysis is presented in the first section as a means for study-ing labor income inequality. The results from earnings func-tions are sometimes interpreted as indicating labor market segmentation in LDCs. The second section evaluates the segmentation literature with an eye toward the question how segmentation theory helps explain incomes and income inequality. After a section on absolute poverty, I offer evi-dence on the dynamic question, To what extent have the incomes of the poor risen with economic growth? The results are heartening–in general, growth reduces poverty–but there are some exceptions. Some countries alleviated poverty substantially despite little economic growth, whereas others had growth with no demonstrable decline in poverty. These findings lead us to ask what accounts for the differences, which is the subject of Chapter 6.

Chapter 6 offers six case studies of distribution and development (Costa Rica, Sri Lanka, India, Brazil, the Philip-pines, and Taiwan), asking four basic questions: Why did some countries do better in alleviating poverty and lowering inequality than others? What structural characteristics dif-ferentiate the successes from the failures? What development strategies and policy packages produce superior outcomes? How do changes in employment opportunities and wage structures relate to the distributional record?

Chapter 7 highlights some of the major conclusions.

Approaches to income distribution and development

Income Distribution and Development

When economic development takes place, how are the benefits of growth distributed? This ~~chapter~~ *section* explores various ways of determining who receives how much of the benefits.

Three general methodological points ~~bear mention at this~~ *are* *here.* ~~stage~~. The first is that the bulk of discussion in this book is in terms of distribution of income. Of course, the benefits of growth may be measured in other ways: by attainment of such basic needs as nutrition, by physical quality of life indicators, by health statistics, by educational levels, as well as by economic measures other than income.[1] A large literature exists on these other indicators.[2] Yet, without dismissing their importance, I feel, as do many other economists, that income is the single best measure of economic condition and that change in income is the single best measure of improvement in that position. Consequently, income distribution – what we mean by it, how we measure it, what we know about it – is the focus of discussion in what follows.[3] *– can be seen*

A second methodological point concerns the essence of economic growth. ~~I see~~ growth as having two kinds of components: Some persons' incomes are raised within economic sectors, and a larger proportion of persons come to be employed within the higher-income sectors. To be relevant to the distributional aspects of growth, any measurement approach must be sensitive both to changes in intrasector income levels and to the changing allocation of the population amongst sectors. None of the income distribution measures in common use was developed with dynamic considerations in mind; accordingly, their suitability for measuring changes over time is open to review from a growth-oriented perspective.

Thirdly, intracountry price differentials, though important

A third methodological point concerns intracountry price differentials.

in LDCs, are largely ignored throughout this book because of lack of data. I think it is better to use the available information, albeit without price corrections, than to do nothing at all.

The first section of this chapter considers several concepts of income distribution, distinguishing the size distribution of income from other concepts. The distinction is also drawn between "income distribution" and "income inequality." The next section presents numerical examples illustrating the various ways income distribution is studied: absolute and relative, inequality and poverty. The final section classifies the various measures into four categories, which form the basis for the subsequent theoretical and empirical analyses of distribution and development, in particular, the more formal welfare economic framework of Chapter 3.

Concepts of income distribution

Many aspects of income distribution are of interest. We may want to know the total amount of income received by an individual or family, where it was earned, how much of it came from different sources or from performing different functions, and what the economically relevant characteristics of the recipients are. With census or survey data on large numbers of income recipients, it is unwieldy to present the details for each household individually.[4] Accordingly, income distributions are presented in summary form, with the observations grouped in some way or other.

Sometimes the income groupings are by income itself. Either income categories are defined and the numbers or percentages of households in each category tabulated, or the households are divided into percentile groupings (deciles, for example) ordered from lowest to highest and the mean income or percentage shares of each presented. These are alternative formats for presenting the *size distribution of income* or, as it is sometimes called, the *personal distribution of income*, that is, how many persons (or families) receive how much income. A recent and extensive compilation of data on size distribution of income around the world is the report prepared by Jain (1975) under the auspices of the World Bank.

At the very outset, it is important to clarify a terminological point that often arises in the study of distribution and development: Despite popular parlance and practice, "income distribution" is *not* the same thing as "income equality" (or "inequality"). To avoid unnecessary confusion on the use of these terms, we should distinguish between them carefully.

At the most elementary level, the *distribution* of any quantifiable magnitude shows the frequency with which the various amounts are distributed in the population or sample under examination. This information may be tabulated in a variety of ways or depicted in histograms or Lorenz curves.[5] The full range of data may be summarized partially by two types of measures: location and dispersion. *Location* measures provide an index of central tendency of where the distribution is located; the mean and median are familiar examples. *Dispersion* measures indicate inequality in the distribution; examples are the range and standard deviation.

Suppose now we want to compare one income distribution with another. Consider the simple case of two countries, one of which has twice as much income as the other, with that extra income distributed proportionately over the population. For example, in two ten-person economies A and B, assume that the income distributions are

$$Y_A = (1, 2, 3, 4, 5, 6, 7, 8, 9, 10)$$

and

$$Y_B = (2, 4, 6, 8, 10, 12, 14, 16, 18, 20)$$

Are the income distributions in A and B the same or different? Economists answer the question ambiguously. On the one hand, the entire income distribution is located in a different position: Everyone in B has twice as much income as in A, and the total is twice as high, too. So in one sense the income distribution is different. On the other hand, in each country the poorest person's income is 10% of the richest person's, the second poorest's 20%, and so on. So in another sense the distribution of income is the same. What this

example illustrates is the difference between the *distribution
of absolute income* and *relative inequality in the distribution
of income*. In this example, absolute income distribution
differs and relative inequality does not. Throughout this
book, the term "distribution" will refer to the entire range of
income values and their observed frequencies; "inequality"
will denote just the dispersion aspect.

It is insightful to contrast the way economists usually
think about income distribution with the way they consider
other economic or social magnitudes, for example, the
distribution of education. For education, our concern is
how many people have attained what level. If at some
future time we find that a larger fraction of the population
achieves literacy, let us say, we are inclined to regard that
country's education system as having done "better." In
making such a judgment, we usually do not think to ask
whether more people had also completed university; nor
do we compute a statistical measure of inequality of educational attainments, such as the variance or a Gini coefficient.
Rather, our strategy is to pinpoint a target group whose
upgrading we care most about and then to measure the rate
of absolute improvement among that target group.

In studies of income distribution, the approach is ordinarily quite different. Most studies ask, Did income distribution
improve? Typically, that question is answered by examining
(1) how the income shares of particular deciles (or other
groupings) changed, (2) how the Lorenz curve shifted, or (3)
whether measures such as Gini coefficients, variance of
incomes or their logarithms, and so on, exhibit greater or
lesser inequality. All these are relative inequality measures.
In effect, then, by beginning with relative inequality measures
rather than with absolute levels, the approach to studies of
the distribution of income reverses the approach to studies of
the distribution of other economic and social goods.

We will return to the distinction between absolute and
relative income distribution measures later in this chapter.

We have been speaking so far only about the size distribution of income, which is the central concern of this book. In
economic analysis, the size distribution of income must be
distinguished from the *functional distribution*, which divides

income according to its source. We may, for example, differentiate among income from labor, capital, land, and transfers. Classical economists devoted most of their attention to functional distribution, having in mind the notion that laborers, capitalists, and landowners represented distinct classes, with relatively little variability within the functional groupings compared with the inequality across them. In present-day analysis, the assumption of within-group homogeneity is untenable. As the data in Chapter 4 show, the principal source of inequality in less-developed countries is the fact that some individuals or households receive more income from the work they perform than do others. This implies that we must look within labor's share to understand economic inequality. Data on functional distribution alone will no longer do.

Other concepts of income distribution are also encountered frequently in the literature. One common distinction is the *rural–urban* dimension. Generally, urban incomes are found to be higher, perhaps twice as high, as rural incomes. In addition, the geographic dimension is sometimes amplified to present information on *interregional* or *interstate* differentials. Data for a large number of countries have been compiled by Williamson (1965). Substantial interregional variations, on the order of three to one or more, are generally noted. We also find data on so-called *homogeneous groups*, obtained by stratifying the sample households according to presumed determinants of income like education, sex, and age. As with functional groupings, if income variation within geographic areas or population groups is large, aggregation causes us to lose important information. For example, in the Latin American context, failure to distinguish *latifundistas* from *minifundistas* would be rather serious when trying to quantify the number of poor households in rural areas or to target them as beneficiaries for public programs.

The challenge confronting income-distribution researchers is that of processing the income data in ways appropriate to the economic problem at hand. In the following section, we take up the question how to measure income distribution changes that take place in the course of economic development.

Measuring income distribution changes: an illustrative example

Dynamic questions of distribution and development are of two sorts. Looking back in time, we might ask, How did the rate and pattern of economic growth in country X lead to the alleviation of poverty and reduction of inequality? Alternatively, looking ahead, we might ask, What would be the effects of alternative growth strategies on country X's poverty and inequality? The two questions reflect the differential concerns of development historians and development planners. Obviously, though, they are closely related, the lessons of the immediate past having a major bearing on perceptions of the fruitfulness of alternative development strategies in the future.

In studies of distribution and development, it is customary to present data on growth of national income and change in relative income inequality. Ordinarily, the judgment is made that *social welfare* (W) depends positively on the *level* of national income (Y) and negatively on the *inequality* in the distribution of that income (I). For example, taking the share of income of the poorest 40% of the population (S) as an index of equality, and the Gini coefficient (G) as an index of inequality, these studies would hold that W is positively related to Y and S and negatively related to G. In the usual terminology, a falling S or a rising G is given the nonneutral term "worsening of the income distribution," and it is generally thought to be a bad thing when rising measured inequality is encountered.

Let us consider a simple hypothetical numerical example showing how these judgments are brought to bear in practice (Table 2.1). Country B grew twice as fast as country A. However, relative income inequality, as measured by the Gini coefficient and income share of the lowest 40%, seems to be worse in country B than in country A; that is, it would appear that the rich benefited at the expense of the poor, whose relative income share deteriorated. A development economist might question whether the higher rate of growth in country B was worthwhile in terms of income distribution, and a well-meaning development planner seeking to give very

Table 2.1. *Example one: relative income inequality*

Country	Rate of growth of national income (%)	Income share of poorest 40%		Gini coefficient	
		Level	% change	Level	% change
Both countries initially		.363		.082	
Country A later	9	.333	−8	.133	+62
Country B later	18	.307	−15	.162	+97

Table 2.2. *Example two: percentage of labor force in high- and low-wage jobs*

Country	% of labor force in		Rate of growth of high-wage jobs ("modern sector labor absorption rate") (%)
	High-wage jobs (real wage = $2)	Low-wage jobs (real wage = $1)	
Both countries initially	10	90	
Country C later	20	80	100
Country D later	30	70	200

high weight to alleviation of inequality might go so far as to choose country *A*'s policies over country *B*'s.

Data on distribution and development may be presented in other ways. Consider now another numerical example for two hypothetical countries at an earlier and a later stage of economic development. Suppose that "the poor" are those who work in low-wage jobs and that "the nonpoor" work at higher wages. A widely accepted social welfare judgment[6] is that welfare is higher when a smaller proportion of the population is poor. Take the income data presented in Table 2.2. In both countries, the poor received the benefits of growth; but in country *D*, twice as many poor benefited. Other things being equal, development economists would almost certainly rate country D as superior, and development planners would seek to find out what had brought about D's favorable experience and to adopt those policies in their own countries. In this second example, the preference is clear-cut, whereas in the previous example, it was open to doubt.

Yet another kind of approach is found in the literature, one that measures the average absolute income (in constant dollars) received by a predetermined share of the population, for example, the poorest 40%. This average income of the poorest 40% is taken as a measure of the poverty status of the population. The welfare judgment is that social welfare is higher when poverty is less by this measure, that is, when the average absolute income of the poorest 40% rises. Consider now Table 2.3. It appears that there was *no* improvement in absolute income of the poorest 40% in either case. One might ask, Why grow if the poor do not share in the benefits of growth? In this third example, E and F both seem to have failed to alleviate poverty.

In point of fact, countries A, C, and E are the same country, countries B, D, and F the same country! The underlying distributions from which the summary statistics in the examples were tabulated are

Initial distribution	$(1, 1, 1, 1, 1, 1, 1, 1, 1, 2)$
A-C-E	$(1, 1, 1, 1, 1, 1, 1, 1, 2, 2)$
B-D-F	$(1, 1, 1, 1, 1, 1, 1, 2, 2, 2)$

The work week is assumed to be forty hours.

Real-world economic development histories and policy projections are often presented in these different ways. Yet, as these examples make clear, how income distribution is measured may dramatically influence our perceptions of the outcome.

The income distribution measures used in the three examples are representative of more general classes:

Example one: *relative inequality approach*, which looks at the income changes of various groups relative to others

Example two: *absolute income approach*, which looks at changes in various groups' incomes; a special case of the absolute income approach is:

Table 2.3. *Example three: average absolute income of poorest 40% of population*

Country	Absolute income of poorest 40% of population ($)
Both countries initially	40
Country E later	40
Country F later	40

        Example two: *absolute poverty approach*, which looks at the proportion who are poor and the incomes received by those who remain poor

        Example three: *relative poverty approach*, which looks at changes in the average absolute income among a fixed percentage at the bottom of the distribution

This taxonomic scheme is developed further in the following section.

Distribution and development: four classes of measures

Relative inequality approach

In most studies of income distribution in less-developed countries, the aspect of income distribution under consideration is relative income inequality. Exemplary of the relative inequality approach to distribution and development is the Nobel Prize–winning work of Professor Kuznets, begun two decades ago.[7] Some of the most influential recent contributions are those of Adelman and Morris (1973), Chenery et al. (1974), and Ahluwalia (1976a). The literature is surveyed by Paukert (1973) and Cline (1975), both of whom also present extensive bibliographies.

    Sometimes, in research on relative inequality, the Lorenz curve itself is taken as the criterion for inequality comparisons. The closer the Lorenz curve is to the forty-five-degree line, the more equal the distribution of income is said to be. The Lorenz criterion provides the following decision rules:

    1. If one Lorenz curve lies wholly above another, then the first situation is deemed more equal than the second.

    2. If the two Lorenz curves coincide, then the two distributions are judged equally unequal.

3. If the two Lorenz curves cross one another, we require further information before making an inequality comparison.

The Lorenz criterion has many adherents in the literature.

Often, in making relative inequality comparisons, Lorenz curves are found to intersect, so that the Lorenz criterion cannot tell us which distribution is more equal. To compare inequality in all circumstances, various indexes have been constructed.

All relative inequality measures in current use are based on the Lorenz curve in two senses: (1) They use the income distribution data depicted by the Lorenz curve to construct an index of income inequality; and (2) like the Lorenz curve, they are mean independent; that is, if everyone's income changes by the same constant percentage, relative inequality is unchanged. The *Gini coefficient* bears the closest relationship to the Lorenz curve, being the ratio of the area between the Lorenz curve and the forty-five-degree line to the total area of the triangle. Next most closely related to the Lorenz curve is the family of *fractile measures,* such as the income share of poorest 40% or richest 5%. Fractile shares can be read directly from the Lorenz curve, but they use only part of the information in it. Finally, there are other relative inequality measures that may be calculated from the data contained in Lorenz curves but do not appear directly. These include many familiar indexes, such as the variance or standard deviation of income or its logarithm, the coefficient of variation, the Kuznets ratio, the Atkinson index, the Theil index, and many others.

It should be noted that the various relative inequality measures are not as objective as may at first appear. Whenever one of these measures is used, certain judgments are made about the desirability of incomes accruing to persons at different positions in the income distribution. Even the Lorenz criterion, which permits us to rank the relative inequality of different distributions in only a fraction of the cases, embodies such judgments. Whenever relative inequality measures are used, researchers are implicitly making *some* value judgments, but it is not clear what these judgments are. Sen (1973) and Fields and Fei (1978) have made some progress toward justifying particular inequality measures axiomatically; but there is still a substantial distance to go before we will know exactly what judgments are being made when a particular inequality measure is used.

Absolute income approach

Income distribution may be measured in absolute as well as relative terms.[8] In a simple descriptive statement such as, "In situation A, everybody has more absolute income than in situation B," the implicit welfare judgment is that more income is preferred to less, ceteris paribus, and therefore A is preferred to B. An additional judgment commonly made is that a dollar of income accruing to a poor person adds more to social welfare than a dollar accruing to a richer person. Formally, without loss of generality, we may order the income recipient units from lowest income to highest. The absolute income approach refers to the general class of studies that treats social welfare in the form

welfare economics

(1) $\quad W = g(Y_1, Y_2, \ldots, Y_n)$ where $g_i \geqslant g_j$ for all j and $g_i > g_j$ for some j.

A well-known example of the absolute income approach is the work of Atkinson (1970). Atkinson suggested that we conceive of social welfare in the economy as the sum of the values placed on each individual's (or family's) income. Hence, the function takes the form

(2') $\quad W = U(Y_1) + U(Y_2) + \cdots + U(Y_n)$

or if the data are grouped into income classes

(2'') $\quad W = \Sigma U(y)f(y), \quad U' > 0, \quad U'' < 0$

where W is social welfare, U is the utility of an individual or family, and f is the number of families with income level y. The form of this function means that each family's utility is a function only of its own income, more income increases utility but at a decreasing rate, all families are treated alike in social welfare judgments, and total social welfare is the sum of each family's well-being. Atkinson did not use this function to evaluate the welfare consequences of economic growth based on absolute considerations, which is our purpose in this chapter. Rather, he explored the making of inequality comparisons with this welfare function as basis. The resultant "Atkinson index of inequality" will be discussed in Chapter 4.

The Atkinson framework (2) represents a special case of the more general absolute income approach (1). Other special cases, to which we now turn, also merit interest.

One serious attempt to integrate absolute income considerations into an analysis of development is found in the work of Ahluwalia and Chenery (1974). Their proposal is to divide society into socioeconomic groups according to assets, income levels, and so on, and to measure the income growth of each. Certain poverty groups–such as small farmers, landless laborers, and the urban underemployed–may be defined. In practice, though, the population is divided into quintile groups. The overall rate of growth of welfare is given by

(3) $G = w_1 g_1 + w_2 g_2 + w_3 g_3 + w_4 g_4 + w_5 g_5$

where g_i is the income growth of the ith quintile, ordered from lowest to highest, and w_i is the welfare weight assigned to the growth of group i's income. The obvious problem at hand is the choice of the welfare weights $w_1, \ldots, w_5$.

Ahluwalia and Chenery suggest three different possible weighting schemes: GNP weights, equal percentage weights, and poverty weights.

GNP weights. Growth of GNP is the most commonly used economic measure. Ahluwalia and Chenery note that the use of GNP corresponds to a special case of (3), namely, when the weights on each quintile's income growth are that quintile's share in total income. Thus a given percentage increase in income of the rich receives more weight than the same percentage increase in income of the poor. For those observers who wish to make welfare judgments favoring income gains among the poor, the GNP weights are not very appealing. Accordingly, Ahluwalia and Chenery suggest two alternatives.

Equal percentage weights. GNP weights give the same gain in social welfare for an additional dollar received by an individual regardless of his position in the income distribution. Suppose instead that we wanted to evaluate equally a given *percentage* increase in income for the rich and poor. Then the weights would be equal to each other; normalizing to one, $w_1 = w_2 = w_3 = w_4 = w_5 = .2$.

Poverty weights. Some observers would not wish to regard a 1% increase in the income of rich and poor equivalently. To give even greater weight to income gains in the poorer quintiles, one might use "poverty weights," which decline monotonically: $w_1 > w_2 > w_3 > w_4 > w_5$. An extreme poverty weight case is where the only income gains that matter are those of the poorest quintile, in which case $w_1 = 1$ and all other weights are equal to zero.

Ahluwalia and Chenery suggest a general principle: "The extent to which a weighted index of growth diverges from the growth rate of GNP and the direction of divergence are measures of the extent and direction to which growth is distributionally biased" (p. 41). I would note in addition that Ahluwalia-Chenery weights are much more meaningful when the income groups are defined *ex ante* than when they are defined *ex post*. This point, as well as the empirical results of their research as applied to less-developed countries, is reviewed in Chapter 5.

Absolute poverty approach

Three other particular cases of the absolute income approach are also of interest. They have in common the property that they concentrate on changes in economic well-being of the poor to the neglect of the rest of the income distribution, and they are referred to collectively as the "absolute poverty approach."

We must first define what we mean by "poverty."[9] Let us regard an individual as poor if his or her income falls below a specified dollar amount, with corresponding figures for families of different sizes. The United States Agency for International Development, for example, makes use of the figure of U.S. $150 per capita in less-developed countries (see AID, 1975); the World Bank uses $50 or $75 (see Ahluwalia, 1974). In other countries, the poverty line is set with respect to minimal nutritional adequacy (see, e.g., Ojha, 1970; and Reutlinger and Selowsky, 1976). Let us choose one of these figures as a poverty line and agree to hold it constant in real terms. Denote the poverty line by $P*$. "The poor" are those whose incomes are less than $P*$.

Proponents of the absolute poverty approach offer various judgments about the extent of poverty (P):

1. P falls when the number (or proportion) of income recipients (individuals or families) with incomes below $P*$ falls.
2. The larger is the average income of those below $P*$, the lower is P.
3. For the same number of poor and the same average income among the poor, the more unequal is the distribution of income among the poor, the more severe is P.[10]

Absolute poverty measures like those just presented have been used in research in the United States for many years; see, for example, Bowman (1973) or Perlman (1976) for summaries of the U.S. literature. But their application to less-developed countries is quite recent.

Despite the attractiveness of these absolute poverty measures, each has certain limitations. The first listed, the "head count," which tells the number of people below the poverty line, fails to gauge the extent of their poverty. The "poverty gap," the second of these measures, gives information on the amount needed to raise the incomes of the poor to the poverty standard, but it does not tell the number of people to whom the gap applies. Finally, the degree of "income inequality among the poor," the third measure, fails to locate the level of their economic malaise, because it measures only dispersion. However, when taken together, changes in these three measures may provide a comprehensive indication of the extent of participation of the poor in economic growth.

One special case of the absolute poverty approach offers considerable promise. A leading growth theorist, Sen (1976a), has combined these measures and argued elegantly for the use of a composite index of poverty. The measure recommended by Sen is

(4) $\pi = H[\bar{I} + (1 - \bar{I})G_p]$

where H = head count of the poor (i.e., how many there are); I = average income shortfall of the poor (i.e., the gap between $P*$ and the average income of those below $P*$); and G_p = Gini coefficient of income inequality among the poor.

The particular way of combining H, $\bar{I}$, and G_p in (4) is justified axiomatically. Given suitably disaggregated data, the severity of poverty in various countries and the extent of their progress in alleviating poverty over time can be measured with the Sen index.

Another special case of the absolute poverty approach is the social organization principle advocated by Rawls (1971).[11] Rawls regards the optimal income distribution as that which makes the worst-off individual(s) in the economy as well-off as possible. Only if the poorest person's economic position is raised is there a welfare improvement. Nobody else's economic position matters to Rawls, nor does inequality. Income distribution need not be exactly equal at the optimum. Inequalities are tolerable if and only if the absolute welfare of the worst-off individual is higher in the presence of inequality than it would be in its absence. This principle of maximizing the welfare of the poorest individual is known as the "maximin principle."

Consider the relationship between the maximin principle and the more familiar Pareto criterion.[12] As shown by Sen (1970), the two criteria may rank two social states differently, as in the following example. Suppose there are two social states X and Y. If state X obtains, individual A has welfare of 10, whereas B has welfare of 1. If state Y obtains, A has welfare of 20, and B's welfare remains at 1. State Y is Pareto superior to X, yet the maximin criterion rates the two indifferently. To avoid this problem, Sen suggests defining a lexicographic ordering as follows:

1. Maximize the welfare of the worst-off individual.
2. For equal welfare of the worst-off individual, maximize the welfare of the second worst-off individual.

   .
   .
   .

n. For equal welfare of the worst-off individual, second worst-off individual, ..., $(n-1)$st worst-off individual, maximize the welfare of the best-off (nth) individual.

In the numerical example just given, Y is preferred to X under this rule, known as the "lexicographic maximin rule."

Note that both the maximin principle and its lexicographic

version are expressed in terms of individuals' welfare and not their incomes. In the special case where individuals' personal welfare functions depend only on their own incomes or if our assessment of an individual's well-being depends only on that person's income, the maximin principle reduces to

(5) $W = g(Y_1), \quad g' > 0$

and the lexicographic maximin principle becomes

(6) $W = g(Y_k \mid Y_1, \ldots, Y_{k-1} \text{ constant})$

The main advantage of absolute poverty indexes is that they provide *direct* measures of changes in the economic position of the poor. Depending on the value judgments of the particular observer, this may be the most important indicator of development progress. The welfare economics of these judgments is deferred until Chapter 3. In contrast, although poverty indicators can be computed from Lorenz curves or Lorenz curve–based inequality measures, the extent of absolute poverty is obtained only indirectly and often with considerable computational difficulty.

Empirical applications of the various absolute poverty indexes to growth in less-developed countries are reviewed in Chapter 5.

Relative poverty approach

In addition to the approaches already considered, there is a newer one being promulgated by researchers at the World Bank and elsewhere known as the relative poverty measure (see, e.g., Chiswick, 1976). This figure is the absolute income (in constant dollars) received by the poorest 40% of the population or some other predetermined percentage.[13] By this approach, economic growth is thought to raise social welfare when the average income of the poorest 40% is higher.

I would submit that the relative poverty approach suffers serious conceptual limitations for measuring who benefits from economic development. The reason is that development processes are typically uneven, and only some of the poor benefit, not all. If we look at those who are the poorest 40% *ex post* at different times, we remove from consideration those who originally *were* in the poorest 40% but who were lifted out because of economic growth. The relative poverty approach is insensitive to the rate of movement out of poverty if more than 40% of the people are poor. It measures only those left behind.

Another kind of relative poverty measure is proposed by Fuchs (1967), who suggests counting the proportion with incomes less than half the median income. This is more an inequality measure than a poverty measure, because if everyone's incomes were to increase by the same percentage, poverty would be unaffected by it. The Fuchs measure has received little attention in the development literature.

Comparing the classes of measures

The numerical examples presented earlier in this chapter may be used to illustrate the differences among the four classes of measures of distribution and development. To summarize the hypothetical "facts" of the example:

Indicator of economic performance	*Change in indicator*
Growth	Higher in *B-D-F* than in *A-C-E*
High-wage employment	Higher in both than initially, faster rise in *B-D-F*
Absolute income among high-wage workers	Unchanged in both cases
Absolute income among low-wage workers	Unchanged in both cases
Absolute poverty	Lower in both than initially, greater reduction in *B-D-F*
Relative inequality	Higher in both than initially, higher in *B-D-F*
Relative poverty	No apparent change in either case

Investigating poverty, inequality, and development according to the various approaches of the preceding section, we come to the following conclusions. By the absolute income and absolute poverty criteria, *B-D-F* clearly dominates *A-C-E* on both growth and distribution grounds. Using the relative inequality criterion, it is difficult to judge: Although *B-D-F* grew faster than *A-C-E*, inequality seems to have worsened.[14] Finally, by the relative poverty criterion, both appear equally unsatisfactory, because neither country seems to have made progress in alleviating poverty; in fact, poverty was being alleviated in both, and at different rates.[15]

The hypothetical data illustrate a basic point: How income distribution is studied – whether in terms of relative income inequality, absolute incomes and absolute poverty, or relative poverty – may lead to fundamentally different judgments about the success or failure of economic growth, even to the point of questioning whether there was any development at all.

The discrepancies among the various approaches are based in part on legitimate differences in value judgments about what aspects of less-developed countries' income distributions are worrisome, and in part on a statistical pattern that in some respects is artifactual. Let us explore these discrepancies further and ask:

1. What is it about the process of economic development that causes the various approaches to differ?
2. In assessing the distributional consequences of growth, do we wish to give greater weight in our judgments to the alleviation of absolute poverty or to the narrowing of relative income inequality?

The answer to the first question is that the discrepancy is produced by the unevenness of economic development itself. Suppose, in keeping with the dualism tradition in the field of economic development, that an economy consists of an advanced "modern" sector and a backward "traditional" sector. The pattern depicted in the example illustrates what I call in Chapter 3 "modern sector enlargement growth," which takes place when an economy grows by enlarging the size of its modern sector, with the incomes (or wages) within the modern and traditional sectors remaining the same. The discrepancy among the various income-distribution measures arises because this type of growth affects only some of the poor, not all. Consequently, those whose situations are not improved by this type of growth, and who therefore remain as poor as before, receive the same dollar amount, but it is a smaller part of a larger whole. From this, it follows that the absolute incomes of the poorest 40% are unchanged and that the Lorenz curve shifts downward at its lower end, so that those Lorenz curve–based measures of relative income inequality that are sensitive to the lower end of the income distribution register a worsening of the income distribution.

We should note that modern sector enlargement growth is not just the figment of an ivory-tower academician's imagination. This pattern is widely regarded as an essential ingredient of development. In their famous book, Fei and Ranis (1964: 7) write:

> The heart of the development problem may be said to lie in the gradual shifting of the center of gravity of the economy from the agricultural to the industrial sector ... gauged in terms of the reallocation of the population between the two sectors in order to promote a gradual expansion of industrial employment and output.

This characterization is echoed by Kuznets (1966). Empirical studies such as that of Turnham (1971) have documented the absorption of an increasing share of the population into the modern sector as growth takes place. In a case study of Indian economic development in the 1950s, Swamy (1967) found that 85% of the change in the size distribution of income was due to intersectoral factors (namely, growth in importance of the urban sector and growing per capita income differential between the urban and rural sectors) and only 15% to changing inequality within the two sectors. Thus modern sector enlargement constitutes a large and perhaps even predominant component of the growth of currently developing countries.

The other question just posed concerns the choice between absolute and relative income measures in determining the beneficiaries of growth. The choice depends on basic ethical considerations. For some observers, the plight of the poor in less-developed countries is objective, to the extent that they do not have command over sufficient resources to feed and clothe themselves and avoid disease. In this way of thinking, poverty is an absolute condition requiring analysis in absolute terms. Predominant emphasis would be given to data on changes in the number who are poor, the average extent of their poverty, and, to a lesser extent, the degree of inequality among them. Others have different concerns and make different judgments. They would give great weight to the subjective feelings of the poor, who may feel relatively worse off if others' economic positions are improving and theirs are not. Observers who feel strongly about such relative income considerations are justified in using relative inequality measures.[16]

What may not be justified, although there are many examples of it in the development literature, is the coupling of a concern about the absolute economic misery of the poor with reliance on calculations of changes in relative inequality over time. I fear that this approach may be mistaken and misleading, quite apart from its logical inconsistency. For just as in the numerical example given in the preceding section, by assigning heavy weight to changes in the usual indexes of relative income inequality, and by interpreting these increases as offsets to the economic well-being brought about by growth, one may overlook important tendencies toward the alleviation of absolute poverty.

Conclusion

This chapter has highlighted the types of issues involved in establishing an income distribution criterion for assessing development progress. The first step was to distinguish between the size distribution of income and other income distribution concepts and to clarify the often-confused notions of income distribution and income inequality. Then we reviewed the tools of analysis of income distribution, both relative and absolute, and illustrated their application with numerical examples. Numerous variants of the four basic approaches–relative inequality, absolute income, absolute poverty, and relative poverty–were presented. The earlier examples were then used to indicate how differences among the various approaches may arise. Clearly, evaluators' basic ethical judgments play an important role in any study of income distribution and economic development. It is to the welfare economics of distribution and development that we now turn.

Growth and distribution: a welfare economic analysis

This section presents a welfare economic analysis of the distributional consequences of growth. We will explore the similarities and differences between the absolute income and poverty and relative inequality approaches for a general dualistic development model and for three stylized special cases. As we will see, these approaches are not always in agreement and, more disturbingly, the most notable discrepancy is found in the most relevant stylized model–growth via the transfer of population from a backward to an enlarging advanced sector. The fact of these discrepancies raises the important question how to measure changing income distribution in a manner consistent with the judgments we wish to make about the alleviation of absolute poverty and amelioration of relative income inequality. A general welfare function is formulated to address these issues. Recent controversies over who received the benefits of growth in two less-developed countries–Brazil and India–are briefly examined in these terms. Finally, income distribution is discussed both as an outcome and as a determinant of the rate and nature of economic growth.

Basic welfare judgments on distribution and development

The purpose of this section is to formalize some of the ideas about income distribution developed in Chapter 2.

Economists are used to regarding social welfare as a positive function of the income levels of the n individuals or families in society before and after development takes place. In empirical studies, the general social welfare function,

(1) $\qquad W = W(Y_1, Y_2, \ldots, Y_n), \quad W_1, W_2, \ldots, W_n > 0$

is too general to be useful, and the Pareto criterion,

(2) $W^A(Y_1^A, Y_2^A, \ldots, Y_n^A) > W^B(Y_1^B, Y_2^B, \ldots, Y_n^B)$

if $Y_i^A \geqslant Y_i^B$ for all i and $Y_i^A > Y_i^B$ for some i,

is too stringent.

For analytical ease, the information contained in the income vector $(Y_1, Y_2, \ldots, Y_n)$ is usually collapsed into one or more aggregative measures. The three classes of measures in most common use are total income (Y) or its per capita equivalent, indexes of relative inequality (I), and measures of absolute poverty (P).

The customary approach to studies of distribution and development, which we earlier termed the relative inequality approach, is to posit (explicitly or implicitly) a social welfare function containing an index of relative inequality as one of its arguments:

(3) $W = f(Y, I),\quad f_1 > 0,\quad f_2 < 0$

where Y is total income and I is an indicator of inequality in its distribution. Theoretical support for the relative inequality approach may be found in the welfare economics literature in the writings of Sheshinski (1972) and Sen (1976b). In the study of distribution and development, the relative inequality approach is best exemplified in the work of Kuznets (1955, 1963, and 1966). Income distribution is said to have "improved" or "worsened" according to Lorenz domination (i.e., whether one Lorenz curve lies wholly above or below a previous one $[L]$) or according to one or more measures of relative inequality, such as the income share of the poorest 40% (S) or the Gini coefficient (G). Thus, formally, relative inequality studies typically make one or more of the following judgments:

(4)   (a) $W = f(Y, L),\quad f_1 > 0,\quad f_2 > 0$
        (b) $W = f(Y, S),\quad f_1 > 0,\quad f_2 > 0$
        (c) $W = f(Y, G),\quad f_1 > 0,\quad f_2 < 0$

As an alternative to the relative inequality approach, some writers have examined the income distribution itself, assigning a lower social welfare weight to income gains of the relatively well-off than to those of the poor. With no loss of generality, we may order the n income-recipient units from lowest to highest. The general class of studies that treats social welfare in the form

(5) $W = g(Y_1, Y_2, \ldots, Y_n)$

where $g_i > g_j$ for all $i < j$, is what we have called the absolute income approach. In the welfare economics literature, the studies of Little and Mirrlees (1969), Atkinson (1970), and Stern (1972) are notable examples. The maximin principle proposed by Rawls (1971), that is, maximizing the income of the worst-off person in the economy, is an extreme version of (5):

(5') $W = g(Y_1), \quad g' > 0$

Finally, for some purposes, we may wish to define a poverty line P^* and concentrate our attention on the group in poverty. This practice, termed the absolute poverty approach, is more common in studies of growth in developed than in less-developed countries. Denoting the extent of poverty by P, absolute poverty studies hold that

(6) $W = h(P), \quad h' < 0$

Usual measures of poverty are the number of individuals or families whose incomes are below that line or the gap between the poverty line and the average among the poor. A new composite poverty measure, the Sen index, is $\pi = H[\bar{I} + (1 - \bar{I})G_p]$, where H is the head count of the poor, $\bar{I}$ is the average income shortfall of the poor, and G_p is the Gini coefficient of income inequality among the poor. Thus alternative forms of the absolute poverty approach are given by

(7)   (a) $W = h(\underline{H}), \quad h' < 0$
        (b) $W = h(\bar{I}), \quad h' < 0$
        (c) $W = h(\pi) = h\{H[\bar{I} + (1 - \bar{I})G_p]\}, \quad h' < 0$

The relative and absolute approaches are often regarded as mutually exclusive, but they need not be. We may formulate a more general welfare function combining these various approaches. Because the distribution of benefits in the course of economic development refers to a phenomenon that takes place over time, it is appropriately measured by a dynamic index. It is important, therefore, to establish a suitably dynamic measure, which we shall do in the context of economic dualism. I now posit a dualistic development model and a general welfare function and develop a number of properties of that welfare function that are desirable for the purpose of evaluating economic development in the dual economy.

A general welfare approach for assessing dualistic development

New

At the forefront of studies of modern economic growth are the dualistic development models of Lewis (1954), Fei and Ranis (1964), and Jorgenson (1961). Although these models differ from one another in a number of important respects, they have in common the division of the economy into a relatively advanced sector and a relatively backward sector, which we shall call "modern" and "traditional" respectively. As with all dualistic models, the working assumption is that the members of each sector are relatively similar to others in that sector and relatively different from those in the other sector. We shall regard the modern sector as synonymous with high wages and the traditional sector as synonymous with low wages. "Wage" and "income" will be used interchangeably.[1]

In the two sectors, workers receive wage rates W^m and W^t respectively.[2] $W^m > P^* > W^t$ where P^* is an agreed-upon absolute poverty line that is constant over time in real terms (with allowance for price changes). The shares of the labor force in the two sectors are f^m and f^t respectively; the total economically active population $f^m + f^t$ is normalized at 1. Economic development consists of changes in W^m, W^t, f^m, and f^t.

Suppose we now want to implement a welfare function of the form

(8) $\qquad W = W(Y, I, P)$

which includes both absolute and relative considerations in the dualistic development model. Total income (Y) is given by

(9) $\qquad Y = Y^m + Y^t = W^m f^m + W^t f^t$

Whichever measure of relative inequality (I) one chooses is functionally related to the distribution of the labor force between the two sectors and to the intersectoral wage structure:

(10) $I = I(W^m, f^m, W^t, f^t)$

The poverty index (P) depends on the wage in the traditional sector and/or the share of the population in that sector:

(11) $P = P(W^t, f^t)$

Substituting (9)–(11) into (8), we have

(12) $W = W[W^m f^m + W^t f^t, \; I(W^m, f^m, W^t, f^t), \; P(W^t, f^t)]$

which we term the "general welfare approach."

We must now specify the relationship between W and its various arguments. In line with the considerations discussed in the preceding section, it is desirable to posit

(A) $\dfrac{\partial W}{\partial Y} > 0$

(B) $\dfrac{\partial W}{\partial I} < 0$

(C) $\dfrac{\partial W}{\partial P} < 0$

Condition (A) relies for its validity on the assumption that the basic goal of an economic system is to maximize the output of goods and services received by each of its members. We should be clear that acceptance of the judgment $(\partial W/\partial Y) > 0$ does *not* require us to accept the stronger quasi-Pareto condition $(\partial W/\partial Y_i) > 0$ for all i, which in our dualistic development models becomes $(\partial W/\partial Y_k) > 0$, $k = m, t$ (this is quasi because it is formulated in terms of incomes rather than utilities). The judgment $(\partial W/\partial Y_m) > 0$ is one that many observers would not want to make, because it implies that even if the richest were the sole beneficiaries of economic growth, society would be deemed better off. No such judgment is imposed in what follows.

Condition (B) requires us first to define what we mean by a more equal relative distribution of income. A generally accepted (although incomplete) criterion is that one distribution A is more equal than another B if A Lorenz dominates B, that is, if A's Lorenz curve lies above B's at at least one point and never lies below it. If A Lorenz dominates B for the same level of income, it means distribution A can be obtained from distribution B by transfering positive amounts of income from the relatively rich to the relatively poor (see Rothschild and Stiglitz, 1973; and Fields and Fei, 1978). The judgment that such transfers improve social welfare dates back at least to Dalton (1920). One possible justification for this principle is diminishing marginal utility of income, coupled with independent and homothetic individual utility functions and an additively separable social welfare function (see Atkinson, 1970). But these assumptions are not necessary for the affirmation of the axiomatic judgment $(\partial W/\partial I) < 0$.

The difficulty with Lorenz domination as a defining criterion for judgments concerning relative inequality is its incompleteness. When Lorenz curves cross, there is nothing to say. We therefore require a more complete relative inequality measure in order to rank various income distributions when Lorenz curves intersect. For this purpose, many indexes of relative income inequality that provide complete orderings have been constructed.

The properties of various inequality indexes have been examined by a number of writers (e.g., Champernowne, 1974; Kondor, 1975; Szal and Robinson, 1977; and Fields and Fei, 1978). It is agreed that a "good" inequality index should have the following properties: *scale irrelevance* (if one distribution is a scalar multiple of another, then they have the same relative inequality), *symmetry* (if one distribution is a permutation of another, then relative inequality in the two cases is the same), and the *Daltonian condition* (if one distribution is obtained from another by one or more income transfers from a relatively rich person to a relatively poor one, then the first distribution is more equal than the second).

Let us now turn to dynamic welfare issues, those concerned with changing incomes within sectors and changing labor-force distributions. For analyzing the growth of a dualistic economy three other properties of relative inequality measures are desirable. The first two are

$$(D) \quad \frac{\partial I}{\partial w^t} < 0$$

and

(E) $\dfrac{\partial I}{\partial W^m} > 0$

These accord with our intuitive notions about relative inequality (in terms of $W^m - W^t$ or W^m / W^t) and will probably not strike the reader as unusual. Then we have

(F) $\dfrac{\partial I}{\partial f^t} = -\dfrac{\partial I}{\partial f^m} \geqslant 0$

This condition holds that when an increasing fraction of the economically active population is drawn into an enlarged modern sector, then, other things being equal, relative inequality should be no greater than before. Because the wage differential between modern and traditional sector workers is being held constant, this is hardly an unreasonable property. Many would wish to go one step further and replace (F) by

(F') $\dfrac{\partial I}{\partial f^t} = -\dfrac{\partial I}{\partial f^m} > 0$

which I myself prefer. Condition (F') states that inequality declines when the fraction of workers in modern sector jobs increases, all other things being equal. The choice between (F) and (F') has no bearing on any of the results that follow; what is important is the exclusion of $(\partial I/\partial f^t) = -(\partial I/\partial f^m) <$ 0. Note that conditions (F) and (F') describe how the *inequality index itself* varies with the levels of development. This does not mean that our feelings about inequality are invariant to income level. For a perceptive analysis of changing tolerance for inequality in the course of economic development, see Hirschman and Rothschild (1973).

Finally, we turn to condition (C), which holds that social welfare (W) is increased as absolute poverty (P) is decreased. Whatever poverty measure(s) we employ should satisfy the properties

(G) $\dfrac{\partial P}{\partial f^t} > 0$

and

(H) $\dfrac{\partial P}{\partial W^t} < 0$

These conditions state that absolute poverty (P) is reduced if there are fewer people in the low-income traditional sector and/or if the wage received by those in the traditional sector is increased, that is, if they become less poor. These concepts are closely related to the "head-count" and "income shortfall" notions discussed earlier. The appeal of these properties is intuitive and requires no further elaboration.

Function (12) and conditions (A)–(H) constitute the general welfare approach. Condition (B) may be modified to

$$(\text{B}')\ \frac{\partial W}{\partial I} = 0$$

for observers interested only in absolute poverty, and (C) might be replaced by

$$(\text{C}')\ \frac{\partial W}{\partial P} = 0$$

for those concerned only about relative inequality. The various approaches for analyzing growth and distribution in the dual economy are summarized in Table 3.1.

As they stand, the welfare functions (4), (5), (7), and (12) are purely static. They are, however, easily made dynamic by differentiating (or differencing) them with respect to time or to their underlying arguments. Changes in W^m, W^t, f^m, and f^t enter directly into (12), indirectly into the others.

The questions that then arise are how the various approaches evaluate distributional change in dualistic economic development and under what circumstances the judgments agree or differ. We address these questions in the next two sections.

Welfare economic analysis of dualistic development: the general case

The overall growth of the dualistic economy is the sum of growth in the two sectors as given by (9). In turn, each sector's growth (or lack thereof) may be partitioned into two components: one attributable to the *enlargement* (or contraction) of the sector to include a greater (or lesser) percentage of the economically active population; the other attributable to the *enrichment* of persons engaged in that sector. If a

Table 3.1. *Various welfare economic approaches for analyzing dualistic economic development*

Relative inequality approach		
General form: (3)	$W = f(Y, I), \quad f_1 > 0, \quad f_2 < 0$	Inequality index
Specific applications: (4)		
(a)	$W = f(Y, L), \quad f_1 > 0, \quad f_2 > 0$	Lorenz criterion
(b)	$W = f(Y, S), \quad f_1 > 0, \quad f_2 > 0$	Income share of poorest 40%
(c)	$W = f(Y, G), \quad f_1 > 0, \quad f_2 < 0$	Gini coefficient
Absolute income approach		
General form: (5)	$W = g(Y_1, Y_2, \ldots, Y_n), \quad g_i > g_j \quad \text{for all } i < j$	Absolute income
Specific application: (5')	$W = g(Y_1), \quad g' > 0$	Rawlsian maximin criterion
Absolute poverty approach		
General form: (6)	$W = h(P), \quad h' < 0$	Poverty index
Specific applications: (7)		
(a)	$W = h(H), \quad h' < 0$	Head count of poor
(b)	$W = h(\overline{I}), \quad h' < 0$	Income shortfall
(c)	$W = h(\pi), \quad h' < 0,$	Sen index
	$\pi = H[\overline{I} + (1 - \overline{I})G_p]$	
General social welfare approach		
General form: (8)	$W = W(Y, I, P), \quad \dfrac{\partial W}{\partial Y} > 0, \quad \dfrac{\partial W}{\partial I} < 0, \quad \dfrac{\partial W}{\partial P} < 0$	General welfare
Specific application: (12)	$W = W[W^m f^{cm} + w^t f^t, \ I(W^m, W^t, f^{rm}, f^t), \ P(W^t, f^t)],$	General welfare, dualistic
	$\dfrac{\partial W}{\partial Y} > 0, \quad \dfrac{\partial Y}{\partial I} < 0, \quad \dfrac{\partial W}{\partial P} < 0,$	
	$\dfrac{\partial Y}{\partial W^{rm}}, \ \dfrac{\partial Y}{\partial W^t}, \ \dfrac{\partial Y}{\partial f^{rm}}, \ \dfrac{\partial Y}{\partial f^t} > 0,$	
	$\dfrac{\partial I}{\partial W^{rm}} > 0, \quad \dfrac{\partial I}{\partial W^t} < 0, \quad \dfrac{\partial I}{\partial f^{rm}} = -\dfrac{\partial I}{\partial f^t} \leq 0,$	
	$\dfrac{\partial P}{\partial W^t} < 0, \quad \dfrac{\partial P}{\partial f^t} > 0$	

dualistic economy is growing successfully, one or more of the following must be happening: (1) the fraction of workers in the modern sector is increasing; (2) those in the modern sector receive higher average incomes than before; or (3) the incomes of those who remain in the traditional sector may rise.   Although every successfully developing country experiences some or all of these phenomena to varying degrees, some pursue more broadly based or more egalitarian courses than do others.

A useful way of examining how different groups benefit from economic growth is to take the first difference of (9), year 1 being the base year and year 2 the terminal year, and to decompose the change in income in the following way:

$$(13) \qquad \Delta Y = (f_2{}^m - f_1{}^m)(W_1{}^m - W_1{}^t) + (W_2{}^m - W_1{}^m)f_1{}^m$$

Modern sector enlargement effect (α)	Modern sector enrichment effect (β)

$$+ (W_2{}^m - W_1{}^m)(f_2{}^m - f_1{}^m) + (W_2{}^t - W_1{}^t)f_2{}^t$$

Interaction between modern sector enlargement and enrichment effects (γ)	Traditional sector enrichment effect (δ)

where α = enlargement of the high-income sector = change in the number of persons in the high-income sector, multiplied by the income differential between the high-income and low-income sectors in the base year; β = enrichment of the high-income sector = change in income within the high-income sector, multiplied by the number of persons who were originally in that sector in the base year; γ = interaction between enlargement and enrichment of the high-income sector = change in income within the high-income sector, multiplied by the change in the number of persons in that sector; and δ = enrichment of the low-income sector = change in income within the low-income sector, multiplied by the number of persons who remained in that sector in the terminal year.   In the general case, a comparative static analysis of (13) reveals:

1. The *modern sector enlargement effect* (α) is greater both the greater the increase in modern sector employment and the greater

the difference between modern sector and traditional sector wage rates.

2. The *modern sector enrichment effect* (β) is greater both the greater the rate of increase of modern sector wages and the more important the modern sector in total employment.

3. The *traditional sector enrichment effect* (δ) is greater both the greater the rate of increase of traditional sector wages and the more important the traditional sector in total employment.

Note that negative enlargement and enrichment effects are both possible. Negative enlargement occurs when a sector shrinks in size; negative enrichment results when real incomes in that sector fall.

Total income growth can be positive while either enlargement or enrichment is negative. For example, a 10% growth rate in a sector might result from either (1) a 20% rise in the size of the sector, coupled with a 10% fall in average wages, or (2) a 20% rise in average wages, accompanied by a 10% decline in number of persons in that sector. This example should make clear that our qualitative judgments about the desirability of any particular sector growth rate depend crucially on the enlargement and enrichment components of that growth; examination of the sector growth rate is not enough.[3]

One immediate application of the decomposition in (13) is to poverty gap analysis. The poverty gap is the total income shortfall of the poor, that is, the sum of the differences between each poor person's (or family's) income and the poverty line, which may be denoted *IS*. The poor may benefit from economic growth in two ways: by more of them (Δf^m) being drawn into an enlarged modern sector (α) or by those remaining receiving higher incomes (ΔW^t) within the traditional sector (δ). The sum $\alpha + \delta$ is then the *ex post* income gain of the poor, and $(\alpha + \delta)/IS$ is an index of an economy's progress toward alleviating absolute poverty. This is one way in which the welfare judgments in (6) and (7) might be implemented. In addition, if the β component is also taken into account, we are able to gauge success in raising incomes more generally, which is what the absolute income approach (5) requires.

Relative inequality judgments may also be made using the decomposition in (13). It would seem natural to compare the share of income growth accruing to the poor $(\alpha + \delta)$ and to the nonpoor (β), but I would be wary of such calculations, because $\alpha + \delta$ will almost inevitably be less than β, for much the same reason that the income share of the poorest $X\%$ must always be less than the income share of the richest $Y\%$.[4]   A more meaningful measure, one that is more sensitive to relative income differentials to begin with, is one that normalizes for the amount of initial income.   Then the *percentage* gains in the two sectors may be calculated as $\beta/Y_1^{\,m}$ and $(\alpha + \delta)/Y_1^{\,t}$ or the equivalent per capita form.

Finally, the general welfare function (12) may be related to the enrichment and enlargement components of growth as follows:

(14)   (a) $\dfrac{\partial W}{\partial \alpha} > 0$

      (b) $\dfrac{\partial W}{\partial \beta} \gtrless 0$

      (c) $\dfrac{\partial W}{\partial \delta} > 0$

The ambiguity in (14b) reflects the fact that, by itself, greater modern sector enrichment increases both total income and income inequality. These changes receive positive and negative weights respectively in welfare judgments according to conditions (A) and (B) of the preceding section, at least among observers who wish to take account of relative inequality changes.   Observers interested only in absolute incomes and absolute poverty face no such difficulty.

For applying the enlargement and enrichment framework to empirical research, the dualistic version developed above may be too restrictive.   Two potentially useful extensions are to allow for more sectors and to recognize the effects of population growth.

Consider first the general n sector case, for instance, a modern urban sector, a traditional urban sector, and a traditional agricultural sector.   With n sectors, national income (Y) is

(15) $Y = \displaystyle\sum_{i=1}^{n} W^i f^i$

The change in national income is

$$(16) \quad \Delta Y = Y_2 - Y_1 = \sum_{i=1}^{n} W_2{}^i f_2{}^i - \sum_{i=1}^{n} W_1{}^i f_1{}^i$$

which, when rewritten as

$$(17) \quad \Delta Y = \sum_{i=1}^{n} (W_2{}^i f_2{}^i - W_1{}^i f_1{}^i)$$

enables us to measure the contribution of the ith sector to total growth. To distinguish each sector's enlargement and enrichment effects and the interaction between them, (17) may be manipulated to yield

$$(18) \quad \Delta Y = \sum_{i=1}^{n} [\underbrace{W_1{}^i (f_2{}^i - f_1{}^i)}_{\substack{\text{Sector } i \\ \text{enlargement} \\ \text{effect}}} + \underbrace{(W_2{}^i - W_1{}^i) f_1{}^i}_{\substack{\text{Sector } i \\ \text{enrichment} \\ \text{effect}}}$$

$$+ \underbrace{(W_2{}^i - W_1{}^i)(f_2{}^i - f_1{}^i)]}_{\substack{\text{Interaction of sector} \\ i \text{ enlargement and} \\ \text{enrichment effects}}}$$

The results of the comparative static analysis of the two-sector case carry over to the n-sector case in an analogous manner.

Besides extensions to more than two sectors, the methodology may be carried over as well to more than two income sources, or to a hybrid classification of sectors and sources. For example, it might be useful to measure income growth in the following six groups:

1. Labor income among modern sector workers in urban areas
2. Labor income among traditional sector workers in urban areas
3. Labor income among traditional sector workers in agriculture
4. Capital income in urban areas
5. Capital income in rural areas
6. Other income

It is also a straightforward matter to give explicit recognition to population growth. Total income growth (ΔY) may be thought of as having two components: a *population growth effect* (P), defined as the expansion of the economy to absorb a growing population at the initial occupational and wage structure, and a *net growth effect* (N), which results from higher wages and a higher proportion of the population employed in high-paying activities. Let f^i be the number of persons in sector i and p the rate of growth of population between years 1 and 2. Then net growth (income growth net of population) is given by

$$(19) \quad N = \Delta Y - P$$

$$= \sum_{i=1}^{n} (W_2{}^i f_2{}^i - W_1{}^i f_1{}^i) - \sum_{i=1}^{n} W_1{}^i f_1{}^i p$$

This can be decomposed into the various net effects as

$$(20) \quad N = \sum_{i=1}^{n} [W_2{}^i f_2{}^i - W_1{}^i f_1{}^i (1+p)]$$

$$= \sum_{i=1}^{n} \{W_1{}^i [f_2{}^i - f_1{}^i (1+p)]\}$$

Sector i net
enlargement effect

$$+ \sum_{i=1}^{n} [(W_2{}^i - W_1{}^i) f_1{}^i (1+p)]$$

Sector i net
enrichment effect

$$+ \sum_{i=1}^{n} \{(W_2{}^i - W_1{}^i)[f_2{}^i - f_1{}^i (1+p)]\}$$

Interaction of sector i net
enlargement and enrichment effects

With such extended methodologies, we are limited only by restrictions of data and our own ingenuity.

Welfare economic analysis of dualistic development: special cases

It is instructive to examine the three limiting cases of dualistic development and then to analyze the growth and distributional patterns that arise. For this analysis, we shall apply the various welfare economic approaches just discussed. This procedure provides valuable theoretical insight into the empirical patterns reported in Chapters 4–6.

First let us take the three limiting cases of dualistic economic development. We might distinguish among three stylized development typologies. In the *modern sector enlargement growth* model, an economy develops by enlarging the size of its modern sector, the wages in the two sectors remaining the same. *Modern sector enrichment growth* occurs when the growth accrues only to a fixed number of persons in the modern sector, the number in the traditional sector and their wages remaining unchanged. Finally, we have *traditional sector enrichment growth* when all the proceeds of growth are divided evenly among those in the traditional sector. The modern sector enlargement growth model most closely reflects the essential nature of economic development as conceived by the existing literature.

Let us now analyze the growth and distributional patterns in each of the three stylized models of dualistic development. The principal results are summarized in Table 3.2.

Traditional sector enrichment growth

In the traditional sector enrichment growth model, incomes in the traditional sector are assumed to rise, incomes in the modern sector remain the same, and the allocation of the labor force between the two sectors also remains the same. The following proposition is easily established:

Proposition 1. Traditional sector enrichment growth results in higher income, a more equal relative distribution of income, and less poverty.

The increase in income and the alleviation of poverty (because each of the poor becomes less poor) are evident. Regarding the relative income distribution, we need only observe that traditional sector enrichment growth has the effect of shifting the kink point on the Lorenz curve vertically, as in Figure 3.1, which establishes Lorenz domination. By inspection, it is apparent that the income share of the poorest 40% (S) increases, and the Gini coefficient (G) (the ratio of the area above the Lorenz curve to the entire triangle) decreases. Hence relative income inequality declines, as was to be shown. By all of the social welfare criteria presented above, this type of growth therefore results in an unambiguous welfare improvement.

Table 3.2. *Summary of distribution and welfare effects in three models of dualistic development*

	Traditional sector enrichment growth	Modern sector enrichment growth	Modern sector enlargement growth		
			Phase 1: $0 \leq f^m < \dfrac{(W^m W^t)^{1/2} - W^t}{W^m - W^t}$	Phase 2: $\dfrac{(W^m W^t)^{1/2} - W^t}{W^m - W^t} \leq f^m \leq 60\%$	Phase 3: $f^m > 60\%$
Growth and distributional effects					
f^m	Unchanged	Unchanged	Rises	Rises	Rises
f^t	Unchanged	Unchanged	Falls	Falls	Falls
W^m	Unchanged	Rises	Unchanged	Unchanged	Unchanged
W^t	Rises	Unchanged	Unchanged	Unchanged	Unchanged
Y	Rises	Rises	Rises	Rises	Rises
π	Falls	Unchanged	Falls	Falls	Falls
L	Lorenz superior	Lorenz inferior	Lorenz crossing	Lorenz crossing	Lorenz crossing
G	Falls	Rises	Rises	Falls	Falls
S	Rises	Falls	Falls	Falls	Rises
Y_{min}	Rises	Unchanged	Unchanged	Unchanged	Unchanged
Welfare effects according to					
Absolute income approach	Unambiguous improvement	Unambiguous improvement	Unambiguous improvement	Unambiguous improvement	Unambiguous improvement
Rawlsian maximin approach	Unambiguous improvement	Unchanged	Unchanged	Unchanged	Unchanged

	1	2	3	4	5
Absolute poverty approach	Unambiguous improvement	Unchanged	Unambiguous improvement	Unambiguous improvement	Unambiguous improvement
Relative inequality approach:					
L	Unambiguous improvement	Lorenz inferior	Lorenz crossing	Lorenz crossing	Lorenz crossing
G	Unambiguous improvement	Ambiguous	Ambiguous	Unambiguous improvement	Unambiguous improvement
S	Unambiguous improvement	Ambiguous	Ambiguous	Ambiguous	Unambiguous improvement
Function (12) and condition (C')	Unambiguous improvement	Ambiguous	Unambiguous improvement	Unambiguous improvement	Unambiguous improvement
General welfare approach (12)	Unambiguous improvement	Ambiguous	Unambiguous improvement	Unambiguous improvement	Unambiguous improvement

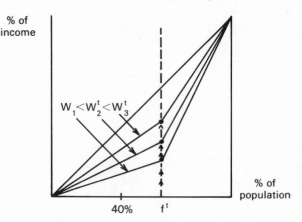

Figure 3.1. Upward vertical shift of the Lorenz curve kink point in the traditional sector enrichment growth model.

Modern sector enrichment growth

In modern sector enrichment growth, incomes in the modern sector rise while incomes in the traditional sector and the allocation of the labor force between the modern sector and the traditional sector remain the same. In this case, we have the following theorem:

Proposition 2. Modern sector enrichment growth results in higher income, a less equal relative distribution of income, and no change in poverty.

Adherents of the more general form of the absolute income approach would regard this type of growth as an unambiguous improvement, although they would have preferred a pattern where less of the benefit accrued to the well-to-do. However, Rawlsians and persons who adopt the absolute poverty criterion would be indifferent to this type of growth, because no poverty is being alleviated.

With respect to relative inequality, the gap between the modern sector wage and the traditional sector wage increases. The kink point on the Lorenz curve shifts vertically downward, as in Figure 3.2, where we see clearly the Lorenz inferiority of the new situation compared with the old. The Gini coefficient rises and the share of the poorest 40% falls.

Those concerned with relative inequality would give positive
weight to the growth in income but negative weight to the
rising relative inequality. Thus the judgments rendered by
the various welfare economic approaches are in disagreement.
The observed discrepancy is not entirely undesirable. It is
quite plausible that some observers may wish to regard the
rising gap between the rich and poor unfavorably, not because the poor have lower incomes, but rather because the
growing income differential might make the poor *feel* worse
off. Some might even wish to allow envy of the rich by the
poor to more than offset the gain in utility of the income
recipients themselves. This is a defensible position–that income growth concentrated exclusively in the hands of the
rich might be interpreted as a situation socially inferior to
one in which the rich have less and the poor the same amount–
but certainly it is an extreme one, based on the primacy of
relative income considerations. In the case of modern sector
enrichment growth, therefore, the differing judgments
according to the welfare functions (4), (5), (7), and (12)
reflect a true difference of opinion.

This is not so in the case of modern sector enlargement
growth, to which we now turn.

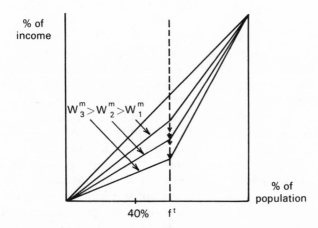

Figure 3.2. Downward vertical shift of the Lorenz curve kink point in
the modern sector enrichment growth model.

Modern sector enlargement growth

As observed earlier, many leading writers in the field hold that countries develop principally by absorbing an increasing share of their labor forces into an ever-enlarging modern sector. As a stylized version of such development, in the modern sector enlargement growth model, incomes in both the modern and the traditional sectors remain the same but the modern sector gets bigger. The numerical example of Chapter 2 illustrated this kind of growth.

In the case of modern sector enlargement growth, we may derive the following results:

Proposition 3. In modern sector enlargement growth: (a) Absolute incomes rise and absolute poverty is reduced; (b) the Rawlsian criterion shows no change; (c) Lorenz curves always cross, so that relative inequality effects are ambiguous; and (d) relative inequality indexes first increase and subsequently decline.

Proofs. (*a*) The proofs of the absolute income and absolute poverty effects are immediate. Clearly, absolute incomes are higher, and because there are fewer poor, poverty is alleviated.

(*b*) In modern sector enlargement growth, there are fewer poor, but those who remain poor continue to be just as poor as before. Until poverty is totally eliminated, the Rawlsian criterion is completely insensitive to modern sector enlargement growth.

(*c*) The crossing of Lorenz curves is demonstrated in Figure 3.3. The explanation is: (i) those among the poor who are left behind owing to the incapacity of the modern sector to absorb everyone have the same incomes, but these incomes are now a smaller fraction of a larger total, so that the new Lorenz curve lies below the old Lorenz curve at the lower end of the income distribution; (ii) each person in the modern sector receives the same absolute income as before, but the share going to the richest $f_1{}^m$ % is now smaller, and hence the new Lorenz curve lies above the old one at the upper end of the income distribution; and (iii) therefore, the two curves necessarily cross somewhere in the middle. Of course, when Lorenz curves cross, welfare judgments based on relative inequality indexes are ambiguous.

(*d*) We shall now demonstrate the inevitability of an initial

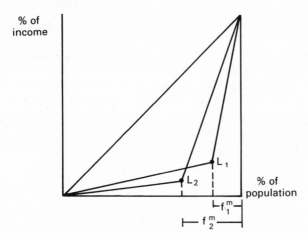

Figure 3.3. The crossing of Lorenz curves in the modern sector enlargement growth model.

increase in relative inequality in the early stages of development, followed by a subsequent decline for the income share of the poorest 40% (S) and the Gini coefficient (G).

Considering S first, it is evident that in the early stages of modern sector enlargement growth, the poorest 40% receive the same absolute amount from a larger whole, and therefore their share falls. However, in the later stages (i.e., for $f^t <$ 40%), they receive all of the income growth, and hence their share rises. This result may be generalized as follows: If our measure of inequality is the share of income accruing to the poorest X%, that share falls continuously in modern sector enlargement growth until the modern sector has grown to include $(1 - X)$% of the population.

For the Gini coefficient, the proof is given in the notes.[5]

Though both measures exhibit the inverted-U pattern in modern sector enlargement growth, the turning points do not coincide. There are three phases: (1) Initially, both G and S show rising relative inequality; (2) then G turns down while S continues to fall; (3) finally S rises while G continues to fall. To indicate the importance of this discrepancy for just these two measures, it is thought that in real terms the modern sector–traditional sector wage gap is something like 3:1.

This implies that phase 2 (falling inequality by G and rising inequality by S) ranges from 37% to 60% of the population in the traditional sector. This range is substantial and may well include many LDCs.

Nearly a quarter century ago, Kuznets (1955) argued that this pattern, known as the inverted U, characterized the historical experiences of a number of then-developed economies. Kuznets's explanation was that the inverted-U pattern was caused by the transfer of workers from the rural sector, where incomes were relatively equally distributed at low levels, to the urban sector, where there was greater income dispersion, owing to the presence of a skilled professional class at the top and poor recent migrants at the bottom. In terms of the development typologies just presented, Kuznets's model is basically one of modern sector enlargement growth with within-sector inequality.

In a further analysis that is not published here but is available upon request, I extend the dualistic development models of this chapter to allow for within-sector inequality. There I repeat a proof I first developed in 1975: that the inverted-U pattern *always* arises in modern sector enlargement growth, even if the *traditional sector has a more unequal distribution of income within it.* This result has been observed by previous researchers, although not for the Gini coefficient.[6]   Where I differ from the others is over the welfare interpretation of these patterns.

Proposition 4. The various welfare approaches give different evaluations of the desirability of modern sector enlargement growth: (a) The absolute income and absolute poverty approaches rate this type of growth as an unambiguous welfare improvement; (b) Rawlsians would be indifferent to this type of growth; (c) the relative inequality approach evaluates this type of growth ambiguously in the early stages but regards it as a good thing once the turning point is reached; and (d) the general welfare approach (12) considers modern sector enlargement growth as an unambiguous improvement regardless of the stage of development.

The proofs of (a–c) are immediate, given the respective welfare functions and the patterns established in proposition 3. Point (d) follows from (12) and conditions (A), (C), (F), and (G). The lack of correspondence between points (c) and (d) merits further attention.

Kuznets, Swamy, Robinson, and many others have interpreted the inverted-U pattern as signifying that in a true economic sense the distribution of income must get worse before it gets better. It would seem at first that a falling share going to the poor (S) or a rising Gini coefficient (G) *should* receive negative weight in a social welfare judgment, possibly negative enough to outweigh the rising level of income. But why? There are at least two possible answers.

Implicitly, we may have in mind that a falling S or rising G implies that the poor are getting *absolutely* poorer while the rich are getting absolutely richer, and many of us would regard this situation as a bad thing indeed. The problem with this notion is that it confuses cause and effect; that is to say, absolute immiserization of the poor would definitely imply falling S and rising G, but as we have just seen, G rises and S falls in the early stages of modern sector enlargement growth without the poor becoming worse off in absolute terms.

Ruling out the necessity of absolute immiserization of the poor as a reason for reacting adversely to a falling S or rising G in modern sector enlargement growth, we may instead have in mind *relative* income comparisons–the idea that a growing income differential between rich and poor reduces poor people's utilities. Yet in the early stages of modern sector enlargement growth, despite the rising Gini coefficient and the falling share of the poorest 40%, the income differential between rich and poor is not changing. Hence:

Proposition 5. For modern sector enlargement growth, the conventional relative inequality measures do not "correctly" measure relative inequality, if the "correct" definition of relative inequality in dualistic development is the intersectoral income difference or ratio (or a monotonic transformation thereof). In the early stages of modern sector enlargement growth, we may be misled into thinking that relative inequality is worsening when in fact the intersectoral income differential is not changing. This same point holds in reverse for relative inequality improvements in the later stages of modern sector enlargement growth. This is because condition (F) is violated.

Proposition 5 implies that rising relative inequality as measured by conventional indexes may be a perfectly natural, and even highly desirable, outcome for this type of development. Put differently, the falling share of the lowest 40% and rising Gini coefficient that arise in this case are *statistical artifacts without social welfare content.* For this type of growth, the specification of social welfare functions like (4) conflicts with our ideas of social well-being as given by (12). This conflict is particularly acute for persons who wish to give heavy weight to relative income considerations. If relative inequality–averse persons compare Gini coefficients or income shares of the poorest 40% at two points when modern sector enlargement growth is taking place, they will be led to social welfare judgments that they themselves would not wish to make. Unfortunately, functions like (4) based on *G* or *S* are being used with increasing frequency in current empirical studies of economic development. The use of functions like (12), based on the enlargement and enrichment components of various sectors' growth experiences, would avoid such difficulties.

Empirical significance

The preceding theoretical analysis has shown that ·nder certain circumstances the absolute poverty and relative inequality approaches may give very different results concerning the distributional effects of growth in the dual economy. In light of these differences, the choice between the two types of measures should be based on the type of welfare judgments the examiner wishes to make. The empirical significance of the choice may be illustrated with reference to two actual cases of particular interest, India and Brazil (see Chapter 6 for further details).

The Brazilian economy achieved a growth in per capita income of 32% during the 1960s, a substantial accomplishment by the standards of less-developed countries. Fishlow (1972), Langoni (1972), and others, in examining the distributional question of who received the benefits of this growth, found greater relative income inequality; from this, they conclude that the poor benefited very little, if at all. Yet when the distributional question is reexamined from an absolute poverty perspective, by looking at the number of very poor and the levels of income they receive, it is found that the average real incomes among families defined as poor by Brazilian standards increased by as much as 60%, whereas the comparable figure for nonpoor families was about 25% (Fields, 1977). At the same time, the percentage of families below the poverty line fell somewhat. It would thus appear that by assigning heavy weight to changes in the usual indexes of relative income inequality, and interpreting these increases as offsets to the well-being brought about by growth, previous investigators may have inadvertently overlooked important tendencies toward the alleviation of poverty.

In the India case, the problem is just the opposite. Bardhan (1974b) reports that relative inequality in India (as measured by the Gini coefficient) exhibited a small but perceptible decline, which some might see as an improvement in income distribution. Yet, owing to the lack of growth of the Indian economy, the percentage of people living in absolute poverty increased in both the urban and the rural sectors.

These examples indicate that the choice of an evaluative criterion does make a very real qualitative difference. It comes down to a choice between welfare judgments that emphasize the alleviation of absolute poverty and those that focus on the narrowing of relative income inequality.

Personally, I am most concerned about the alleviation of economic misery among the very poorest, especially in low-income countries, and therefore give greatest weight to absolute poverty changes. Others with different value judgments, who may be more concerned than I with relative income comparisons or with the middle or upper end of the income distribution, may wish to rely more on one of the other approaches.

The inconsistency between the professed concerns of many researchers for the alleviation of absolute poverty and their reliance on relative inequality measures in empirical research is striking. It is to be hoped that this practice will be less prevalent in the future.

Conclusion

In summary, this chapter has considered [*we considered*] two broad classes of measures that merit serious attention for gauging the distributional effects of economic growth. Relative inequality indexes inherently deal with one person's (or family's) income position in relation to others', whereas absolute poverty measures provide information on that individual's income in relation to a fixed, absolute poverty standard. Thus they are more than just alternative classes of measures of the same thing. Rather, they pertain to fundamentally different phenomena that enter our social welfare judgments to varying degrees. The choice of measure should accord with the type of welfare judgment sought. This chapter has tried to clarify the ethical basis for that choice.

Inequality and development

Relative Inequality

This ~~chapter~~ *section* summarizes the available empirical evidence on the relationship between economic inequality and development. There are three major ~~sections~~ *points*. The first ~~looks at~~ the size distribution of income across countries at a point in time and relates countries' income inequality to their economic characteristics. The second ~~section examines inequality changes within LDCs and~~ *point* looks for relationships between changes in inequality and such economic factors as the stage of economic development and the rate of growth. The third section decomposes ~~LDC inequality,~~ *point* analyzing various statistical approaches for ascertaining the sources of inequality within a country at a single point in time and reviewing the major results and patterns emerging from empirical research.

Inequality at different stages of development: cross-sectional evidence

This section summarizes studies that look at size distribution of income across countries at more or less the same point in time. These studies share a common methodology, consisting basically of looking at a cross section of countries and (1) measuring the degree of inequality in each, (2) measuring other characteristics of each country (e.g., level of GNP, its rate of growth, importance of agriculture in total product, etc.), and (3) relating the level of inequality to that economy's characteristics, using correlation or regression analysis. Among the questions to be addressed are how relative inequality differs for countries at different stages of development, whether any particular relationship between inequality and level of development arises, if such a relationship is inevitable, and the extent to which inequality is correlated with other aspects of a country's economic situation. The answers to these questions are valuable in providing clues on how to reduce inequality and alleviate poverty in the course of economic development.

Cross-sectional studies of inequality and level of development

The pathbreaking work in this area is that of Kuznets (1955). Measuring inequality by the income shares of various quintiles, Kuznets compared India, Ceylon, Puerto Rico, the United Kingdom, and the United States and observed greater inequality in the developing countries. Some of his data are given in Table 4.1. Kuznets explains the difference between less-developed and developed countries this way:

> The former have no "middle" classes: there is a sharp contrast between the preponderant proportion of the population whose average income is well below the generally low countrywide average, and a small top group with a very large relative income excess. The developed countries, on the other hand, are characterized by a much more gradual rise from low to high income shares, with substantial groups receiving more than the high countrywide income average, and the top groups securing smaller shares than the comparable ordinal groups in underdeveloped countries. [1955:22]

Viewed from this perspective, the variations in inequality reflect real differences across countries in participation in the "advanced" or "modern" sectors of the economy.

A few years later, Kravis (1960) presented evidence on patterns of inequality in eleven countries.[1] Taking the United States as a standard for comparison, he found higher inequality than that of the United States in Italy, Puerto Rico, El Salvador, and Ceylon; comparable inequality to that of the United States in Great Britain, Japan, and Canada; and less inequality than in the United States in Denmark, the Netherlands, and Israel. Thus, like Kuznets, Kravis found that less-developed countries had relatively greater inequality than did more-developed countries.

At about that same time, Oshima (1962) suggested that inequality increases up to and through the semideveloped stage and declines once a country is fully developed. But this speculation was not tested, owing to data limitations.

The pattern of greater relative income inequality in less-developed countries than in the developed countries was

Table 4.1. *Relative inequality in various countries in about 1950*

| Country/date | Income share (%) | | Ratio |
	Poorest 60%	Richest 20%	Richest 20%/ poorest 60%
India (1949–50)	28	55	1.96
Ceylon (1950)	30	50	1.67
Puerto Rico (1948)	24	56	2.33
United States (1950)	34	44	1.29
United Kingdom (1947)	36	45	1.25

Source: Kuznets (1955:20–21).

confirmed for eighteen countries in a subsequent paper by Kuznets (1963) (see Table 4.2). His findings include:

1. The shares of the upper income groups are distinctly larger in the less-developed countries (LDCs) than in the more-developed countries (DCs).
2. Although the shares of the lowest-income groups in some LDCs are lower than in some DCs, the differences are much narrower than for the shares of the upper-income groups.
3. It follows from (1) and (2) that the shape of the income distribution curve is different in LDCs than in DCs.

These findings are depicted in Figure 4.1. Finding (1) is illustrated in the upper right corner, finding (2) in the lower left. At either end of the income distribution, the Lorenz curve for the typical LDC lies below that for the typical DC. On the likely assumption that the two curves do not intersect in the middle, it would follow that the Gini coefficient of inequality would be greater in LDCs than in DCs. The data show an average Gini coefficient of .44 for the LDCs covered by the data, .37 for the DCs (Kuznets, 1963:17).

On that evidence, Kuznets was led to the view that the *level* of economic development (as measured by gross national product per capita) is a major determinant of the extent of income inequality in a country. The specific nature of that dependence has come to be known as the *inverted-U hypothesis*, which states that relative income inequality rises during the early stages of development, reaches a peak, and then declines in the later stages. Much research effort has gone into attempts to confirm or refute the inverted-U pattern.

Table 4.2. Inequality in eighteen countries in the 1940s and 1950s

Country/date	Shares of ordinal groups							
	0%–20%	21%–40%	41%–60%	0%–60%	61%–80%	81%–90%	91%–95%	Richest 5%
India (1955/6)	—	—	14.8	33.5	19.7	13.6	9.6	23.6
Ceylon (1952/3)	5.1	9.3	13.3	27.7	18.4	13.3	9.6	31.0
Northern Rhodesia (1946)	—	—	—	—	—	—	—	45.3+
Southern Rhodesia (1946)	—	—	—	—	—	—	—	65.3
Kenya (1949)	—	—	—	—	—	—	—	50.9+
Mexico (1957)	4.4	6.9	9.9	21.2	17.4	14.7	9.7	37.0
Colombia (1953)	—	—	—	31.4	12.2	8.0	6.8	41.6
El Salvador (1946)	—	—	—	32.2	15.7	8.5	8.1	35.5
Guatemala (1947/8)	—	—	13.2	28.8	15.8	11.6	9.3	34.5
Barbados (1951/2)	3.6	9.3	14.2	27.1	21.3	17.4	11.9	22.3
Puerto Rico (1953)	5.6	9.8	14.9	30.3	19.9	16.9	9.5	23.4
Italy (1948)	6.1	10.5	14.6	31.2	20.4	14.4	10.0	24.1
Great Britain (1951/2)	5.4	11.3	16.6	33.3	22.2	14.3	9.3	20.9
West Germany (1950)	4.0	8.5	16.5	29.0	23.0	14.0	10.4	23.6
Netherlands (1950)	4.2	9.6	15.7	29.5	21.5	14.0	10.4	24.6
Denmark (1952)	3.4	10.3	15.8	29.5	23.5	16.3	10.6	20.1
Sweden (1948)	3.2	9.6	16.3	29.1	24.3	16.3	10.2	20.1
United States (1950)	4.8	11.0	16.2	32.0	22.3	15.4	9.9	20.4

Source: Kuznets (1963:13).

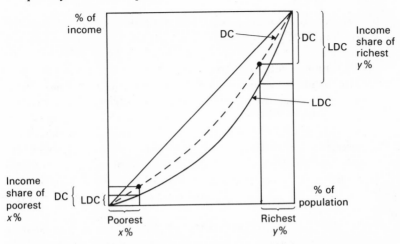

Figure 4.1. Patterns of relative inequality in developed countries (DC) and less-developed countries (LDC).

One line of research has regarded the hypothesis dynamically, testing it by measuring relative inequality at several points in the course of a given country's economic development. Kuznets himself assumed that LDCs had greater inequality in their earlier stages of development, because everyone was thought to be more or less the same, that is, equally poor. No data were available to test this speculation. Even today, for only a handful of less-developed countries are there data on the distribution of income at several points in time. Economists have had to perform in-depth analyses of individual countries to test the inverted-U hypothesis. This motivation appears explicitly in a number of studies of growth and distribution, for instance, in the work of Fei, Ranis, and Kuo (1978:17) on Taiwan. They write:

> The key question that is raised again and again is whether or not the beginnings of rapid growth in the developing economy must necessarily be associated with a worsening distribution of income [meaning here increasing relative inequality, not absolute immiserization] ... The careful examination of even one successful counter-example to any such "historical necessity" should prove useful in its own right. But beyond that, a fuller understanding of some of the underlying causal relationships ... will hopefully provide us with some policy relevant conclusions concerning the precise conditions under which "things do not have to get worse before they can get better."

Evidence on changing relative inequality in the course of economic development is now available for a small number of countries. Consideration of those findings is deferred until the following section of this chapter.

The other way of viewing the inverted-U hypothesis is as a cross-sectional statement, whereby countries at intermediate stages of development are thought to have more unequal distributions of income than do richer or poorer countries. Such a pattern is generally supported by Kuznets' studies from the 1950s and 1960s. More recently, several new and more comprehensive data sets have been .compiled, which give further credence to the inverted-U pattern. Some of the major studies are reviewed here.

In the late 1960s and early 1970s, Adelman and Morris gathered new data for forty-three developing countries. Their 1973 book presented considerable evidence on the correlates of relative income inequality.[2] By means of analysis of variance, they found six factors to be important in explaining variations in relative income inequality, one of which was the level of economic development.[3] We will return to the correlates of inequality later in this section.

A short while later, Paukert (1973) refined Adelman and Morris's estimates. He discarded information that he thought to be particularly unreliable, added some new countries where good data had recently become available, and presented summary information on the size distribution of income in fifty-six countries. The Gini coefficients and gross domestic product per capita are presented in Table 4.3. For each of several alternative relative inequality measures,[4] Paukert found that inequality begins at a comparatively low level, reaches a peak in countries with per capita incomes of $301–$500, and then diminishes at higher incomes. Thus the inverted-U pattern is reconfirmed.

Most recently, new intercountry evidence has been reported by Chenery and Syrquin (1975) and Ahluwalia (1974 and 1976a and b) at the World Bank, and by Lydall (1977) for the International Labour Office. Using updated data compiled by Jain (1975) for sixty-two countries, these authors also found the inverted-U pattern in the cross-sectional studies.[5] Other variables related to inequality are discussed

Table 4.3. *Gini coefficient of inequality and gross domestic product per capita*

Country and level of GDP per head	Gini ratio	GDP per head in 1965 (U.S. $)
Under $100		
Chad (1958)	.35	68
Dahomey (1959)	.42	73
Niger (1960)	.34	81
Nigeria (1959)	.51	74
Sudan (1969)	.40	97
Tanzania (1964)	.54	61
Burma (1958)	.35	64
India (1956-7)	.33	95
Madagascar (1960)	.53	92
Group average	.419	78.3
$101-$200		
Morocco (1965)	.50	180
Senegal (1960)	.56	192
Sierra Leone (1968)	.56	142
Tunisia (1871)	.53	187
Bolivia (1968)	.53	132
Ceylon (Sri Lanka) (1963)	.44	140
Pakistan (1963-4)	.37	101
South Korea (1966)	.26	107
Group average	.468	147.6
$201-$300		
Malaya (1957-8)	.36	278
Fiji (1968)	.46	295
Ivory Coast (1959)	.43	213
Zambia (1959)	.48	207
Brazil (1960)	.54	207
Ecuador (1968)	.38	202
El Salvador (1965)	.53	249
Peru (1961)	.61	237
Iraq (1956)	.60	285
Philippines (1961)	.48	240
Colombia (1964)	.62	275
Group average	.499	244.4
$301-$500		
Gabon (1960)	.64	368
Costa Rica (1969)	.50	360
Jamaica (1958)	.56	465
Surinam (1962)	.30	424
Lebanon (1955-60)	.55	440

Table 4.3. (*cont.*)

Country and level of GDP per head	Gini ratio	GDP per head in 1965 (U.S. $)
Barbados (1951-2)	.45	368
Chile (1958)	.44	486
Mexico (1963)	.53	441
Panama (1969)	.48	490
Group average	.494	426.9
$501-$1,000		
Republic of South Africa (1965)	.58	521
Argentina (1961)	.42	782
Trinidad and Tobago (1957-8)	.44	704
Venezuela (1962)	.42	904
Greece (1957)	.38	591
Japan (1962)	.39	838
Group average	.438	723.3
$1,001-$2,000		
Israel (1957)	.30	1,243
United Kingdom (1964)	.38	1,590
Netherlands (1962)	.42	1,400
Federal Republic of Germany (1964)	.45	1,667
France (1962)	.50	1,732
Finland (1962)	.46	1,568
Italy (1948)	.40	1,011
Puerto Rico (1963)	.44	1,101
Norway (1963)	.35	1,717
Australia (1966-7)	.30	1,823
Group average	.401	1,485.2
$2,001 and above		
Denmark (1963)	.37	2,078
Sweden (1963)	.39	2,406
United States (1969)	.34	3,233
Group average	.365	2,572.3

Source: Paukert (1973:tab. 6).

later in this chapter in the section on economic structure and inequality.

In summary, the cross-section data on income inequality at different stages of development reveal two patterns: higher inequality on the average in the less-developed countries than in the developed countries; and within the less-developed countries, lower average inequality in the very poorest countries than in the less poor ones. Let us now explore further the relationship between income inequality in a country and the level of its economic development.

On the inevitability of the inverted U

The evidence on relative inequality patterns presented in the last section was disturbing to many development economists. The prevailing view as recently as 1975 was that income distribution must get worse before it gets better. Considerable pessimism was expressed over the supposed trade-off between growth and income equality. Some were even skeptical about the welfare implications of the development process itself.[6]

There are two immediate problems with this inference. One is that the conclusion is based on cross-section data rather than on analysis of historical trends over time. For this reason, Adelman and Morris, for example, in the introduction to their book, use words like "preliminary," "exploratory," and "tentative" to describe their efforts. But having voiced these words of caution, they and others like them proceed to conclusions about the process of economic development by viewing countries at different stages of development. Making inferences from cross-section data about dynamic growth processes is a well-established practice pioneered at Harvard and practiced by many over the last two decades.[7] The maintained assumption of such analyses is that currently developing countries will follow much the same patterns in their development experiences as are found in the cross section. This assumption requires a leap of faith that many, myself included, are hesitant to make.

A second problem with the inverted U is that we are dealing with averages among *groups* of countries and not, for the most part, with the information on individual countries themselves. Table 4.3 and Figure 4.2 present Paukert's data. In Figure 4.2, the individual data are indicated by asterisks and averages for each income class by large dots. Even casual inspection suggests much more variation in relative inequality *within* countries grouped by gross domestic product per capita than *between* them. That is, level of income is only an imprecise predictor of income inequality in a country.

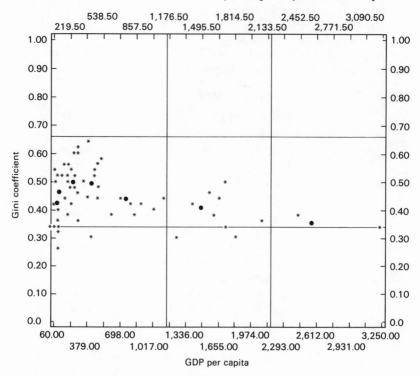

Figure 4.2. Gini coefficient and gross domestic product per capita, 56 countries. Computed from data in Paukert (1973: 114–15).

Before regarding the inverted-U pattern as inevitable, even in the cross section, we need to know how well the inverted U fits the data. To explore this question, let us work directly with the individual country data rather than with the grouped data. By means of multiple regression analysis, we may determine (1) whether an inverted U is the appropriate characterization of the relationship between inequality and level of income, and (2) whether any particular pattern of inequality change over time is inevitable. On both accounts, the evidence suggests that income distribution need *not* get worse before it gets better.

In the individual country data collected by Paukert, we may define six dummy variables denoting income class, the first for gross domestic product (GDP) per capita between

$101 and $200, the second for GDP per capita between $201 and $300, and so on. (The reason for defining only six dummy variables when there are seven categories is to avoid perfect multicollinearity in the regression equation.) For each, let us assign the value one if the country's GDP places it in that category, and zero otherwise. If we then run a multiple regression with the Gini coefficient of inequality as the dependent variable and these six dummies as independent variables, the coefficients on the dummy variables may be interpreted as the average effect on the Gini coefficient of being in that income group rather than in the $0-$100 per capita income group. If the inverted-U hypothesis is correct, these coefficients will be positive and increasing up to some point, and declining thereafter.

The results of the regression based on the figures for fifty-six countries are

$$\text{Gini} = .418 + \underset{(.042)}{.050Y_{\$101-200}} + \underset{(.039)}{.080Y_{\$201-300}}$$
$$+ \underset{(.040)}{.076Y_{\$301-500}} + \underset{(.045)}{.019Y_{\$501-1,000}}$$
$$- \underset{(.039)}{.019Y_{\$1,000-2,000}}$$
$$- \underset{(.057)}{.052Y_{\$2,001+}}, \quad R^2 = .22$$

where Y denotes GDP per capita (standard errors in parentheses). The pattern of regression coefficients is consistent with the pattern predicted by the inverted-U hypothesis, that is, rising significantly to a peak between $200 and $500 and then falling. Cline (1975) reports substantially similar results using Adelman and Morris's data, rather than Paukert's, and using instead as the measure of inequality (I) the ratio of the income share of the top quintile to the share of the bottom quintile. Using a parabolic form,[8] Cline found:

$$I = 7.23 + \underset{(.0096)}{.0258\text{GNP}} - \underset{(.000005)}{.000014\text{GNP}^2}, \quad R^2 = .12$$

The terms producing the inverted U have the expected signs and both are statistically significant. Thus a statistically significant increase in inequality at the early stages of development is found. Initially increasing inequality is also found by

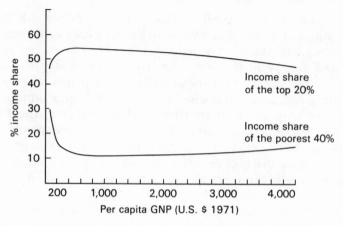

Figure 4.3. Predicted income shares in a cross section of countries. *Source*: Ahluwalia (1974:15).

Lydall (1977) and by Ahluwalia, (1974 and 1976a and b), using a larger sample of countries and using as inequality measures the income shares of the lowest 40% and top 20% and the Gini coefficient. An inverted U (albeit skewed) is found by both authors. Ahluwalia's predicted values are shown in Figure 4.3.

These empirical findings need to be evaluated carefully. The evidence *does* show the highest relative inequality in the group of lower-middle-income countries than elsewhere. However, this pattern is far from inevitable. Concerning the inevitability issue (the view that income distribution *must* get worse before it gets better), we should note how little of the variance in relative inequality is explained by income level. At most one-fourth of the intercountry variation in inequality is explained by income level. This means, very simply, that the inverted U *is* avoidable.

In the perspective of the overall economic development literature, it should not be too surprising to find that income level fails to provide a satisfactory explanation for the degree of inequality in a country. These results are consistent with the writings of many leading development economists (e.g., Fei and Ranis, 1964; Kuznets, 1966; and Adelman and Morris, 1973) who have been saying that the income distribution is determined as much or more by the *type* of economic development and the policies followed in a given country as by the *level* of development. One can hope, therefore, that appropriate public policy can be designed so as to avoid a deterioration in the relative distribution of income and to effect an improvement in the economic status of the poor.

Further empirical research has shown that intercountry variations in inequality are systematically related to structural differences in the countries' economies. Evidence from the most important empirical studies is reviewed here.

Economic structure and inequality

To understand better the observed cross-sectional pattern, a number of authors have tried to relate the income distribution observed in a country to that country's economic characteristics. Four particularly noteworthy studies are reviewed in this section.

Adelman and Morris (1973). Perhaps the best-known work in this area is that of Adelman and Morris (1973), based on cross-sectional observations for forty-three less-developed countries. To measure income inequality, they used three alternative figures: the income share of the lowest 60%, the income share of the middle quintile, and the income share of the richest 5%. Potential explanatory variables included economic, sociocultural, and political influences:

Economic influences: extent of factor endowments, sectoral productivity in agriculture, sectoral productivity in industry, allocation of resources between sectors, a population variable, economy-wide resource productivity, extent of income redistribution through taxation, and a measure of country size and orientation of development strategy

Sociocultural influences: urbanization, literacy, importance of the indigenous middle class, social mobility, and cultural and ethnic homogeneity

Political influences: importance of participant political institutions, aspects of colonial experience, and key characteristics of political leadership

The statistical methodology used was an analysis-of-variance technique akin to stepwise multiple regression. The specific procedure followed–Automatic Interaction Detection–allows for nonlinear effects of the various explanatory variables, but it does so on purely statistical rather than economic grounds.

They report six variables to be important in determining the distribution of income in a country. In order of decreasing influence, they are

1. "Rate of Improvement in Human Resources," as measured by school enrollment rate
2. "Direct Government Economic Activity," defined as high for mixed economies with large government role and low for predominantly private enterprise systems
3. "Socioeconomic Dualism," which may be classified according to level of technology, type of economic organization, or life-style
4. "Potential for Economic Development," taken as a discriminant score from earlier work in evaluating development potential
5. "Per Capita GNP," apparently entered linearly
6. "Strength of Labor Movement," which is high when the labor movement is well established, active, and free of government control

Interestingly, no significant relationship is found between relative income inequality and short-term economic growth rates, short-term economic improvements in tax and financial institutions, or short-term increases in agricultural or industrial productivity. The interested reader is referred to their book for the proxy variables used and their specific definitions.

What does it mean for "rate of improvement in human resources" or "direct government economic activity" to be related to inequality in an important way? Adelman and Morris's criterion of importance is that the variable in question explain more of the variance in income distribution than any other candidate variable, or at least contribute significant additional explanatory power. But what is the direction of the contribution? Which variables contribute to equality and which to inequality? It is not obvious a priori what the answer should be. In fact, an examination of Adelman and Morris's figures 1 and 2 shows that "dualism," "development potential," and "natural resources" are *positively* related to inequality and that "GNP," "human resources," "government economic activity" and "middle class" are *negatively* related to inequality.

The Adelman–Morris exercise has been subjected to a great deal of criticism, including doubts about the quality of the underlying data, discomfort over the lack of a well-defined theoretical framework, and skepticism about the appropriateness of the statistical methodology employed.[9] Were we to explore these criticisms, we would drift far away from the thrust of this section. I will just record my concurrence with many of these criticisms and my hesitancy in accepting Adelman and Morris's conclusions on the importance of the six factors listed and the unimportance of others not in that list.

Let us now turn to other studies of the determinants of inequality.

Chiswick (1971). A second study of causes of relative inequality, conducted contemporaneously with the work of Adelman and Morris but less well known, is that of Chiswick (1971). Drawing on the human capital literature, he postulates a model in which differences in the earnings of individuals are accounted for solely by differences in their training. Chiswick deduces that variability in earned income should be functionally related (positively) to four factors:[10]

1. The inequality of investment in human capital
2. The average level of investment in human capital
3. The average level of the rate of return to human capital investment
4. The inequality in the rate of return to human capital investment

Therefore, in order to understand the impact of economic development on income inequality, we should see how each of these variables is influenced by growth.

Chiswick hypothesizes that human capital level should be positively related to inequality, all other things being equal. The level of training generally increases with growth. We would therefore expect a positive relationship between level of economic development and amount of inequality. Empirically, the gross relationship between per capita income and inequality is not positive but negative. But Chiswick's hypothesis is not necessarily refuted, because it is ceteris paribus, not mutatis mutandis. Turning to inequality in training, it is plausible that this would decrease with level of development. Chiswick writes: "If . . . the more advanced nations have a smaller inequality of wealth, more effective minimum schooling laws, and larger schooling subsidies for lower grades or for youths from poor families, we would expect their inequality of schooling to be lower than in less developed areas" (p. 26). Another factor is the lack of school spaces in poor countries, which leads to wide disparities in schooling attainments. Thus the effect of development, acting through inequality in training, would be to decrease earnings inequality. In regard to rates of return, the effect of the level of development on the average is unclear, but inequality in rates of return should be greater in less-developed countries, one reason being the lack of development of the capital market. From this point of view as well, then, development would tend to lessen the dispersion of earned income.

These hypotheses were subjected to empirical testing in a cross section of nine countries, four of which are less developed. Unfortunately, there is a scarcity of data to test the model, and what data there are (from Lydall, 1968) prove inconclusive. Chiswick relates inequality to three variables.[11] The variable measuring *inequality of educational attainments* is statistically significantly related (with the correct sign) to earnings inequality in two out of three cases. The variables for *average per capita GNP* and *rate of growth of GNP* prove to be insignificant, with one exception. Thus the hypotheses derived from the human capital model of earnings inequality receive only limited empirical support. Whether this weakness is owing to limitations of the data or to difficulties with Chiswick's formulation is a question awaiting additional examination.

Ahluwalia (1974 and 1976a and b). More recent work was done at the World Bank by Ahluwalia. His information is cross-country data from sixty-two countries. As alternative measures of relative income inequality, he uses the percentage income shares of the top 20%, middle 40%, lowest 40%, and lowest 60%. His multiple regressions produce the following results:

1. As we have seen, a statistically significant relationship arises between these income shares and the logarithm of per capita GNP, entered linearly and quadratically. The form of

the relationship supports the inverted-U pattern. The relationship between inequality and GNP is skewed asymmetrically to the right.

2. There does not appear to be an independent short-term relationship between the level of inequality and the rate of growth of GNP.

3. Other explanatory variables are found to be associated with income inequality. These are the rate of expansion of education, the rate of decline of demographic pressures, and changing economic structure. More specifically, improvement in literacy, reduced rate of growth of population, reduced share of agriculture in national product, and shifting of population to the urban sector are found to reduce relative income inequality in the cross section. Also, socialist countries have less inequality than nonsocialist ones.

The relationships on the correlates of inequality merit some discussion. Ahluwalia offers interesting speculations on the economic mechanisms underlying the observed patterns. *Education,* he says, will create a more skilled labor force. This, in turn, "will produce a shift from low paid, unskilled employment to high paid, skilled employment. This shift, it is argued, produces higher labour incomes, a reduction in skill differentials, and an increase in the share of wages in total output" (1976b:322). Hence inequality will diminish as education expands. Regarding the positive relationship between *population growth* and inequality, Ahluwalia suggests two possibilities:

Perhaps the most important link between population growth and income inequality is provided by the fact that different income groups grow at different rates, with the lower income groups typically experiencing a faster natural rate of increase in population . . . A second link between population growth and inequality is suggested by the fact that higher growth rates of population imply greater pressure of labour supply on other productive factors with a consequent deterioration in the share of labour in total output. [1976b:326-7]

Urbanization is also found to be associated with lesser inequality. Ahluwalia's interpretation is this:

Given the dualistic nature of the development process, a higher rate of urbanization, other things being the same, reflects a wider access to productive employment opportunities in the expanding nontradi-

tional sector and a correspondingly lower pressure of population in
the rural areas. Both forces can be expected to operate in favour of
the lower income groups. [1976*b*:320]

In regard to the *share of agriculture* in total production, the
statistical results indicate greater inequality in countries
where agriculture's share is lower. Ahluwalia suggests the
possibility that "as the relative size of agricultural activity
diminishes, compared to nonagricultural activity, there is a
shift towards greater concentration of income and wealth
because the nonagricultural sector typically promotes larger
size production units for both institutional and technological
reasons" (1976*b*:321). Another possibility that I would offer has to do with modern sector enlargement, the type of
growth described in Chapter 3, in which modern industrial
sectors expand to absorb greater percentages of the population while backward sectors, including agriculture, diminish
in importance. This type of growth is inherently uneven.
The income shares of the highest income groups increase,
because there are now more high-income people, whereas
the income shares of those left behind are correspondingly
reduced. When inequality is measured by income shares of
particular percentile groups–Ahluwalia's method-*ex post*
inequality is greater. Finally, *socialist countries* have lower
inequality ceteris paribus. "This is precisely what one would
expect, given the absence of the disequalising effect of
income from property (i.e. land and capital), which is typically
highly concentrated" (1976*b*:327).

Subject to the limitations of the underlying data, which
Ahluwalia is forthright in discussing, the research is thought-
fully done and offers a reasonable set of stylized facts about
the patterns of relative income inequality and their correlates
in the cross section. Ahluwalia also devotes considerable
attention to understanding the economic mechanisms underlying the observed patterns. The interested reader would do
well to study his papers carefully.

Chenery and Syrquin (1975). While Ahluwalia was doing
his research on the relationship between income distribution
and level of development, related work was undertaken as
part of a larger effort by Chenery and Syrquin (1975), also

at the World Bank. They conceive of development as "a multidimensional transition from one relatively constant structure to another." Their overall design was to explore the correlations between income level and each of ten dimensions of structural change. In regard to income distribution, the cross-sectional data reveal the inverted-U pattern, but only a small fraction of intercountry variation in inequality is explained by income level. To investigate the unexplained residual, they then introduce "proxy variables . . . for several of the factors that are thought to have some effect on income distribution: *education* (measured by school enrollment), *dualism* (measured crudely by the share of primary exports), and the *extent of the agricultural sector* (measured by the share of primary production)" (p. 61). These variables are all found to have statistically significant effects; primary export share contributed positively to inequality, and school enrollment and primary production negatively. For the income share of the poorest 40%, 24% of the variance is explained by income level and these three proxy variables; for the income share of the highest 20%, the proportion of variance explained is 52%. These results are broadly similar to those reported in the other studies, although somewhat different explanatory variables are used.

A final word

In summary, the extent of relative inequality is known to be related to the level of per capita national income and to various structural measures. Specific conclusions are collected at the end of this chapter.

Relative inequality trends in less-developed countries

The evidence on historical trends in income distribution within a country over time is scattered and has not yet been synthesized for the twenty or so less-developed countries for which intertemporal data are available. Much of the research is as yet unpublished, and many more studies are now in progress. This section reviews the evidence on relative inequality changes within specific less-developed countries.

Review of major multicountry studies

Kuznets's study of nine now-developed countries. As with the cross-sectional data on inequality, the pathbreaking contribution on changes over time is that of Professor Kuznets. In his famous 1963 paper, Kuznets investigated how the structural changes associated with economic growth affect the size distribution of income and how the process of economic growth is in turn affected by the income distribution. His ultimate conclusion is a disappointing one:

> We cannot say that a somewhat less (or more) unequal size distribution might not have contributed to even faster growth. We know far too little of the interplay between relative income position, the average income and its rate of growth, and the responses of man as producer, consumer, saver, and investor to answer such questions seriously. [p. 69]

That assessment remains equally valid today.

Although Kuznets was unsuccessful in establishing a firm relationship between aggregate income growth and the distribution of that income, his work produced many interesting hypotheses of pieces of data. Of great value, for example, were his estimates of income distribution, going back to the mid-1880s, in nine now-developed countries. The highlights of his income-distribution estimates are shown in Table 4.4.

Kuznets's data show that for two countries (Prussia and Saxony in the late 1800s), the income share of those at the top of the income distribution had either risen or remained the same. However, in the other countries (United Kingdom, Germany, Netherlands, Denmark, Norway, Sweden, and the United States), the data show a steady *decline* in relative inequality, as measured by the income shares of the top 5% and lowest 60%. Interestingly, this is not the usual lesson drawn from Kuznets's research. He is widely thought to say that "income distribution must get worse before it gets better" (the inverted-U hypothesis discussed in the cross-sectional context in the first section of this chapter). And indeed he does say that. Writes Kuznets (1963:67): "It seems plausible to *assume* that in the process of growth, the earlier periods are characterized by a balance of counteracting forces that may have widened the inequality in the size distribution of income for a while" (emphasis added). Indeed, it *is* an

Table 4.4. *Long-term estimates of shares of ordinal groups in selected countries*

United Kingdom — Decline

		Bowley		Clark	Seers		Lydall		
Dates		1880	1913	1929	1938	1947	1938	1949	1957
Income before tax:									
Richest 5%		48	43	33	31	24	29	23.5	18
Richest 20%		58	59	51	52	46	50	47.5	41.5
Income after tax:									
Richest 5%					26	17	24	17	14
Richest 20%					48	39	46	42	38

Prussia — Rising inequality at first, possible decline later

	Procopovitch				Reich Statistical Office	
Dates	1854	1875	1896	1913	1913	1928
Richest 5%	21	26	27	30	31	26
Richest 20%		48	45	50	50	49
Poorest 60%		34		33	32	31

	Mueller				
Dates	1873–80	1881–90	1891–1900	1901–10	1911–13
Richest 5%	28	30	32	32	31

Table 4.4. (cont.)

Saxony — Changes in inequality over time: Slight increase at first, then decline

	Procopovich			Reich Statistical Office		Mueller		United Nations		Wochenbericht	
Dates	1880	1896	1912	1913	1928	1928	1936	1936	1950	1955	1959
Richest 5%	34	36	33	33	28	20	23	28	24	18	18
Richest 20%	56	57	55	54	50			53	48	43	43
Poorest 60%	27	26.5	27	28	31			26.5	29	34	34

Germany–West Germany — Changes in inequality over time: Decline

Reich Statistical Office

	1913	1928	1928 (adj.)
Dates	1913	1928	
Richest 5%	31	27	21
Richest 20%	50	49	45
Poorest 60%	32	31	34

Netherlands — Changes in inequality over time: Decline

	1938	1949	1954
Dates	1938	1949	1954
Richest 5%	19	17	13
Richest 20%	49	45.5	38.5
Poorest 60%	31	34	40

Denmark — Decline

Zeuthen I

Dates	1870	1903	1925
Richest 5%	36.5	28	26
Richest 10%	50	38	36
Richest 20%			
Poorest 60%			

Zeuthen II

Dates	1903	1925
Richest 5%	30	26
Richest 10%	39	37
Richest 20%	55	53
Poorest 60%	31	25

Bjerke

Dates	1939	1949	1955
Richest 5%	24.5	19	17.5
Richest 10%	35	29.5	27.4
Richest 20%	51	45	44
Poorest 60%	27	32	32

Norway — Decline

Dates	1907	1938	1948
Richest 5%, country districts	27	20	14
Richest 5%, cities	28–32	22	19

Sweden — Decline

Bentzel

Dates	1930	1935	1945
Earned income before tax			
Richest 5%	30	28	24
Richest 20%	59	58	52
Poorest 60%	19	19	23

United Nations

Dates	1935	1945	1948	1948	1954
Total income before tax					
Richest 5%	28	23.5	20	20	17
Richest 20%	56	51	47	45	43
Poorest 60%	23	26	29	32	34

Table 4.4. (cont.)

82

Country	Changes in inequality over time		Successive dates and entries

United States — Decline

Total income after tax

Richest 5%	25.5	21	17
Richest 20%	54	48	43
Poorest 60%	23	28	32

Kuznets

Dates	1913–19	1919–28	1929–38	1939–43	1944–8
Income before tax					
Richest 1%	14	14	13	11	9
Richest 5%	24[a]	25	25	21	17
Income after federal tax					
Richest 1%	13	13	12	9	6
Richest 5%	22[a]	24	24	18	14

Department of Commerce

Dates	1929	1935–6	1941	1944–7	1950–4	1955–9
Income before tax						
Richest 5%	30	26.5	24	21	21	20
Richest 20%	54	52	49	46	45	45
Poorest 60%	26	27	29	32	33	32

Income after federal tax				
Richest 5%	29.5	21.5	18	18
Richest 20%	54	47	43	44
Poorest 60%	26.5	30	34	34

[a]1917–19.
Source: Kuznets (1963:tab. 6).

assumption, at least as far as I can tell from a careful reading
of Kuznets's 1963 paper and his 1955 work. Yet these two
papers are among the best known in the income-distribution
field and are widely cited as providing empirical support for
the inverted-U hypothesis.

   Kuznets's writings naturally stimulated a great deal of
interest among development economists who were concerned
that along with economic growth might come rising inequality
as a necessary evil. Recognizing that Kuznets's work was
limited to currently developed countries, researchers asked
about the facts of the matter in the countries that were still
less developed. Several such studies have appeared in the
1970s. We now consider the evidence from the most important of the multicountry studies.

Weisskoff's study of Puerto Rico, Argentina, and Mexico. The
first multicountry historical study of the patterns of income-
distribution change in less-developed countries was the paper
by Weisskoff (1970) on Puerto Rico, Argentina, and Mexico.
This paper offers a brief discussion of the traditional measures
of relative income inequality, including the Gini coefficient,
Kuznets ratio, coefficient of variation, variance of the logarithms of income, the standard ordinal shares. After reviewing the strengths and weaknesses of these measures, Weisskoff
examines the empirical evidence and concludes: "In each of
the three developing countries, we noted that equality of
income declined as the level of income rose over time"
(p. 317). (Note that it is equality which is said to decline, not
inequality. Weisskoff's conclusion has been echoed by others. For instance, Cline (1975:377) writes: "These studies
show . . . an increase in concentration in Puerto Rico from
1953 to 1963, and in Argentina from 1953 to 1961; and in
Mexico, a shift of income away from both the bottom 50%
and the top 5% towards the upper middle class, from 1950
to 1963." Weisskoff's paper concludes with some speculations on the causes for the alleged increases in inequality.
   Weisskoff's data are reproduced in Table 4.5.[12] It is
interesting to note, in contrast to Weisskoff's interpretation
of his own numbers, that *the numerical results are in fact
quite mixed.* In each country, at least one of the relative

Table 4.5. *Measures of income growth and inequality in Puerto Rico, Argentina, and Mexico*

Country/date	Gini ratio	Coefficient of variation	Standard deviation of logs	Income share of richest 5% (%)	Income share of poorest 40% (%)
Puerto Rico(1953)	0.415 ↑	1.152 ↓	0.736 ↑	23.4 ↓	15.5 ↑
Puerto Rico(1963)	0.449	1.035	0.843	22.0	13.7
Argentina(1953)	0.412 ↑	1.612 ↑	0.626 ↑	27.2 ↑	18.1 ↑
Argentina(1959)	0.463 ↓ ↑	1.887 ↓ ↓	0.675 ↓ ↑	31.8 ↓ ↑	16.4 ↓ ↑
Argentina(1961)	0.434	1.605	0.653	29.4	17.4
Mexico(1950)	0.526 ↑	2.500 ↓	0.718 ↑	40.0 ↓	14.3 ↑
Mexico(1957)	0.551 ↓ ↑	1.652 ↓ ↓	0.879 ↑ ↑	37.0 ↓ ↓	11.3 ↑ ↑
Mexico(1963)	0.543	1.380	0.976	28.8	10.1

Note: Arrows indicate direction of change in inequality according to the indicated measure.
Source: Weisskoff (1970:tabs. 1, 2).

inequality measures shows an increase and at least one other one a decline. The discrepancy between the different inequality measures arises because in each of the three countries the Lorenz curves for the respective time periods cross. Before concluding that inequality rose or fell in a particular country, each reader should carefully examine the properties of the various inequality measures and compare the measures' implicit value judgments with the value judgments he would wish to make.[13] This counsel of caution contrasts with the lesson Weisskoff wishes us to draw.

Taken together, Kuznets's and Weisskoff's results painted a bleak picture. These findings, along with growing bodies of evidence from cross-sectional studies, led many observers in the early 1970s to the view that there may be a conflict between the rate of growth of income and equality in the distribution of that income. If so, this would be a harsh dilemma. Further investigation was in order, and it was soon forthcoming.

Ahluwalia's multicountry study. In an influential paper in an influential volume, Ahluwalia (1974) presented evidence

on changing income shares of the poorest 40% of the population in the economies of eighteen countries, all but a few of
which are less developed.   His study relies on the most
extensive compilation of data yet available on income distribution.[14] As reported by Cline (1975:377):

> Ahluwalia shows that there is no generalized deterioration in distributions
> over time. Of thirteen developing countries for which intertemporal
> data are available (mostly for the decade of the 1960s), six showed
> increasing concentration (India, Peru, Panama, Brazil, Philippines,
> Mexico); six registered decreasing concentration (Taiwan, Sri Lanka,
> Iran, Colombia, Costa Rica, El Salvador); and one showed constant
> concentration (Korea).

What emerges, then, from this multicountry evidence is that
*there is no systematic pattern relating changes in income
inequality to economic growth per se.*
      Another related question is whether there is a relationship
between changing relative inequality and the *rate* of development.   Ahluwalia offers data on growth and the lowest 40%,
shown in Figure 4.4.   Contrary to the prevailing way of
thinking on a supposed trade-off between rate of economic
growth and equality of income distribution, the data tell
another story.   Writes Ahluwalia (1974:13):

> The scatter suggests considerable diversity of country experience in
> terms of changes in relative equality. Several countries show a deteriora-
> tion in relative equality but there are others showing improvement . . .
> *there is no strong pattern relating changes in the distribution of income
> to the rate of growth of GNP.*   In both high-growth and low-growth
> countries there are some which have experienced improvements and
> others that have experienced deteriorations in relative equality. [Em-
> phasis added]

In short, Ahluwalia found no particular relationship between
changes in relative inequality and economic growth. Just as
cross-sectional data were found to disprove the suspicion that
inequality must inevitably increase in the early stages of
economic development before it subsequently declines (see
the first section of this chapter), so too is this notion disproven in the experiences of those less-developed countries
for which we have data over time.

Conclusion from multicountry studies.   The multicountry
data presented by Kuznets, Weisskoff, and Ahluwalia suggest

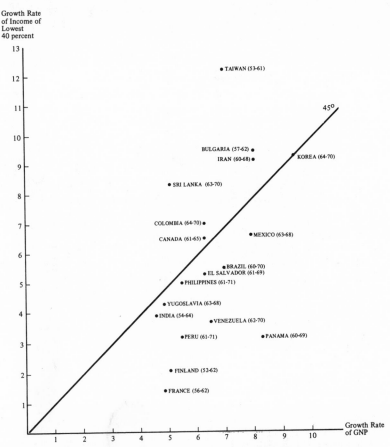

Figure 4.4. Growth and the lowest 40%. *Source*: Ahluwalia (1974:14).

that the supposed "harsh dilemma" of having to choose between rapid economic growth in the aggregate and equality in the distribution of income might be avoided. This result is supported by other studies of changing income distribution in individual countries. Several of these studies are summarized here.

Evidence from studies of individual countries

There are more than twenty less-developed countries for which data on relative inequality have been published for two or more points in time. Table 4.6 summarizes the

Table 4.6. *Economic growth and changing inequality in less-developed countries*

Country/date	Development characterization	GNP per capita (U.S. $ 1970)	Growth experience	Inequality change	Principal information sources
Argentina (1953–61)	Upper level of development, subsistence agriculture relatively unimportant, moderate growth, rising inequality overall, falling inequality during period of stabilization (1959–61)	$1,640	Problems with balance of payments and inflation; severe recession in 1959, recovery by 1961; real GDP growth of 3%–4% per year on the average	*Families* Gini coefficient: 1953 .413 1959 .463 1961 .435 Income share of richest 10%: 1953 37.0% 1959 42.3% 1961 39.1% Income share of poorest 10%: 1953 3.2% 1959 3.0% 1961 2.9% Inequality rose	ECLA (1969); Weiss-koff (1970)
Bangladesh (1963/4–73/4)	Extremely poor; very little growth, if any; rising inequality and poverty	$80	Moderate progress until the War of 1971, absolute immiserization since	*Households* Gini coefficient, rural: 1963/4 .33 1966/7 .31 1968/9 .27 1973/4 .38 Gini coefficient, urban:	Alamgir (1975 and forth-coming)

Brazil (1960–70)	$760	Middle level of development, moderate economic growth, rising inequality, emphasis on industrialization	Economic slump early in 1960s, stabilization between 1964 and 1967, rapid economic growth after 1967	*Individuals* Gini coefficient: 1963/4 .41 1966/7 .38 1968/9 .37 1973/4 .39 Rising inequality	Fishlow (1972); Langoni (1972 and 1975)
Costa Rica (1961–71)	$710	Upper-middle level of development, rapid economic growth, falling inequality, growth of export-oriented commercial agriculture	Sustained economic growth of GDP between 6% and 7% per annum since 1950s	*Individuals* Gini coefficient: 1960 .57 1970 .63 Income share of richest 3.2% 1960 27% 1970 33% Inequality rose *Families* Gini coefficient: Early 1960s .52 Early 1970s .45 Income share of richest 5%: Early 1960s 35% Early 1970s 23% Income share of poorest 40% Early 1960s 14% Early 1970s 15% Inequality fell	Céspedes (1973); ECLA (1969)
El Salvador (1945–61)	$350	Low level of development, moderate rate of GDP growth, continued large	Real GDP grew 5% per year, 1960–70	*Individuals* Share of richest 20% 1945 52.9%	ECLA (1971)

Table 4.6. (*cont.*)

Country/date	Development characterization	GNP per capita (U.S. $) 1970	Growth experience	Inequality change	Principal information sources
	agricultural sector, extreme concentration of land ownership, increasing inequality			1961 61.4% Share of poorest 60% 1945 32.2% 1961 20.8% Inequality rose	
India (1960/1–68/9)	Extremely poor, very slow growth, indications of constant or slightly falling inequality and rising poverty	$120	Slow, susceptible to large fluctuations on account of weather	*Families* Gini coefficient, rural: 1960/1 .321 1963/4 .297 1967/8 .293 1968/9 .310 Gini coefficient, urban: 1960/1 .350 1963/4 .360 1967/8 .345 1968/9 .350 Mixed evidence	Bardhan (1974*b*); other estimates also available
Mexico (1963–75)	Rapid growth, imbalanced; rising inequality; little trickle-down to poorest 40%	$890	Growth in excess of 8% per annum between 1968 and 1975, some-	*Individuals* Gini coefficient: 1963 .53 1968 .58	Felix (1977); Gollás (1978)

Country (period)	Income	Description	Growth	Findings	Source
Pakistan (1963/4–69/70)	$120	Moderate growth, diversified, with progress in agriculture; falling inequality and poverty	Sluggish growth in the 1950s, growth of GNP of 5.4% per annum in the 1960s ... what higher in the beginning of the period than in the end	1975 .58 Income share of poorest 40%: 1963 11.1% 1969 10.5% 1975 — Income share of richest 10%: 1963 49.9% 1969 51.0% 1975 — Inequality rose *Households* Gini coefficient for income, rural households: 1963/4 .357 1969/70 .294 Gini coefficient for income, urban households: 1963/4 .400 1969/70 .374 Gini coefficient for income, national: 1963/4 .361 1969/70 .327 Inequality fell	Ayub (1977)
Philippines (1961–71)	$280	Low level of development, rapid growth, rising relative inequality, narrow participa-	Average annual growth rates of real GDP:	*Families* Gini coefficient: 1961 .50	ILO (1974); Mijares and

Table 4.6. (cont.)

Country/date	Development characterization	GNP per capita (U.S. $) 1970	Growth experience	Inequality change	Principal information sources
	tion of the poor in economic development		1950-60 6.4% 1960-5 5.1% 1965-73 5.8%	1971 .49 Ratio of income of richest 20% to poorest 20%: 1961 13.4 1971 14.2 Inequality rose	Belarmino (1973)
Puerto Rico (1953-63)	Upper level of development, rapid growth, modern sector enlargement and industrialization, rapid growth, increasing inequality as measured by Gini coefficient but not by other measures, a heavy out-migration	$1,700	Real per capita GDP growth of 68% over this period	*Families* Gini coefficient: 1953 .415 1963 .449 Share of richest 5%: 1953 23.4% 1963 22.0% Share of poorest 10%: 1953 2.1% 1963 1.6% Mixed evidence	Puerto Rico (1960 and 1970); Weiss-koff (1970)
Singapore (1966-75)	Rapid growth, increasing share of manufacturing and construction, falling inequality and poverty	$1,830	Average annual rate of growth of GDP equal to 13% between	*Individuals* Gini coefficient: 1966 .498 1975 .448	Rao and Rama-krishnan (1977)

		GNP per capita	Economic growth		Income distribution	Inequality trend	Sources
Sri Lanka (1953–73)	Poor, slow growing, falling inequality and poverty, welfare-state policies	$120	Slow growth throughout, inward orientation after 1960, persistent balance-of-payments difficulties	1966 and 1973, recession in 1974 and 1975	*Spending units* Gini coefficient: 1953 .46 1963 .45 1973 .35 Income share of richest 10%: 1953 40.6% 1963 36.8% 1973 28.0% Income share of poorest 10%: 1953 1.9% 1963 1.5% 1973 2.8%	Inequality fell	Karunatilake (1975); Jayawardena (1974)
Taiwan (1950s–70s)	Upper middle level of development, rapid economic growth, falling inequality, development of rural industry and commerce	$660	Moderate growth in 1950s, exceptionally rapid sustained growth in 1960s and 1970s		*Households* Gini coefficient: Early 1950s .5 1968–72 .3 Ratio of income share of richest 10% to poorest 10%: 1964 8.6 1972 6.8	Inequality fell	Kuo (1975); Fei, Ranis, and Kuo (1978)

Notes: Countries excluded because of poor-quality, noncomparable, or unverifiable data: Colombia, Malaysia, Mexico (1950 and 1957 estimates omitted), Tunisia, Panama, Venezuela, Peru, Thailand, and Korea.

Years set with a slash (for instance, 1963/4) indicate fiscal years, whereas ranges of years separated with a dash (as in 1953–61) indicate a span of time from a base year to a terminal year. This distinction is maintained in subsequent tables and in the text.

evidence on growth experience and inequality change in these countries.[15]

According to the best available data, it appears that inequality rose in seven countries (Argentina, 1953-61; Bangladesh, 1963/4-73/4; Brazil, 1960-70; El Salvador, 1945-61; Mexico, 1963-75; the Philippines, 1961-71; and Puerto Rico, 1953-63); fell in five (Costa Rica, 1961-71; Pakistan, 1963/4-69/70; Singapore, 1966-75; Sri Lanka, 1953-73; and Taiwan, 1950s-70s); and exhibited no unambiguous trend in one country (India, 1960/1-68/9), though perhaps a slight decline may be inferred.

The most impressive feature of Table 4.6 is the lack of any pronounced pattern. It is sometimes thought that the increase or decrease in inequality would be associated with such economic conditions as the initial level of inequality, the level of economic development, or the rate of economic growth. The absence of systematic relationships among these variables suggests otherwise. Growth itself does not determine a country's inequality course. Rather, the decisive factor is the *type* of economic growth as determined by the environment in which growth occurs and the political decisions taken.

To account for changes in inequality in a country, many questions need to be answered. What is the nature of the economic system? Is growth oriented toward current consumption or toward investment for the future? In designing policies and programs, how much weight is given to improving the economic positions of the poor? Are development resources spread evenly throughout the country, or are resources channeled toward particular activities and localities? Does the country give predominant emphasis to enlarging its modern industrial sector or upgrading traditional agriculture? Does the country rely heavily on international trade, or is it a more closed economy? If international trade is important, is the trade regime one of import substitution or export promotion?

At present we know too little about these matters to be able to generalize. Studies of the distribution of the benefits of economic growth have only recently begun to appear. Six case studies are presented in Chapter 6. Some hypotheses derived from those and other country studies are suggestive and warrant further examination.

One issue is the nature of the economic system itself. Ahluwalia (1974) found that socialist countries had more equal income distributions than nonsocialist countries, even after standardizing for differences in level of GNP, rate of expansion of education, rate of decline of demographic pressures, and changing economic structure. That is, equality in size distribution of income is responsive to political choice and is not strictly determined by growth rates or levels of development. Are socialist countries able to maintain comparatively equal distributions or equalize incomes even further? Communist China is thought to have eliminated abject poverty (Reynolds, 1975b) by redistributing income and assets from the upper classes; but pronounced regional disparities remain (Lardy, 1978). Information on gross national product in China is nonexistent. In Tanzania, which has been following an avowedly socialist course since 1967, there are no reliable national income-distribution data to speak of. It has been suggested, though, that income inequality declined and the economy grew moderately (Green, 1974). Developments in Cuba are less favorable. After the revolution, there was redistribution of income, assets, and government spending. Although inequality was diminished, Cuba experienced zero growth for more than a decade leading even sympathetic observers (e.g., Seers, 1974:268) to suggest that "very drastic redistribution, especially if it takes the form of abolishing incentives, may interfere with the reduction of poverty." In summary, what little evidence there is suggests that newly socialized countries have achieved greater equality than nonsocialist countries at similar stages of development, but their growth records are far from exemplary, or at least have been until now.

A second question of some interest is whether broad-based development strategies are consistent with rapid economic growth. The case of Taiwan is frequently cited as a success story. Taiwan has simultaneously one of the highest growth rates and one of the most equal distributions of income of any country in the world. In his analysis of the Taiwanese experience, Ranis (1978) contends that Taiwan's success is the outcome of specific policies: a long-standing land reform, early concentration on raising agricultural productivity, development of nonagricultural rural activities, investment in the rural infrastructure, avoidance of premature capital intensity, and the switch from import substitution to exporting of labor-intensive goods. By international standards, Taiwan pursued an exceptionally broadly based development strategy. In future research, it would be interesting to identify other countries that followed similarly broad development strategies and compare these countries' income-distribution experiences with Taiwan's.

A third concern is the relationship between countries' industrialization and international trade policies on the one hand and changes in economic inequality on the other. In a penetrating study of these relationships, Little, Scitovsky, and Scott (1970) infer from seven case studies that less-developed countries deliberately tended to choose pro-industrial development strategies. Central to this type of development strategy was imposition of import restrictions on manufacturing goods by means of tariffs, controls, and multiple and overvalued exchange rates. The authors argue that this type of economic development pattern had a variety of adverse effects: worsening relative income inequality, diverting domestic savings from agricultural production, promoting overutilization of capital and underutilization of labor, exacerbating balance-of-payments problems, and leading to the neglect of comparative advantage. With respect to relative inequality, our concern in this chapter, the arguments are that import substitution produced extra profits in the industrial enclave without benefiting the majority in agriculture, turned the terms of trade in favor of manufactured goods for which those in agriculture then had to pay more, lowered the prices (in domestic currency) that agricultural producers could receive by selling their products in world markets, and favored the already favored sectors while leaving the backward sectors behind. Direct evidence in support of these propositions is weak, the reason being that data on the size distribution of income were not available (except for Mexico) at the time of the Little, Scitovsky, and Scott study. A major challenge facing development economists today is the task of measuring the size of the effects of various industrial and trade policies on the size distribution of income. More recent studies have made some progress in this direction; see Bruton (1977), Krueger (1978), and Bhagwati (1978), for references to the latest literature.

A fourth issue is the contribution of education to in-equality. Some argue that education is vital and that more education will both raise growth and reduce inequality.[16] Others argue that education exacerbates inequality: by per-petuating economic status across generations,[17] by acting as a mechanism for "cultural imperialism,"[18] and by taxing everyone regressively to pay for the education of the rich.[19] The debate is particularly heated in Brazil, which concurrently underwent rapid economic growth, rising income inequality, and an expanded educational system. Langoni (1972 and 1975) contends that much of the increase in growth and employment can be explained by increased numbers of highly educated workers receiving higher wages because of their higher productivity. He attributes growing relative income inequality in Brazil in large part to the realization of quasi rents by persons possessing scarce human capital. That inter-pretation has been challenged by Fishlow (1973*a* and *b*), Wells (1974), and others for several reasons, including the fact that income differentials between university graduates and secondary graduates have widened and the observation that average social rates of return are estimated to be highest at the lowest educational levels; yet Brazilian policy favors educational investment at the upper levels. Personally, I would think that education helps lessen inequality when it is concentrated at the elementary level. This is because the beneficiaries of an enlarged primary educational system will include disproportionately large numbers of children of the poor and because the per pupil cost of elementary schooling is only a small fraction of the cost per student in higher edu-cation, and so many more children can benefit.

Finally, an interesting hypothesis is suggested by Berry's (1974) work on Colombia, which presents income-distribution estimates for an unusually long time span, three decades.[20] Berry observes a "probable" increase in inequality in periods of rapid economic growth and a reversal in slow growth periods. The data are of admittedly dubious quality, having been pieced together synthetically from a variety of sources. It is questionable, therefore, whether the hypothesis of a relationship between increasing inequality and rapid growth is valid even for Colombia, let alone for other countries. Then too, even if Berry's hypothesis were borne out empirically, it would be difficult to distinguish cause from effect. Still, the very possibility that inequality may change procyclically is worth bearing in mind and testing on data for other countries.

A final word

In summary, relative inequality changes have been estimated for more than twenty LDCs. No systematic pattern of change appears, let alone any necessary pattern. These and other specific results are summarized at the end of this chapter.

Decomposing LDC inequality

In the preceding sections, we examined the evidence from cross-sectional and intertemporal studies of the determinants of income inequality. Those studies share a common methodological feature: The *country* is the unit of analysis and the goal of the research is to look at macroeconomic characteristics to help explain why the level of national inequality is what it is.

In the last few years, another type of approach has been followed, which looks instead at inequality *within a country,* and measures the contribution of the various components to total inequality.[21]   This latter type of approach, using a variety of methodologies, has decomposed inequality by economic sector (e.g., urban vs. rural), income source (e.g., income from labor vs. capital vs. land vs. transfers), or family characteristics (including attributes of the workers, their jobs, and regional and other locational considerations). This mode of inquiry is potentially of great value for understanding the *structure* of inequality and inequality *changes* over time and for identifying the most important factors that cause some individuals or families to receive higher incomes than others.

This section explores the decomposition type of inequality analysis.   I review the alternative decomposition methodologies that have been set forth in the literature and the problems to which they have been applied and summarize the principal findings of empirical decomposition studies.

Types of decomposition problems

Decomposition problems are of three general types: functional decomposition by income source, functional decomposition by economic sector, and microeconomic decomposition by income-determining characteristics. Let us now review each.

Decomposition by functional income source. The starting point for source decompositions is the assumption that income determination can best be studied by disaggregation by a small number of functional income sources. Take as an example the familiar functional division of income into income from labor, income from capital, and (at the micro level) income from transfers. The question asked by source decompositions is, Of total inequality, how much is attributable to income from labor, how much to income from capital, and how much to income from transfers? Source decomposition procedures quantify these effects and further show how each source's contribution to overall inequality depends positively on the degree of inequality of each income source, the importance of that income source in total income, and the extent of correlation between income from that source and total income.

Decomposition by economic sector. Sectoral decompositions divide the economy into economic sectors (e.g., agriculture vs. nonagriculture). Generally, these sectors are thought to be mutually exclusive, so that all of the household's income is treated as agricultural or nonagricultural. The question asked by sector decompositions is, Of total inequality, how much is attributable to variability in agricultural incomes, how much to variability in nonagricultural incomes, and how much to between-sector inequality?

Sector and source decompositions have been presented independently here, as is the practice in the literature. This distinction, though convenient, is not necessary. The economy could very easily be divided into segments defined by source–sector combinations, e.g., rural labor income, urban labor income, rural capital income, and so on.

Source and sector decompositions have in common the property that total inequality is completely accounted for by the several components, in much the same way that total national income is completely accounted for by summing income from consumption, investment, government expenditures, and net exports. The characterization of source and sector decompositions as accounting procedures is deliberate. For just as decompositions of national income into consumption, investment, government, and export components cannot explain why national income is what it is, neither can source and sector decompositions explain why national income inequality is what it is. The value of these decompositions is that they gauge the relative importance of various sources and sectors to overall inequality, and thereby direct our attention to potentially fruitful areas of research.

Suppose, for instance, we find, as indeed the data to be presented show, that the primary contribution to overall income inequality is made by variation in labor income. This suggests that a valuable next step in understanding overall income inequality would be to study those economic forces that might determine the amount and distribution of labor income. In this connection, many characteristics of family members and their jobs become important. Note that microeconomic data on the individual households and their family members are needed to explore the determinants of income from labor or any other source or sector. Let us now consider what types of decompositions can be performed when such microeconomic data are available.

Decomposition by income determinants. A now large number of studies of less-developed countries have shown that households' overall incomes and labor market earnings are systematically related to a number of family characteristics: the number of labor-force participants, their incidence of unemployment, their personal characteristics (such as education and age), the family's location (by region, size of place, or rural or urban situation), the nature of their jobs (including occupation, industry, and employer's characteristics).[22] In a few of these studies (see the section on the survey of empirical findings later in this chapter), attempts have been made to decompose income inequality according to income determinants.

Determinant decompositions ask the question, Of total inequality, how much inequality is associated with variation in income determinant 1, how much with income determinant 2, and so on, and how much is not associated with any of the explanatory variables? The presence of an unexplained component is one important difference between the determinant decompositions and the other types of decompositions. Another important difference is that determinant decompositions provide much more insight into causal factors underlying the distribution of income than is the case with decompositions by source and/or sector.

We now turn to the different types of decomposition methodologies.

Decomposition methodologies

Four different decomposition methodologies are in current use: Gini decompositions, Theil decompositions, analysis of variance, and decomposition of the Atkinson index. We consider these in turn, highlighting their conceptual features.[23]

Gini decomposition. The Gini coefficient is the most popular measure of relative income inequality, owing to the ease of interpreting it (in relation to the Lorenz curve). Gini decomposition procedures have been devised by Rao (1969), Fei and Ranis (1974), Fei, Ranis, and Kuo (1978), Pyatt (1976), and Mangahas (1975), among others; several of these applications were derived independently. In addition to the empirical applications of these authors, Gini decompositions have been applied in research by Mehran (1974), Ayub (1977), and Fields (1979).

For purposes of discussion, let us suppose there are three income sources–wage income, property income, and transfer income–and that the sum of these is the total income for each family and for the economy as a whole. A decomposition by additive factor components is presented here.

With the Gini coefficient as our measure of inequality, it might be thought that the Gini for the economy as a whole would be a weighted average of the factor Ginis for the individual components, the weights being given by the factor share of that income in the total. This is, however, incorrect, because the overall Gini coefficient requires the households to be ranked in increasing order of income, and the different component incomes (wage, property, transfer) may not be monotonically related to one another or to the total.

To indicate the correct relationship between the overall Gini coefficient and the factor Ginis, let us order the families according to total income. For each factor income source, we may then compute a so-called pseudo-Gini coefficient, that is, the Gini coefficient that would be obtained if households in that sector were not ordered with their incomes monotonically increasing.[24] The overall Gini for the economy (G) turns out to be a weighted average of the pseudo-Ginis for the ith income source $(\bar{G}_i)$ with the weights given by the factor share of that income source (ϕ_i):

(1) $G = \bar{G}_1\phi_1 + \bar{G}_2\phi_2 + \bar{G}_3\phi_3$

Fei, Ranis, and Kuo (1978) have shown that the pseudo-Gini for the ith source $(\bar{G}_i)$ is equal to the product of the true Gini for that source (G_i) and a relative correlation coefficient (R_i),

(2) $\bar{G}_i = G_i R_i$

where for each factor, the relative correlation coefficient is the ratio of two other correlations:

(3) $R_i = \dfrac{\text{cor}(Y_i, \rho)}{\text{cor}(Y_i, \rho_i)} = \dfrac{\begin{array}{c}\text{coefficient of correlation between factor}\\ \text{income amount and total income rank}\end{array}}{\begin{array}{c}\text{coefficient of correlation between factor}\\ \text{income amount and factor income rank}\end{array}}$

To further explain (3), consider the R_i for labor income. The numerator of (3) is the correlation between labor income in dollars (Y_i) and the family's total income position (ρ), ordered from lowest to highest. The denominator of (3) relates the dollar labor income figure (Y_i) to that family's labor income rank (ρ_i).

Substituting (2) and (3) into (1) and dividing through by G, we obtain

(4) $100\% = \phi_1\dfrac{G_1\,\text{cor}(Y_1,\rho)}{G\,\text{cor}(Y_1,\rho_1)} + \phi_2\dfrac{G_2\,\text{cor}(Y_2,\rho)}{G\,\text{cor}(Y_2,\rho_2)} + \phi_3\dfrac{G_3\,\text{cor}(Y_3,\rho)}{G\,\text{cor}(Y_3,\rho_3)}$
$= FIW_1 + FIW_2 + FIW_3$

the *FIW*s denoting the so-called factor inequality weights

of labor, property, and transfer income respectively. Overall inequality in an economy is seen to depend on the degree of inequality of each income source, the extent of correlation between income from that source and total income, and the importance of that income source in the total.

The Gini coefficient has also been decomposed in other ways. For example, Mangahas (1975) decomposed inequality into rural and urban components as follows:

$$(5) \qquad G = \sum_j \theta_j G_j + \sum_{i > j} \phi_i \phi_j (D_{ij}/\overline{Y}),$$

where G = overall Gini coefficient, G_j = Gini coefficient among those in group j, θ_j = family income in group j as proportion of total family income, ϕ_j = families in group j as proportion of all families, $\overline{Y}$ = mean income, and D_{ij} = Gini difference. The first summation measures within-sector inequality, and the second, between-sector inequality. Another breakdown was offered by Pyatt (1976), who interpreted the Gini coefficient as the expected value of a game in which a randomly drawn individual compares his income with others'.

Other decomposition procedures partition total inequality differently. These are reviewed here.

Theil decomposition. A decade ago, Theil (1967) set forth a readily decomposable inequality measure, which he subsequently (1972) illustrated with a number of empirical applications. Because an exact decomposition is possible, the Theil index has received widespread use. Among the studies of LDCs performing Theil decompositions are those by Fishlow (1972), van Ginneken (1975), Chiswick (1976), Uribe (1976), and Altimir and Piñera (1977).

The Theil index of inequality is derived rigorously from the notion of entropy in information theory. The fundamental idea of information entropy is that occurrences that differ greatly from what was expected should receive more weight than events that conform with prior expectations. The entropy index gauges the expected information content from the various outcomes, with the weights depending on the likelihood of each.

Building on this concept of entropy, the Theil index (T) of income inequality is formally the expected information of the message that transforms population shares into income shares. Mathematically, its algebraic formula is given by

$$(6) \qquad T = \sum_{i=1}^{n} q_i \log \frac{q_i}{1/n}$$

where n = number of individuals or households, and q_i = income share of ith individual. Theil (1972:100) notes that T equals the mean product of income and its own logarithm. Why this should be used as measure of economic inequality is far from transparent.

In any case, the main attraction of the Theil index lies not in its intuitive justification but rather, as remarked, in its decomposability. Theil decompositions are well suited for estimating the contribution of different groups to total inequality; examples of such groups are economically distinct regions of a country or population subgroups divided into educational and/or age categories.

Various decomposition formulas are given in Theil (1972: 100), Fishlow (1972:395), Chiswick (1976:9), Szal and Robinson (1977:524), and Altimir and Piñera (1977:14), among other places. Fishlow, for instance, gives two alternative decomposition procedures:

$$(7) \qquad I_{ijk} = \sum_i y_i \cdot \cdot \log \frac{y_i \cdot \cdot}{x_i \cdot \cdot}$$
$$+ \sum_i y_i \cdot \cdot \left(\sum_j \frac{y_{ij} \cdot}{y_i \cdot \cdot} \log \frac{y_{ij} \cdot / y_i \cdot \cdot}{x_{ij} \cdot / x_i \cdot \cdot} \right)$$
$$+ \sum_i \sum_j \frac{y_{ij} \cdot}{y_i \cdot \cdot} \left(\sum_k \frac{y_{ijk}}{y_{ij} \cdot} \log \frac{y_{ijk} / y_{ij} \cdot}{x_{ijk} / x_{ij} \cdot} \right)$$

and

$$(8) \qquad I_{jk} = \sum_j y_j \cdot \log \frac{y_j \cdot}{x_j \cdot} + \sum_k y \cdot_k \log \frac{y \cdot_k}{x \cdot_k}$$
$$+ \left(\sum_j \sum_k y_{jk} \log \frac{y_{jk}}{x_{jk}} \right.$$
$$\left. - \sum_j y_j \cdot \log \frac{y_j \cdot}{x_j \cdot} - \sum_k y \cdot_k \log \frac{y \cdot_k}{x \cdot_k} \right)$$

where y are the income shares and x the population shares, and the subscripts i, j, and k refer to income class, sector, and education, respectively. Equation (7) decomposes total inequality into between-group and within-group components, whereas (8) decomposes the between-group component according to the variation among the means of the various groups.

Another decomposition procedure, substantially similar in nature, is the analysis of variance, which we now examine.

Analysis of variance (ANOVA). ANOVA procedures have a long history in social scientific analysis, but their applications to economic problems are quite limited. In particular, on the problem of economic inequality in less-developed countries, work is just beginning; see Langoni (1972 and 1975), Chiswick (1976), Fields (1979), and Fields and Schultz (forthcoming).

The basic idea of analysis of variance is to decompose the variance of a dependent variable, which is the sum of squared deviations from the overall mean divided by the sample size, into two types of effects: those caused by variation between different groups and those caused by variation within each of the groups. For example, if the dependent variable is the logarithm of income in each of a number of households and the independent variable is the region of the country in which these households are located, the total sum of squares (SS) of income is expressed as

(9) $\qquad SS_y = SS_{\text{between}} + SS_{\text{within}}$

where

$$SS_y = \sum_j \sum_i (Y_{ji} - \bar{Y})^2$$

in which $\bar{Y}$ is the overall mean of log income Y in the entire sample, the is are households, and the js are various regions;

$$SS_{\substack{\text{between} \\ \text{regions}}} = \sum_j N_j (\bar{Y}_j \cdot - \bar{Y})^2$$

in which $\bar{Y}_j \cdot$ is the mean log income in region j, and N_j is the number of sample households in region j;
and

$$SS_{\substack{\text{within} \\ \text{regions}}} = \sum_j \sum_i (Y_{ji} - \bar{Y}_j \cdot)^2$$

In other words, equation (9) tells us the relative importance of income inequality within regions as compared with diversity in mean incomes across regions.

In the example of the preceding paragraph, the only explanatory factor was region. ANOVA may also handle multiple explanatory variables, say region and education. We then obtain a breakdown such as

(10) SS_y = SS owing to region
              + SS owing to education
              + SS owing to interaction between region and education
              + SS within region–education groupings

A decomposition like (10) tells us whether income inequality is greater across regions or across educational groups and whether the effects of region and education on income are independent of one another; it also tells the relative importance of variations across these groupings as compared with the variations within them. Both gross and marginal effects may be estimated. Additionally, and quite importantly, tests of statistical significance are available for each factor.

Finally, a major advantage of analysis-of-variance techniques is that, because they are very much like multiple regressions, they indicate the quantitative importance of each category of each explanatory variable. Thus we can learn from ANOVA decompositions how much difference it makes to income if the family is located in one region rather than another or if the family head has an additional year of education. No other decomposition procedure yields such information.

Atkinson index. The inequality index proposed by Atkinson (1970) represents the cumulative deviation of the actual income distribution from the "equally distributed equivalent income," which is the "level of income per head which if equally distributed would give the same level of social welfare as the present distribution" (p. 250). Without repeating the algebraic derivation, the index is given by

(11) $I = 1 - \dfrac{1}{\mu} \left[\sum_i f(Y_i)(Y_i)^{1-\epsilon} \right]^{1/(1-\epsilon)}$

where μ = mean income, Y_i = income of ith income recipient, and ϵ = parameter of relative inequality aversion, as specified by the observer. It is clear with the Atkinson index (and implicit with the other measures) that value judgments are an integral part of inequality measurement. If the population is divided into mutually exclusive and jointly exhaustive groups, the Atkinson index is readily decomposable into within-group and between-group components, as follows:

(12)   (a) $I = I_B + I_W$

       (b) $I_B = 1 - \dfrac{1}{\mu} \left(\sum_j \lambda_j \mu_j^{1-\epsilon} \right)^{1/(1-\epsilon)}$

where λ_j = share of jth group in total population, μ_j = mean income of jth group, and μ, ϵ = as before. The kind of decomposition into within-group and between-group components closely parallels similar breakdowns of other inequality indexes.

The Atkinson index is sometimes criticized as subjective, because a value judgment (on the magnitude of the inequality aversion parameter) must be made in order to calculate the index. Yet the Atkinson index only does explicitly what other inequality measures do implicitly: pass judgment on the desirability of income gains at different points in the same income distribution. An index like

(13) $I^* = 1 - \dfrac{1}{\mu} \left[\sum_i f(Y_i) \right]$

may *look* more objective, but it is not: This is merely the Atkinson index with ϵ arbitrarily set equal to one.

The value judgments implicit in the familiar inequality indexes (like the Gini coefficient, Theil index, and log variance) are only partially understood. In recent years, the properties of these measures have been scrutinized with some care. The next section reports on some of the relevant considerations.

Choice of decomposition procedure

In weighing the advantages of the various decomposition procedures for empirical research, three central issues arise: the properties of the inequality measure itself, the richness of the information derived from the decomposition, and the suitability of the measure for the different decomposition problems.

Properties of the different measures of inequality. One way of choosing which inequality measure to decompose is to consider the measure's basic nature. In this respect, the Gini decomposition and analysis of variance applied to the logarithms of income come out ahead. The Gini coefficient is easily conceptualized in terms of the Lorenz curve. The variance has a familiar basis in standard statistical analysis; furthermore, income distributions are approximately log normal in shape, so that analysis of the log variance is conceptually appealing. The difficulty with the Atkinson index is that it is derived from a welfare framework with which many students of inequality may disagree.[25] Finally, the Theil index, despite its wide usage as a measure of inequality, has no clear interpretation.

Another selection criterion is the usefulness of the inequality measure in making inequality comparisons. Among the desirable axioms for this purpose are:[26]

A1. *Axiom of scale irrelevance.* If one distribution is a scalar multiple of another (i.e., each person's income in the first case is *x*% of his income in the second), then the two distributions have the same degree of inequality. Put somewhat differently, the degree of inequality in the distribution of income is measured independently of the level of income.

A2. *Axiom of symmetry.* If two income distributions are identical except that different families receive the income in the two cases, then the two distributions have the same degree of inequality. This follows from the principle of treating all individuals and families alike with regard to income distribution.

A3. *Axiom of rank-preserving equalization.* If one distribution is obtained from another by the transfer of a positive amount of income from a relatively rich family to a relatively poor one, while their relative rank in the distribution is preserved, then the new distribution is more equal than the old. (Although few persons are likely to quarrel with this axiom, it should be noted that some additional, nontrivial assumptions about the nature of judgments of social well-being are necessary to guarantee that a "more equal" distribution is always regarded as "better.")

The Gini coefficient, Theil index, and Atkinson index

satisfy these axioms. The variance does not fulfill the axiom of scale irrelevance. However, scale irrelevance and the other axioms are satisfied by the variance of the logarithm of income (commonly known as the log variance). Hence all four of the inequality measures considered are suitable by the axiomatic criterion for decomposition analysis.

Another consideration of some importance is the sensitivity of the different measures to income changes at various points in the distribution. Persons whose value judgments lead them to give greatest weight to the economic position of the poor may wish to choose that inequality measure which is most sensitive to inequality associated with low-income groups. Observations on the several inequality measures may be found in Sen (1973), Weisskoff (1970), Szal and Robinson (1977), and Chiswick (1976), among others, but perhaps the most thorough analysis of this question is in the work of Champernowne (1974). He found, among other things, that the variance of the logarithms of income is most sensitive to inequality associated with poverty, the Theil index is most sensitive to inequality associated with the very rich, and the Gini coefficient is most sensitive to inequality in the middle of the income distribution. For observers whose main concern is with the low-income population, analysis-of-variance procedures would appear more appropriate.

Let us now take up a number of other considerations relevant to the choice of decomposition procedure.

Decomposition output. Here is a list of desirable outputs from decomposition exercises:

1. Decomposes overall inequality into within-factor and between-factor components
2. Measures the gross contribution of each explanatory factor to total inequality
3. Tests the statistical significance of these main effects
4. Measures the marginal contribution of each explanatory factor
5. Tests the statistical significance of the marginal effects
6. Measures the effects of interactions between pairs of explanatory factors (and higher-order combinations if needed)
7. Tests the statistical significance of the interaction effects
8. Estimates the magnitude of the effect on income of each category of each explanatory variable

ANOVA does all eight of these; Theil decompositions do only
1, 2, 3, 4, and 6; and Gini and Atkinson decompositions only
1 and 2. Thus, in comparison with other available decomposition procedures, ANOVA provides richer information on
the sources of inequality.

*Different decomposition procedures for different decomposi-
tion problems.* Consider first the problem of decomposing
inequality by functional income source. As described above,
procedures for using the Gini coefficient for this problem
have been worked out in considerable detail. Particularly
helpful is the technique for constructing factor inequality
weights and the breakdown of those weights into factor share,
factor Gini, and correlational components (see equation [4]).
In principle, ANOVA, Theil, and Atkinson procedures could
be used similarly, but I have not yet seen them used in this
way.

For the sectoral decomposition problem, which analyzes
between- and within-sector inequality, each of the four
procedures appears satisfactory. The choice among them
therefore is partially dependent on the properties discussed
above and is partially a matter of convenience (depending,
for example, on the availability of computer programs for
the different procedures).

Finally, with respect to decompositions by income-determining factors, ANOVA and Theil techniques come out
ahead. Both these procedures give a clear picture of the
importance of each explanatory factor (e.g., education and
region) in determining overall inequality, while at the same
time gauging the unexplained residual. Gini decompositions,
on the other hand, deal with deviations from predicted values
in a quite cumbersome way, the difficulty being inherent in
the Gini coefficient itself.[27] The Atkinson index has not
been applied to this problem, as far as I know.

In the income-determinant problem, how do we choose
between analysis of variance and Theil decompositions?
I would say that two considerations work strongly in favor
of ANOVA.[28] One advantage of ANOVA is the use of log
variance as the measure of inequality. The parallel between
ANOVA and multiple regressions explaining the logarithm of

income permits a richer characterization of the income determination process than does Theil.[29] We can learn, for example, by how much rural residence reduces income.[30] A second positive consideration is the availability of statistical significance tests for ANOVA but not for Theil. Thus, using ANOVA, we can compare the likelihood that the estimated contribution of an explanatory variable like region or education is a "true" effect with the alternative possibility that the apparent relationship is due to chance sampling. This permits us to bring the full logic of conventional statistical analysis to bear on the problem of ascertaining the determinants of inequality. From a causal (as opposed to an accounting) perspective, this is valuable indeed.

Summary. Many decomposition properties of the several inequality measures have been considered in this section. These considerations are summarized in Table 4.7. All in all, analysis-of-variance procedures based on the logarithms of income have the most desirable properties with no offsetting limitations. The use of ANOVA procedures in future research on the determinants of LDC inequality appears warranted.

Concerning the choice of decomposition procedures for the types of problems under consideration, I would conclude: (1) The Gini decomposition technique is a proven method for the source problem; (2) for the sector problem, the choice of technique is a matter of some indifference, with the available computer software possibly proving decisive, and (3) analysis of variance dominates for decomposing inequality into the contributions of various determinantal factors.

Survey of empirical findings in LDCs

The various techniques for decomposing inequality have been applied to analyses of the structure of inequality by income source, economic sector, and income-determining characteristics in a number of LDCs.[31] Some patterns seem to be emerging from these studies. This section reviews the major results.

Source decompositions. The pioneering work on source decompositions in less-developed countries is that of Fei and

Table 4.7. *Summary of properties of four inequality measures relevant to decomposition*

	Inequality measure			
Property	Gini	Theil	Log variance	Atkinson
Decomposability	Yes	Yes	Yes	Yes
Intuitively appealing as a measure of inequality	Yes	No	Yes	Dubious
Axiomatically justified as a measure of inequality	Yes	Yes	Yes	Yes
Sensitivity to inequality associated with poverty	No	No	Yes	Yes
Ranks contribution of various determinants of inequality	Yes	Yes	Yes	Yes
Quantitative estimates of the magnitude of inequality determinants	No	No	Yes	No
Tests of statistical significance for estimated effects of various factors	No	No	Yes	No
Computer packages readily available	No	No	Yes	No

Ranis (1974) and Fei, Ranis, and Kuo (1978) in their study of Taiwan. Their methodology was followed in subsequent research on Pakistan by Ayub (1977) and on Colombia by Fields (1979).

The source decompositions are based on the Gini coefficient. Taiwan's overall Gini is .28, which is among the lowest of all countries in the world (see Table 4.3). The source decomposition tells us which of five income sources (wage, mixed,[32] property, gifts, and other) accounts for how much of the overall inequality. In the absence of microeconomic data, the decomposition was conducted across income groups.[33]

The natural way to start is by looking at the Gini coefficients of the individual income sources. The reported factor Ginis are given in row 1 of Table 4.8. Fei and Ranis report that property and gift income have the highest factor Ginis and therefore are least equally distributed; mixed and other

Table 4.8. *Decomposition of inequality in Taiwan, 1972*

	Wage	Mixed	Property	Gifts	Other	Total
Factor Gini	.2518	.2968	.4020	.3965	.2925	
Factor share	.582	.275	.093	.046	.004	1.000
Factor inequality weight	.5187	.2882	.1322	.0584	.0024	1.000

Source: Fei and Ranis (1974).

are in an intermediate position; and wage income is most equally distributed. From this, we might be inclined to conclude that property and gift income account for the largest part of overall inequality and wage income the least. In actuality, these inferences would be mistaken, the reason being that we have omitted two important factors from consideration, namely, the factor shares, which tell us the importance of that factor in total income,[34] and the correlations between factor income and total income, which tell us the degree to which that factor augments total inequality or offsets the inequality attributable to other sources.[35]

When one looks at the factor shares in row 2 of Table 4.8, one sees that wage income is the most important source of income by far, mixed income is in an intermediate position, and property and gift income are relatively unimportant. As the decomposition procedure (equation [4]) showed, total inequality is a weighted average of inequality in the individual factor incomes. In the case of Taiwan, wage income is relatively equally distributed but has the largest factor share; property and gift income are relatively unequally distributed but have small factor shares; and mixed and other sources are in the middle in both respects.

The factor inequality weights presented in row 3 measure each factor's contribution to total inequality. The data show that wage income is the source of more than half of total inequality, whereas property and gifts combined account for less than 20%; the rest is accounted for by mixed income, some substantial but unknown part of which reflects returns to labor.

The same basic decomposition methodology has been ap-

plied to the cases of Pakistan (Ayub, 1977) and urban Colombia (Fields, 1979) with quite similar qualitative results.[36]
Both Ayub and I found: (1) higher factor Gini coefficients
for nonlabor income sources than for labor incomes;[37] (2)
the reverse ordering for factor income shares;[38] and (3) the
overwhelming importance of labor incomes (including wage
employment and self-employment) in accounting for overall
inequality.[39]

Individually and together, the results for Taiwan, Pakistan,
and Colombia give a common impression about the contribution of the various income sources to overall inequality:
The bulk of income inequality is attributable to labor income.
The high factor inequality weights for labor incomes suggest
that the principal inequality-producing factor is that some
people receive a great deal more income for their work than
do others. This has important implications both for research
(researchers should study the labor market) and for policy
(policy makers should create more well-paying jobs). The
intuitive prior notion that the most unequally distributed
factors (property, gifts, etc.) contribute the most to total
inequality is found to be false in each case.

Sector decompositions. Sector decomposition studies do
three things: They measure the inequality within each sector
or region of an economy, indicate the importance of within-
sector inequality for all sectors taken together, and determine
the amount of inequality accounted for by between-sector
variation. The available studies decompose inequality within
a country and within regions of the world.

Within-country sector decompositions have been carried
out, using the Gini coefficient, by Mehran (1974) for Iranian
cities, by Mangahas (1975) for areas and regions of the
Philippines, and by Pyatt (1976) for urban and rural locations
in Sri Lanka. In other studies – by Fishlow (1972 and 1973*a*)
and Langoni (1972 and 1975) in Brazil, van Ginneken (1975)
in Mexico, Chiswick (1976) in Thailand, Fields (1979) and
Fields and Schultz (forthcoming) in Colombia, and Altimir
and Piñera (1977) in Chile, Panama, and Venezuela–regional
or urban-rural decompositions were undertaken as part of
a larger exercise; these studies used Theil decompositions

or analysis of variance. Without exception, the result emerges that variations *within* sectors or regions are far more important in accounting for inequality than variations *between* sectors.[40]

Another result of the within-country sector decompositions is that inequality is found to be greater within urban than within rural areas. See, for example, Mangahas (1975:295) for the Philippines; Pyatt (1976:tab. 3) for Sri Lanka; Fei, Ranis, and Kuo (1978:diagram 2) for Taiwan; Ayub (1977: tab. 12) for Pakistan; and Fields and Schultz (forthcoming: tab. 3) for Colombia. These results accord with the findings of Kuznets (1955) and many other income inequality studies.

Sector decompositions have also been applied to studies of inequality in the world. First Theil (1972) and after him Uribe (1976), using the same methodology, examined the structure of inequality within a number of countries and across countries. Theil's analysis covered all parts of the world, whereas Uribe's was limited to Latin America. Both studies found more intra- than intercountry inequality.[41]

In summary, the sector decomposition studies report more inequality *within* sectors or countries than *across* them. As with the source decomposition literature, these studies clearly demonstrate the importance of going down to the household level in order to understand the determinants of incomes and income inequality.

Determinant decompositions. Eight studies decomposing inequality in less-developed countries by income determinants are surveyed here. The countries covered are Brazil (two studies), Mexico (two studies), Thailand, Taiwan, Colombia (three studies), Argentina, Costa Rica, Chile, Panama, Peru, and Venezuela. Three of the four statistical decomposition methodologies (all but the Atkinson index) have been used. The results of these studies are summarized in Table 4.9.

The available studies exhibit several similarities: (1) Large effects are found for personal attributes; (2) of the personal attributes considered, education and age contribute roughly equal explanatory power; (3) large effects are sometimes found for employment aspects; (4) of the employment aspects considered, the most important correlate of income is

Table 4.9. *Decomposition of inequality in ten less-developed countries by income determinants (rank ordering of findings)*

Country/date	Author and decomposition methodology	Factors considered, in order of importance		

Brazil (1960) — Fishlow (1972), Theil decomposition

1. Education
2. Age
3. Sector
4. Region

Brazil (1960 and 1970) — Langoni (1975), multiple regression approach to analysis of variance (ANOVA)

Factor	1960 rank	1970 rank
Education	1	1
Region	2	3^a
Age	3	2
Sex	4	3^a
Activity	5	3^a

Thailand (1971, urban) — Chiswick (1976), Theil decomposition and ANOVA

Factor	Theil, gross explanation	Theil, marginal explanation	ANOVA, gross explanation	ANOVA, marginal explanation
Age	1	2	2^b	3^b
Education	2	1	1^b	1^b
Sex	3	4	3^c	2^b
Farm occup.	4	5	4^d	4^b
Type of earnings	5	3	5^d	5^b

Taiwan (1966) — Fei, Ranis, and

1. Education

116

			Gross explanation	Marginal explanation
Colombia (1967/8, urban)	Kuo (1978), Gini decomposition	2. Age 3. Sex		
Colombia (1973)	Fields (1979), ANOVA	1. Education 2. Age 3. City		
Colombia (1973)	Fields and Schultz (forthcoming), ANOVA	1. Education[b] 2. Age[b] 3. Region[b] 4. Urban–rural[b] 5. Type of employment[b]		
Colombia (1974, urban)	Altimir and Piñera (1977), Theil decomposition	Education Occupation Age Kind of econ. activity Employment status Sex Time worked	1 2 3[a] 3[a] 5 6 7	1 4[a] 4[a] 2 3 7 6
Mexico (1968)	van Ginneken (1975), Theil decomposition	1. Education 2. Urban–rural 3. Age 4. Sector of activity 5. Occupation		

117

Table 4.9. (cont.)

Country/date	Author and decomposition methodology	Factors considered, in order of importance		
			Gross explanation	Marginal explanation
Mexico (1970)	Altimir and Piñera (1977), Theil decomposition	Education	1	2
		Occupation	2	3[a]
		Age	3	1
		Sex	4[a]	6
		Employment status	4[a]	5
		Kind of econ. activity	6	3[a]
			Gross explanation	Marginal explanation
Costa Rica (1966/7)	Altimir and Piñera (1977), Theil decomposition	Education	1[a]	2
		Occupation	1[a]	3
		Age	3	1
		Sex	4[a]	4[a]
		Employment status	4[a]	6[a]
		Kind of econ. activity	6	6[a]
		Time worked	7	4[a]

Chile (1971)

Altimir and Piñera (1977), Theil decomposition

	Gross explanation	Marginal explanation
Occupation	1	1
Age	2	2
Employment status	3	4^a
Sex	4	4^a
Kind of econ. activity	5	3
Time worked	6	6
Education	—	—

Panama (1972)

Altimir and Piñera (1977), Theil decomposition

	Gross explanation	Marginal explanation
Education	1	1^a
Occupation	2	3^a
Time worked	3	3^a
Age	4	1^a
Kind of econ. activity	5	3^a
Employment status	6^a	6^a
Sex	6^a	6^a

Peru (1970)

Altimir and Piñera (1977), Theil decomposition

	Gross explanation	Marginal explanation
Education	1	2
Occupation	2	4^a
Age	3	1
Kind of econ. activity	4^a	4^a
Employment status	4^a	6
Sex	4^a	7
Time worked	7	3

Table 4.9. (cont.)

Country/date	Author and decomposition methodology	Factors considered, in order of importance		Gross explanation	Marginal explanation
Venezuela (1971)	Altimir and Piñera (1977), Theil decomposition	Education		1	2
		Occupation		2	3
		Age		3	1
		Employment status		4	4
		Sex		5	7
		Time worked		6	5
		Kind of econ. activity		7	6

[a] Contributions of these variables were virtually identical.
[b] Statistically significant effect at .01 level.
[c] Statistically significant effect at .05 level.
[d] Not statistically significant effect at .05 level.
Note: If no [b], [c], or [d] appears, no test of statistical significance is possible.

occupation; (5) regional effects are found to be of some importance, but these effects are not major ones; and (6) intraregional inequality dominates interregional inequality.[42]

The considerable importance of personal attributes in the decomposition studies accords with the findings of income- and earnings-generating functions; see Chapter 5. In those studies, personal characteristics are found to explain as much as 60% of the variance in the logarithms of income. Little is gained by adding information on the employer or the place of residence.

The decomposition findings of Altimir and Piñera differ from the others in attributing a large role to employment variables, particularly occupation. Their results on this point are suspect because of the decomposition equivalent of simultaneous equations bias. It seems warranted to conclude that occupation and other employment variables help exlain income inequality but that these variables have lesser effects than do personal variables.

Other sources also suggest the limitations of analyses of income distribution at the sectoral level. Webb (1976), for instance, reports that the poor in Lima are found scattered in many different sectors – commerce, manufacturing, transport, construction, public service, modern sector firms or occupations, and miscellaneous services – each sector containing at least 10% of the poor. More generally, it would appear that to predict an individual's income, we can do much better knowing his education and age than which economic sector he is located in.

Decompositions of inequality by income-determining characteristics, such as those summarized in Table 4.9, are potentially of great usefulness in analyzing LDC wage structures. Economic theory does not yet offer a comprehensive explanation for income inequality. However, we do have partial explanations based on considerations of labor demand, labor supply, technological variability, and institutional influences. Attempts to integrate these various strands of analysis into a unified theory of the determinants of wages and size distribution of income and to implement such a theory empirically have met with only partial success. The empirical results of decomposition studies may aid in the inductive development of a more comprehensive view of this vitally important process.

A final word

In summary, the decomposition studies have proven of great help in establishing the proximate causes of inequality within less-developed countries. We turn now to a synthesis of the main lessons from the various kinds of relative inequality studies.

Conclusion

On inequality at different stages of development

Research studies suggest that the relationship between relative inequality and per capita GNP tends to have an inverted-U shape: Among groups of countries in the cross section, inequality rises in the early stages of economic development and falls in the middle and later stages. In all cases, the proportion of variation in inequality explained by income level is small, which suggests that the initial stage of rising inequality is avoidable. Various authors have found that the usual concomitants of economic development – in particular, improved education, declines in the importance of agriculture, urbanization, and reduced population growth – significantly lower relative income inequality in the cross section. None of the existing studies finds a statistically significant relationship between the level of inequality and the rate of short-run economic growth. They also fail to establish any substantial importance of tax systems and agricultural productivity improvements for inequality. None of these correlates of inequality is decisive, in the sense of accurately discriminating between high- and low-inequality countries.

On inequality change in less-developed countries

We now have studies of changing relative inequality in the actual economic development histories of more than twenty less-developed countries. Examining the experiences of the thirteen countries for which data sources appear to be reliable, we may conclude that inequality has risen in slightly more countries than it has fallen in. No necessary pattern emerges. ~~Earlier, we saw~~ that the *level* of inequality in a *cross section* of countries tends to be systematically related to several aspects of countries' economic structure, but none of these factors was found to be decisive. When it comes to *changes* in inequality, the evidence is similarly mixed. Scattered studies provide some information on the association between changes in the various determinants of incomes and changes in income inequality. No general relationship has ~~thus far~~ been encountered between changing inequality on the one hand and initial level of inequality, level of GNP, or rate of growth on the other. A thoroughgoing analysis of the relation between changing income distribution and countries' development policies and performances worldwide is yet to be undertaken. Some evidence for a limited sample of countries is presented in Chapter 6.

On decomposing LDC inequality

From our examination of three types of decompositions of inequality and four methodologies for decomposition analysis and our review of the findings of empirical studies in less-developed countries, several methodological and empirical conclusions emerge.

The three decompositions–by functional income source, by economic sectors, and by income-determining characteristics–are basically quite different. Source and sector decompositions give an accounting for income inequality, whereas determinant decompositions are interpreted causally.

The various decomposition methodologies–by Gini coefficient, Theil index, analysis of variance, and Atkinson index–are suited for different types of problems. For the source problem, the Gini decomposition technique is an effective method. In analysis of inequality within and among mutually exclusive sectors, any of the available techniques, though they are not entirely interchangeable, will serve more or less satisfactorily. For gauging the causal importance of various explanatory factors, analysis of variance can do more than any of the other approaches.

Source decomposition studies point to variation in labor incomes as the predominant factor accounting for income inequality. To understand the structure of income inequality in LDCs, knowledge of the determinants of incomes from wages and self-employment becomes paramount, as does an understanding of the functioning of LDC labor markets.

Sector decomposition studies indicate substantially more inequality within regions than across them. This finding implies the need to look within regions for other sources of income variability, at the level of either the worker or his job.

From studies that decompose inequality by income-determining characteristics, we find that more inequality is attributable to variation in personal characteristics than to the sector of employment or locational aspects. The most powerful personal characteristics explaining inequality are education and age; occupation, economic sector, and location have lesser effects.

Singly and together, decomposition studies in less-developed countries lead to an inescapable conclusion: the primary importance of income variation according to attributes of individuals and the secondary role of variation between economic segments grouped according to sector of the economy or functional income source. Given this overall conclusion, the need for further microeconomic income determination studies at the level of the household stands out. Sectoral considerations may have a role to play in determining LDC inequality, too, explaining why some individuals with a given set of personal attributes (education, age, sex, etc.) receive higher incomes than others. These microeconomic factors are treated further in Chapter 5. These studies, when combined with more macroeconomic analyses, may shed additional light on the systemic forces generating inequality in LDCs.

Absolute income, absolute poverty, and development

Absolute poverty

In this ~~chapter~~ section, distributional aspects of development are studied in absolute terms. The first section examines absolute incomes and their correlates and introduces earnings functions. This discussion is followed in the next section by an analysis of the question, How segmented are LDC labor markets? The third section addresses absolute poverty, including various definitions of absolute poverty, counts of the numbers of people failing to attain basic standards of living, and profiles of poverty populations. The chapter continues in the fourth section with a review of the evidence on changing absolute income and poverty in the course of economic development. Conclusions are in the last section.

Absolute incomes and earnings functions

With the rising concern for income distribution in less-developed countries, it is incumbent upon students of economic development to gain a clear understanding of the determinants of incomes at the individual and household levels. Studies decomposing income inequality were reviewed in Chapter 4. Those studies demonstrate that in the countries for which we have information, variations in labor income account for a larger fraction of total income inequality than do variations in all other income sources combined. This is partly because labor's functional share is higher than any other, partly because, for most individuals and families in LDCs, labor is the predominant if not sole income source. Both total income and labor income are in turn associated with economically relevant characteristics of individuals and of their jobs. Hence an understanding of labor income inequality and its correlates is central to the study of income distribution in developing countries.

How are we to deal with this fact of demonstrated importance – that some persons receive much higher wages (or self-employment income) than do others? Standard development economics, with its emphasis on functional distribution of income and its usual assumption of labor-force homogeneity, cannot provide a sufficient answer. We must look elsewhere.

Fortunately, we may turn for help to another field of economics: labor economics. A now-standard tool of labor economics is the earnings function,[1] which is a functional relationship between the income of a recipient unit (typically an individual, though sometimes a family) and the factors thought to determine that unit's income. Earnings functions have been applied increasingly in the last decade to the study of developing countries, and this is an area where intellectual arbitrage has had a high payoff.

Earnings functions permit answers to questions like the following: How important is it to one's income to have one more year of education? to work in a capital-intensive industry? to be a member of a labor union? The importance of these factors is judged in two different ways: information evaluation and quantitative estimation. From an informational point of view, the proportions of income variance explained by each of the variables are used to indicate the value of information about the person or his job – the value of knowing, for example, a person's education, whether he is a union member, or how capital intensive his industry is. For quantitative estimation, we may measure how large is the effect on income of a particular income determinant; this yields such information as the rate of return on the marginal year of education, the percentage income gain owing to unionism, or the incremental wages paid by capital-intensive industries.

In earnings-function analysis in developed countries, the preferred income variable is usually taken to be the hourly wage. But in the context of less-developed countries, it is hazardous to estimate the hourly wage. In part, this is because a large fraction of the labor force is self-employed rather than working for wages. Also, many people simply do not know how many hours they work, because in low-income countries' labor markets, periods of work and nonwork may be interspersed and fully occupy the day. For these reasons, it may be preferable to use total labor earnings (per day, week, or month) rather than the hourly wage as the income concept under analysis.

In specifying the functional form of the earnings function, a number of considerations suggest the advisability of a semilog form, that is, regressing the *logarithm* of earnings on such potential explanatory variables as years of education, union membership, and capital intensity of the industry. One justification for the logarithmic specification is that it follows directly from human capital–theoretic reasoning. But even if one is skeptical of human capital models, the logarithm of income may be justified on other bases, among them the fact that income distributions are approximately log-normally distributed; the ability to interpret each regression coefficient in a semilog regression as a percentage effect on income of a unit change in the explanatory variable; and the empirical finding in earnings-function studies that the semilogarithmic form provides a better fit to the data than other functional forms involving the same variables. For a thorough discussion of these specification issues, see Mincer (1974).

What factors ought to enter into earnings functions as explanatory variables? Here is a list of some of the variables that have been considered and found to be significant determinants of income in LDCs:

Job characteristics: occupation, union membership
Employer characteristics: industry, profits, capital intensity, cost structure, industrial concentration, firm size, foreign ownership
Personal characteristics: education, training, age, experience, socioeconomic origins, ability and intelligence, race, sex, migration history
Location: region, urban–rural
Compensating factors: safety, other working conditions, fringe benefits, employment stability, cost-of-living differences
Complementary factors of production: land ownership, ecological zone, availability of capital, access to credit

This list could be expanded ad infinitum. Innumerable

tabulations of incomes and earnings cross-classified by these characteristics may be found. The available evidence is surveyed in a recent paper by Psacharopoulos (1978).

Commonly, the explanatory variables are entered into earnings functions in a rather ad hoc manner. Economic theory does not yet offer a comprehensive explanation for income inequality. There are, however, partial explanations based on considerations of labor demand (see Welch, 1970; and Johnson, 1970), labor supply,[2] technological variability,[3] institutional influences,[4] and compensating differentials.[5] One recent review (Sahota, 1978) listed eight theoretical approaches: the ability theory, the stochastic theory, the individual choice theory, the human capital theory, theories of educational inequalities, the inheritance theory, the life-cycle theory, and public income redistribution theories. Some of these strands of analysis have been synthesized in empirical work.[6] However, the construction of a unified theory of the determinants of wages and size distribution of income has so far eluded economists.[7] The formulation of such a theory merits high priority.

One particularly noteworthy distinction in the empirical literature is between studies that emphasize firms' characteristics as determinants of earnings and those that emphasize workers' characteristics. In the former type of study, factors such as the value added per worker, largeness and foreign ownership of the firm, and presence or absence of a labor union are thought to be the principal determinants of wages. Other studies, many but not all of which are in the human capital tradition, give greater weight to the characteristics of workers. This type of research looks to an individual's education, labor market experience, and similar personal characteristics in attempting to explain his or her income.

An important feature of these two types of studies is that they usually have been done in isolation from one another. Now, however, attempts are being made to integrate them. Among the LDCs where integrated studies of this type (largely unpublished as yet) are under way are Tanzania, Malaysia, Peru, Chile, and Colombia.[8]

From a policy perspective the findings matter a great deal. Different policies are in order if the cause of low incomes is lack of skills rather than lack of demand for skilled people, or if people are poor because the only available work is in low-paying sectors rather than because they are discriminated against by virtue of things like race or sex. Knowledge of the determinants of wage structures helps suggest policy areas that would be most fruitful in raising the incomes of the poor.

From an analytical point of view, the finding that incomes and earnings are associated with more than just the personal characteristics of the individual is provocative. It suggests the incompleteness, if not the downright incorrectness, of the main theory of the size distribution of income, which is the human capital model. As an adjunct or even replacement for human capital theory, some analysts of LDC labor markets have turned to segmentation theory. An analysis of labor market segmentation follows.

On labor market segmentation

Labor market segmentation is increasingly being offered as an explanation of inequality and poverty in LDCs. The goal of this section is to evaluate the segmentation literature.[9] The plan is first to define segmentation in the labor market, then to review theories of how the labor force is segmented, and finally to consider evidence on the existence of segmentation.

What is labor market segmentation?

To answer what segmentation is, it may be helpful to discuss what it is not. Consider, therefore, the standard textbook model of a nonsegmented (i.e., homogeneous) labor market.

In the simplest textbook model, supply and demand for labor determine the volume of employment and the wage rate paid. If all firms and workers are homogeneous, the labor market processes and outcomes are the same for everyone. In particular, this means that all workers receive the same wage and the only unemployment is frictional.

Heterogeneity of outcome is the essential characteristic of many definitions of labor market segmentation. One definition of segmentation is that given by Edwards, Reich, and Gordon (1975:xi):

The *labor market* consists of those institutions which mediate, effect, or determine the purchase and sale of labor power; the *labor process* consists of the organization and conditioning of the activity of production itself, i.e., the consumption of labor power by the capitalists. Segmentation occurs when the labor market or labor process is divided into separate submarkets or subprocesses of segments, distinguished by different characteristics, behavioral rules, and working conditions. [Emphasis in the original]

A similar conception of segmentation as observable differences among groups appears in Freedman (1976).

According to these authors, segmentation is easy to document. By the preceding definitions, certain observations-professionals earn more than manual laborers, better-educated workers receive higher incomes than less-educated workers, unionized industries pay a wage premium over nonunionized ones, urban incomes are higher than rural incomes, and men are paid more than women-are prima facie evidence of labor market segmentation.

These definitions and this type of evidence are unsatisfactory. No attempt is made to standardize for any possible compositional differences between groups. In the case of educational differences, allowance should be made for the period of time when the better-educated individuals were in school and not receiving income; in the case of male-female differences, it is desirable to standardize for length, quality, and continuity of labor-market experience; and so on.

The absence of standardization is an important conceptual deficiency in some writings on segmentation, one that is rectified in other work. Thus, Souza and Tokman (1977:8), for instance, claim: "For segmentation in the labor market to exist, persons *with equal abilities* ought to receive different incomes depending on the stratum of the productive units in which they work" (translation mine, emphasis added). Similarly, Mazumdar and Ahmed (1977:1) write: "A rather stringent definition of labor market segmentation is that a difference in earnings can be attributed to 'institutional' factors after we have allowed for variations in measurable human quality factors like education and experience." Both pairs of authors present empirical results (for several Latin American cities and for Malaysia, respectively) that are consistent with the existence of segmentation as they have defined it. Critics of the notion of segmentation would contest this kind of evidence, arguing that the included variables (things like years of education and age) fail to capture many other important human capital characteristics, such as quality of schooling, continuity of experience, extent of on-the-job training, and such personal characteristics as intelligence and motivation.

If all there were to the concept of segmentation were the claim that different groups are rewarded differently in the labor market, there would be little controversy, because equality of outcome obviously does not obtain in modern economies. Segmentation theory, however, goes further by contending that labor markets function in a particular segmented fashion. We take up segmented market theories next.

Theories of labor market segmentation

Labor market segmentation theories argue that labor markets are restrictive – restrictive in the sense that some individuals are prevented from acquiring more education, moving to higher-paying locations, or in other ways taking action aimed at increasing their attractiveness to the market. As Flanagan (1973:253) writes: "The crux of any theory of labor market segmentation is the mechanism or institutional barriers which truncate competition by precluding mobility between the various labor market segments."

One segmentation theory is the dual labor market approach advanced by Doeringer and Piore (1970). As described by Wachter (1974:639), the dual labor market model advances four hypotheses:

First, it is useful to dichotomize the economy into a primary and a secondary sector. Second, the wage and employment mechanisms in the secondary sector are distinct from those in the primary sector. Third, economic mobility between these two sectors is sharply limited, and hence workers in the secondary sector are essentially trapped there. Finally, the secondary sector is marked by pervasive underemployment because workers who could be trained for skilled jobs at no more than the usual cost are confined to unskilled jobs.

One consequence of the dual labor market theory is that poverty is thought to result from a shortage of good jobs rather than from a shortage of work effort and skill.

Another segmentation theory is the radical model advanced by Gordon (1972), Reich (1971), and others. In the radical approach, labor market segmentation is the outcome of forces fundamental to the nature of the economic system. Segmentation exists, radicals argue, because it is functional and essential to the maintenance of a system of monopoly capitalism. Segmentation is analyzed within this model using a broad historical approach in which considerations of relative power are central.

In response to the challenges posed by these and other segmentation theories, orthodox economists have extended the conventional framework to build more complete models. These newer orthodox models extend the logic of profit (or income) maximization to a more complex setting. Among the real-world complexities that are introduced are barriers to mobility and entry. These include the combined effects of inertia, ignorance, prejudice, misinformation, and psychic and monetary costs in a world where limitations may be imposed by discrimination, unions, and government regulations.

Orthodox and segmentation theories have the same ana- lytical core: the postulate of maximizing behavior by indi- vidual agents. So the contribution of segmentation theory lies not in the novelty of its behavioral assumptions but elsewhere. As Gordon (1972:14) writes: "Orthodox analysis ... tended to take market structure for granted and probe the determinants of behavior within those given structures. Some economists sought to develop economic models which dealt directly with these basic concerns about the relation- ship between labor market structure and income." This suggests that the heart of the distinction between orthodox theories of labor markets and segmentation theories may well lie in the nature of the questions that they address, rather than in their way of conceptualizing the behavior of individ- uals and firms. Segmentation theorists address fundamental questions: Why is discrimination in the economic system perpetuated? Why is poverty transmitted across generations? Why do labor movements in many countries accept the legitimacy of the prevailing economic order? These root questions about operation of labor markets have not received much attention among orthodox economists, nor have the relevant variables been endogenized by them. I predict that in the 1980s much will be learned from those among us who sympathetically blend orthodox and segmentation models and questions.

Evidence on labor market segmentation

Income studies have now been done with varying degrees of sophistication for a large number of countries. *That* there are differences in labor market returns cannot be disputed. *Why* there are differences is the matter for debate. Are persons *with the same characteristics* rewarded differentially depending on where they are employed? In empirical research, an affirmative finding would be taken as evidence of labor market segmentation, at least according to the Edwards-Reich-Gordon, Freedman, Souza-Tokman, and Mazumdar-Ahmed definitions.

Take, for example, the possibility that labor market segmentation is associated with region. Multivariate questions like the effect of region on the incomes of workers with given education and experience are answerable empirically, but only within a multivariate framework. In most countries, questions of this sort cannot be answered, because the correlates of income are typically presented in simply univariate tables. Questionnaires on individual income recipient units are ordinarily needed, preferably in computer-readable form.

Given data on individual recipient units, researchers can explore in much greater depth the sources of inequality. It is possible to ascertain the relative importance of each of several variables in explaining income, following decomposition procedures like those described in Chapter 4. Studies including the ones summarized in Table 4.9 have shown that, despite large differentials in income *between* one geographic area and another, the great bulk of income inequality is *within* geographic areas rather than between them. To a lesser extent, this is also true of divisions of the labor force according to education or any of the other correlates of income. Simply put, no one variable-nor set of explanatory variables combined-is decisive in predicting income with a high degree of precision. One research task for the future is to consider the unexplained variation and to see what accounts for the residual.

The nondecisiveness of the available variables in determin-

Table 5.1. *Income differences in urban Colombia*

Group	Mean income (pesos per 3 months)
All urban manufacturing workers	6,570
Education breakdown	
Primary	3,820
Secondary	8,020
Higher	16,180
Sector breakdown (selected industries)	
Clothing	4,100
Transportation	5,920
Foodstuffs	6,730
Textiles	8,200
Electrical machinery	8,240
Chemicals	12,320

Source: Fields (1978).

ing income has important implications for labor market segmentation. In urban Colombia, the income differences shown in Table 5.1 have been observed. Some might interpret these data as convincing evidence of labor market segmentation by education and economic sector. Yet when the individual data are plotted, as in Figures 5.1–5.3, we see that there is much overlap between one education or industry group and another. Given the more disaggregated presenta-

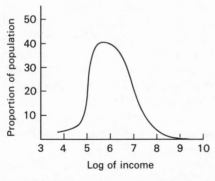

Figure 5.1. Distribution of (log) income for urban Colombia manufacturing workers, full sample. *Source*: Fields (1978: 87).

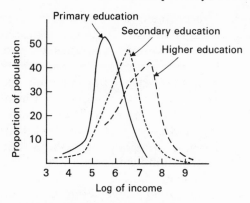

Figure 5.2. Distribution of (log) income by education group. *Source*: Fields (1978: 87).

tion of the available data, we should be much less willing to conclude that the Colombian labor market is segmented, at least in these dimensions.

It also bears mention that the literature offers many examples of tests for labor market segmentation that are methodologically inappropriate. A particularly serious error is to look at the determinants of income for low-income workers and to infer from the small magnitudes of regression coefficients or analysis-of-variance effects that income is not

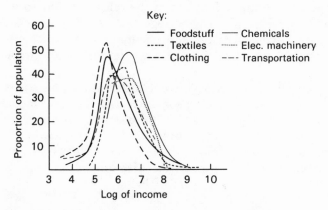

Figure 5.3. Distribution of (log) income by industry group. *Source*: Fields (1978: 87).

affected by education. This problem (known in econometrics as "truncation bias") is found in some of the segmentation literature.[10] It arises when a sample is stratified by the dependent variable (in this case, income). The independent variable (here, education) has two effects: It determines the probability of a particular individual's being included in the sample, and it determines the income that individual receives if he is included. Among the less-educated workers, many will have low enough incomes to qualify for the sample. However, among highly educated individuals, only those with unusually low incomes are selected. Not surprisingly, with such a sample, the estimated effect of education on income understates the true effect. Nothing can be learned about labor market segmentation from such invalid "evidence." Equally invalid are similar tests conducted within low-income occupations (e.g., among small farmers in poor countries)[11] or within low-income neighborhoods (e.g., in urban ghettos or squatter settlements).[12] Stratification according to endogenous variables is erroneous and misleading. This is not to refute the existence of labor market segmentation in these countries but rather to call into question the evidence offered in support of it.

Heterogeneity of income and employment opportunities can be studied more fruitfully by disaggregating by exogenous rather than by endogenous variables. Standardization by age, sex, education, and race may be relevant. But to deal satisfactorily with the many endogenous variables associated with income (e.g., industry and occupation), more comprehensive structural models of the wage-determination process are needed.

The central issue facing income-distribution analysts, be they orthodox or segmentation theorists, is why income differences exist. Are they due to systematic forces or to luck? to productivity differentials or to discrimination? to characteristics of workers or of their jobs? What is the role of compensating differentials (for ease and pleasantness of work, differential safety, costs of living, risks of unemployment, and so on)? To what extent do current differentials reflect life-cycle factors and present value considerations? How much is due to barriers to mobility? to barriers to entry?

Despite what is known of some of these questions, we are disappointingly far from knowing the answers to others. There are abundant opportunities for enriching the study of low-income countries by bringing to bear the analytical tools of supply and demand from economics, stratification theory from sociology, and systems approaches from political science (just to name a few). As concerned world citizens, we can use these tools to advance our understanding of the determinants of poverty and economic malaise and thereby take the first step toward their eradication.

Absolute poverty: definitions, numbers, and profiles

Earlier in this book, I argued that a country's progress in alleviating poverty is best gauged by a measure designed especially for that purpose. Several such absolute poverty measures are now in existence. The objective of this section is to consider how to use them to implement the absolute poverty approach to the study of economic development.

Much of the pioneering work on absolute poverty in the context of LDCs has been done by Indian economists.[13] It is fitting that researchers from India would be at the forefront of this effort. The extent of absolute poverty in India is staggering: about 240 million people with incomes below U.S. $50 per *year*, and about 360 million below U.S. $75. Estimates of the extent of absolute poverty in the less-developed countries of the world are presented later in this section.

In broad outline, the absolute poverty approach to the study of economic development requires that we first define a time-invariant measure of economic position, which we agree to call the poverty line. Suppose we choose real income as the appropriate measure of economic position. Next we must obtain information on the number of income-recipient units (persons or families) with incomes below that line and the average income among them. In addition, we may wish to know the degree of income inequality among the poor. After that, we may want to characterize the poor: their personal characteristics, job attributes, and so on. Finally, so that we can measure the extent to which poverty has been alleviated (or not) in a particular country's economic development, we must have sufficiently comparable and detailed figures on the size distribution of income for at least two time periods, and preferably more. Let us consider each of these points.

Defining the absolute poverty line

Conceptually, the absolute poverty line should be defined in such a way that we would have little hesitancy in regarding an individual or family with income below that figure as poor. A straightforward way of doing this is to establish a dollar income figure, chosen in as scientific a way as possible. In the United States, for example, the poverty line was derived by ascertaining the amount of money needed to purchase a nutritionally adequate diet consistent with the food preferences of the poorest groups in the population, and then multiplying this figure by a factor of three, because the poor spend about one-third of their incomes on food (Orshansky, 1965). To cite some LDC examples, the poverty line in Brazil is taken to be the minimum wage in the Northeast (Brazil's poorest region), adjusted in other parts of the country for cost-of-living differences (Fishlow, 1972); another LDC example, based on consumption rather than income, is found in Musgrove and Ferber (1976). In both cases, the specific income figure depends on family size. In India, the Planning Commission used a figure of Rs. 20 per month (in 1960–1 prices) per capita as the nutritionally minimal standard. This figure was modified by other researchers: Dandekar and Rath (1971) took Rs. 15 per capita per month for rural poverty and Rs. 22½ for urban, whereas Bardhan (1970 and 1974b) used Rs. 15 and Rs. 18 respectively.[14] The World Bank has estimated the population below U.S. $50 per capita per year (Ahluwalia, 1974), whereas the U.S. agency for International Development (AID, 1975) has suggested an international poverty line of U.S. $150 per capita per year. Both sets of estimates are based on official exchange rates.[15]

These various definitions raise a number of conceptual issues, some of which have not yet been satisfactorily resolved. The following discussion is brief, so as not to divert us too much from the more substantive issues. Readers seeking more in-depth treatment of these issues are referred elsewhere.[16]

Choice of recipient unit. Economics tries to measure material (if not spiritual) well-being. Yet there is no consensus among economists on whether the appropriate unit of measurement is the family or the individual.

Among those who regard the family as the appropriate unit is Simon Kuznets (see, in particular, Kuznets, 1976). Perhaps the most important justification for looking at families rather than individuals is the fact of widespread income sharing within families. Both economically active and dependent persons are included. The family is the unit that decides how to allocate the distribution of goods and services among its members. Another reason for choosing the family as a recipient unit is the difficulty in many situations of attributing incomes or earnings to a specific individual, as in family-run farms or businesses. Still another is that property is jointly held, so that the income from that property is jointly received and not assignable to any one family member. Finally, a family member or members may engage in economic activity specifically to supplement another member's income or to replace the loss of that income, as studies of "additional worker effects" bear witness.[17]

On the other hand, there are counterarguments for preferring individuals as the recipient unit under investigation. It has been argued that families may systematically distribute their resources inequitably–in favor of the head of household and at the expense of other family members (see, e.g., Srinivasan, n.d.; McGreevey, 1976; and Johnson and Whitelaw, 1972). Then too, from the perspective of income, the labor market employs individuals and rewards each individual according to his characteristics. Finally, certain key indicators of economic development–for example, the composition of employment, rates of infant mortality, and school achievement ratios–pertain exclusively to individuals.

My overall inclination is to use family income data where available to measure the fraction in poverty and their income shortfall and to use individual characteristics to try to characterize the poor. In practice, data are often limited, and we must use what we have.

Absolute poverty versus relative poverty. The poverty line should bear a reasonable relationship to living standards in the country in question. By U.S. standards, virtually the entire population of some countries would be classified as poor, whereas by Indian standards, virtually no one in the United States would qualify as absolutely poor. But recognizing that the definition of poverty within a country is chosen relative to that country's economic level is very different from using a relative poverty measure for that country. Relative poverty measures-such as the average absolute income received by the poorest 40% of the population or the fraction of the population with incomes less than half the mean-are not suitable, at least for most applications, for reasons given in Chapter 2.

Direct method versus income method. One issue for debate is whether it is better to try to measure the consumption of particular goods and services directly or to use income as a proxy. Those who advocate direct measurement see directness as a virtue. Death because of material deprivation is the most compelling form of poverty. Dietary inadequacy is next. The direct method enables us to identify those who are not eating enough. The direct method also permits us to measure cumulative deficiencies in some concrete fashion.[18] In similar fashion, we can quantify the number who live in substandard housing, who have not received education, or who lack access to health care.

The income method is less precise. Skeptics may contend that although a certain dollar amount of income is required to buy the basic necessities of life, there is no assurance that a person (or family) with that income in fact purchases those goods.[19] The income method is also less graphic. Problems arise in deciding how to include all the components of full income and how to evaluate these components properly. These problems may at times induce an ugly cynicism.[20] Finally, there is a fine, albeit meaningful, conceptual difference between the direct and the income method.[21]

I see considerable merit in both the income and the direct consumption methods of defining and measuring poverty. Both measures are informative and should be used whenever possible.

Incidence versus duration. Most research on poverty in LDCs is concerned with the incidence of poverty. This provides information on the number who are poor at any given time, the extent of their income shortfall, and their socioeconomic characteristics; but by focusing attention on those who are poor at any given time, we lack data on the flow of individuals (or families) into or out of poverty. Flow data also prove insightful. In the United States, for example, we know that the majority of those who are poor this year were poor last year and that three or four times as many persons experience a spell of unemployment during the year as are unemployed at any one time. A useful area of future research in LDCs would be to explore the duration of poverty over time and the determinants of mobility out of poverty (or lack of such mobility). For research in this area, the framework suggested by Robinson and Dervis (1977) might be helpful.

Consumption vs. income. As an indicator of poverty, it is better to have data on consumption than on income for at least three reasons. For one thing, consumption directly measures the flow of utility-producing inputs. Income, in contrast, measures the ability to purchase those inputs. Typically, our concern is with what is in fact consumed. Secondly, income is measured over a short length of time: week, month, or year. During such periods, some persons' incomes may be unusually low because of stochastic events (illness, drought, temporary fall in world price for the crop grown) or because of life-cycle effects (very young or very old age). A better measure of permanent economic position, it is argued, is the present value of lifetime income. In the absence of reliable data on lifetime income, economic theory suggests the use of current consumption as an indicator of permanent income (Friedman, 1957). Thirdly, prices may differ substantially across regions, or goods may not be available at the prevailing price, either of which cases would lead to a divergence between distribution of income and distribution of consumption.

We often cannot get reliable information on consumption. When households are asked how much they consume, a frequent response is, "I spend what I make." Consumption information usually must be obtained from detailed household budget studies, which because of their high administrative costs are not in wide use. More often than not, the distribution of income is all we can get for a country; so a poverty definition must be income- rather than consumption-based.

Although the issue of consumption versus income may be important in identifying *which specific* individuals or families are poor at any particular time, I doubt whether the choice makes much difference in determining *how many* are poor in any one year or how that number has changed over time. The ideal would be to look at consumption *and* income data and reconcile any conflicting indications that might emerge.

Conclusions on defining the absolute poverty line. All the income adjustments, classifications, and other fine points mentioned are useful and indeed indispensable in measuring the true extent of the poverty problem in LDCs. This holds whether we are interested in the distribution of income within a given country at a point in time, or in a time-series analysis of that country's development path, or in a cross section of many countries at different stages of development. These adjustments define an ideal: what information we would like to have and what we ought to do with it.

With all the attention paid to theoretical complexities and definitional problems, I fear we may be moving quite far from where we want to be. The major goal in measuring absolute poverty is to quantify the extent of economic misery in a country or in the world so as to be able at a later time to assess progress toward its alleviation and, more generally, to learn how the benefits of economic development are distributed. In other words, we ultimately want to assess *changes* in income distribution over time. In time-series comparisons, whatever biases and limitations there are in our definitions of poverty and in the data used to measure it at one time may reappear the next time. If so, the indicated changes in the unadjusted data, for all their imperfections, are likely to parallel the changes in the "ideal" distribution of income.[22]

Provided that the poverty line is appropriate to living standards in the country under investigation, I see little value in worrying about what the exact dollar figure should be. Absolute income standards like $150 per capita or the minimum wage in the country are quite reasonable bench marks.

What is important, indeed crucial, about the absolute poverty line in a dynamic development context is that it be held *constant in real terms* (i.e., after adjusting for inflation). No other adjustment (e.g., for productivity growth; see Bacha, 1976) is appropriate.

In empirical research, as a check on the arbitrariness of any given poverty line, one might experiment with simple multiples of that line, as Bardhan (1974*b*) did in India, to test whether similar changes in the incidence and severity of poverty are found. In this way, disputes over the correctness of any specific poverty line definition are minimized and attention is directed where it should be, namely, at the constancy of the line itself and the distribution of the population around it.

This is not to say that more refined definitions and better data are not of great importance, for indeed they are. What I mean to be arguing is that in the interim, pending further improvements, in countries with comparable and reliable censuses or surveys, I think we would do better to look at the data on distribution of income and consumption to try to measure progress toward alleviating poverty than to look at nothing at all. Thus, I would conclude that the usual types of figures on incomes, although not ideal in many respects, may serve as a useful guide to changes in the economic position of the poor.

The available empirical information on changing poverty over time in LDCs is synthesized in the later section of this chapter entitled "Economic growth, absolute income, and absolute poverty." But before turning to those data, we look at two other issues: the number who are poor in the world and profiles of the poor at present.

Absolute poverty numbers

The numbers on absolute poverty in the world are mind-
numbing. I shall not try to articulate the dimensions of
human suffering that they represent. The numbers speak
for themselves.

Table 1.1 presented one compilation of data on absolute
poverty in LDCs. The coverage of the table was limited to
the thirty-seven countries that received foreign assistance
from the U.S. Agency for International Development and for
which income-distribution data were available. Absolute
poverty was defined as a per capita income less than $150
(in 1969 prices). In those countries alone, the number of
poor approached 800 million–nearly 80% of their populations. Other data have been gathered by the World Bank
and are reproduced in Table 5.2. The table includes poverty
rates for forty countries whose combined population totaled
1.2 billion. In those countries, some 30% had incomes below
$50 per capita per year, and another 20% had annual incomes
between $50 and $75. That is, nearly 600 million people
received less than $75 per year just in the countries tabulated.
Furthermore, China is omitted from these data owing to lack
of statistics. With the addition of China, the number of
absolutely poor would be several hundred million greater.

Who are the poor? What characterizes them? We take
this question up next.

Absolute poverty profiles

Who are the poor? What are their socioeconomic characteristics? How do they earn their livings? Where and how do
they work? These are questions that need to be answered in
order to understand the causes of poverty and to design
antipoverty policies. This section draws together some of
the available information on "profiles of poverty" in LDCs,
that is, the socioeconomic makeup of the poor.

Many socioeconomic characteristics are considered: sex,
race, age, family size, occupation, education, and so on. The
overriding concern, as far as the poverty profile is concerned,
is to bring together the available information for a number of
countries and to point out patterns where they exist.

It is not practicable to employ an internationally constant

Table 5.2. *Estimates of population below poverty line in 1969*

Country	1969 GNP per capita	1969 population (millions)	Population below $50		Population below $75	
			Millions	% of total population	Millions	% of total population
Latin America						
Ecuador	264	5.9	2.2	37.0	3.5	58.5
Honduras	265	2.5	.7	28.0	1.0	38.0
El Salvador	295	3.4	.5	13.5	.6	18.4
Dominican Republic	323	4.2	.5	11.0	.7	15.9
Colombia	347	20.6	3.2	15.4	5.6	27.0
Brazil	347	90.8	12.7	14.0	18.2	20.0
Jamaica	640	2.0	.2	10.0	.3	15.4
Guyana	390	.7	.1	9.0	.1	15.1
Peru	480	13.1	2.5	18.9	3.3	25.5
Costa Rica	512	1.7	a	2.3	.1	8.5
Mexico	645	48.9	3.8	7.8	8.7	17.8
Uruguay	649	2.9	.1	2.5	.2	5.5
Panama	692	1.4	.1	3.5	.2	11.0
Chile	751	9.6	a	a	a	a
Venezuela	974	10.0	a	a	a	a
Argentina	1,054	24.0	a	a	a	a
Puerto Rico	1,600	2.8	a	a	a	a
Total	545	244.5	26.6	10.8	42.5	17.4

Table 5.2. (cont.)

Country	1969 GNP per capita	1969 population (millions)	Population below $50		Population below $75	
			Millions	% of total population	Millions	% of total population
Asia						
Burma	72	27.0	14.5	53.6	19.2	71.0
Sri Lanka	95	12.2	4.0	33.0	7.8	63.5
India	100	537.0	239.0	44.5	359.3	66.9
Pakistan (E&W)	100	111.8	36.3	32.5	64.7	57.9
Thailand	173	34.7	9.3	26.8	15.4	44.3
Korea	224	13.3	.7	5.5	2.3	17.0
Philippines	233	37.2	4.8	13.0	11.2	30.0
Turkey	290	34.5	4.1	12.0	8.2	23.7
Iraq	316	9.4	2.3	24.0	3.1	33.3
Taiwan	317	13.8	1.5	10.7	2.0	14.3
Malaysia	323	10.6	1.2	11.0	1.6	15.5
Iran	350	27.9	2.3	8.5	4.2	15.0
Lebanon	570	2.6	a	1.0	.1	5.0
Total	132	872.0	320.0	36.7	499.1	57.2

146

Africa					
Chad	75	3.5	1.5	43.1	2.7	77.5
Dahomey	90	2.6	1.1	41.6	2.3	90.1
Tanzania	92	12.8	7.4	57.9	9.3	72.9
Niger	94	3.9	1.3	33.0	2.3	59.9
Madagascar	119	6.7	3.6	53.8	4.7	69.6
Uganda	128	8.3	1.8	21.3	4.1	49.8
Sierra Leone	165	2.5	1.1	43.5	1.5	61.5
Senegal	229	3.8	.9	22.3	1.3	35.3
Ivory Coast	237	4.8	.3	7.0	1.4	28.5
Tunisia	241	4.9	1.1	22.5	1.6	32.1
Rhodesia	274	5.1	.9	17.4	1.9	37.4
Zambia	340	4.2	.3	6.3	.3	7.5
Gabon	547	.5	.1	15.7	.1	23.0
South Africa	729	20.2	2.4	12.0	3.1	15.5
Total	303	83.8	23.8	28.4	36.6	43.6
Grand total	228	1,200.3	370.4	30.9	578.2	48.2

[a] Negligible.
Source: Ahluwalia (1974).

Table 5.3, part A. *Poverty profiles in selected less-developed countries*

Brazil (1960) — Fishlow (1972)

Section	Category	Poor families (%)	All other (%)
Education (Of household head)	None	64	35
	Primary	35	55
	Lower sec.	1	5
	Upper sec.	0	2
	University	0	2
Age (Of household head)	14–29	17	20
	30–60	70	60
	61+	13	14
Sex (Of household head)	Male	83	92
	Female	17	8
Family size (No. in family)	1	4	6
	2–3	18	33
	4–5	27	32
	6+	51	29
Family composition (No. children 0–14)	0	15	35
	1–2	29	39
	3–4	29	39
	5+	27	7
Number of workers or earners (No. workers per family)	0	11	3
	1	62	59
	2	15	21
	3+	12	17

Malaysia (1970) — Anand (1977)

Section	Category	Incidence of pov. (%)
Education (Of household head)	None	49.0
	Some primary	39.1
	Completed primary	32.8
	Lower secondary	11.7
	Some upper sec.	5.2
	Certificate V or higher	2.1
Age (Of household head)	Under 20	31.5
	20–9	27.4
	30–9	38.5
	40–9	40.4
	50–9	34.3
	Over 60	39.0
Sex (Of household head)	Male	34.6
	Female	44.9
Family size (Household size, selected)	1	23.5
	2	23.2
	4	31.8
	6	41.8
	8	45.6
	10+	45.7
Family composition (No. children 0–14)	0	20.7
	1	30.7
	2	35.2
	3	41.5
	4	48.4
	5+	53.5
Number of workers or earners (No. earners)	0	99.0
	1	41.9
	2	31.1
	3	22.4
	4+	13.3

Taiwan (1972), Kuo (1975)

Of family head	Poor groups (%)	All groups (%)
Illiterate	81.0	12.3
Primary	14.1	51.4
Secondary	0	29.1
College	4.9	7.2

Of family head	Poor groups (%)	All groups (%)
Male	50.9	93.3
Female	49.1	6.7

No. employed	Poor groups (%)	All groups (%)
0	67.9	1.8
1	18.2	42.2
2	13.9	32.2
3+	0	23.8

Thailand (1968/9), Meesook (1975)

Of head	Incidence of pov. (%)
None	21.4
P1–MS2	26.1
MS3–	
MS4	1.1
MS5+	1.8

Of family head	Poor groups (%)	All groups (%)
Under 30	4.9	10.5
30–50	0	65.0
50–60	18.7	18.4
60+	76.4	6.1

Of head	Incidence of pov. (%)
Under 20	8.7
20–9	23.4
30–9	31.2
40–9	24.9
50–9	17.4
60+	17.3

Of head	Incidence of pov. (%)
Male	24.6
Female	18.2

No. of children 0–14	Incidence of pov. (%)
0	7.2
1	11.0
2	21.0
3	26.6
4	36.7
5+	42.0

No. of members	Incidence of pov. (%)
1	1.1
2	5.9
3	8.8
4	18.6
5	20.5
6	27.9
7	32.1
8+	34.8

No. of earners	Incidence of pov. (%)
1	26.9
2	19.7
3	15.4
4	10.8
5+	13.7

Pakistan (1969/70), Iqbal (1977)

No. of members	Relative incidence of pov.
1	2.1
2	1.7
3	1.7
4	1.7
5	1.0
6	.7
7+	.3

No. of earners	Relative incidence of pov.
1	1.3
2	.8
3	.5
4	.2
5+	.1

Table 5.3, part A. *(cont.)*

Country/ date	Source of data	Education	Of head — Average disposable income per household (Rs.)	Age	Sex	Family size	Family composition	Number of workers or earners
India (1964/5)	Bardhan (1974[b]); DaCosta (1971)	Illiterate	1,186					
		Primary	1,489					
		Above primary, below matric-ulation	2,358					
		Matric-ulation and inter-mediate	2,803					
		Prof./tech. cert.	2,630					
		College grad., arts and science	5,432					
		Prof./tech. degree	6,776					
		Postgrad-uate	12,015					

150

Table 5.3, *part B*

Country/date	Labor force status		Occupation	Sector of employment			Rural–urban			Regional data			Miscellaneous data		
		Poor families (%)	All other (%)		Sect. distribution of economically active	Poor families (%)	All other (%)	Location of family	Poor families (%)	All other (%)	Region of family	Poor families (%)	All other (%)	Migratory status of household head	Poor families (%)	All other (%)
Brazil (1960)	Household head economically active	83	92		Agriculture and extractive	68	49	Urban	40	54	North-east	43	15	Migrant rural area	14	14
					Industry	10	15	Rural	60	46	East	40	38	Migrant urban area	19	37
	Occupation of household head	Poor families (%)	All other (%)		Commerce	5	11				South	17	47	Non-mig.	67	49
	Employer	1	4		Services	9	8									
	Self-employed	51	45		Transport and communic.	5	8							No. of children in school	Poor families (%)	All other (%)
	Employee, private sector	37	38		Professional, gov't. etc.	2	8							0	67	67
	Employee, public sector	3	9											1	13	16
	Share-cropper	8	4											2	10	9
														3+	10	8

151

Table 5.3, *part B. (cont.)*

Country/ date	Labor force status		Occupation		Sector of employment		Rural–urban		Regional data		Miscellaneous data	
	Employment status of household head	Incidence of pov. (%)	Of household head	Incidence of household pov. (%)	Sect. of household head	Incidence of pov. (%)	Location	Incidence pov. (%)	Region (selected)	Incidence of pov. (%)	Race	Incidence of pov. (%)
Malaysia (1970)	Employer	5.1	Prof. & tech.	6.7	Agriculture	61.5	Urban	15.8	Johore	32.9	Malay	51.4
	Employee	26.3	Adm. & mgr.	4.4	Agric. production	46.2	Rural	44.6	Kedah	48.6	Chinese	14.7
	Own account	50.1	Clerical	2.7	Mining	18.1			Kelantan	65.2	Indian	24.8
	Housewife/house-worker	30.5	Sales workers	20.0	Manufacturing	21.8			Penang	29.7	Other	40.3
	Unemployed	38.0	Service workers	14.9	Construction	21.5			Perak	34.5		
			Farmers	61.9	Public utilities	21.0			Selangor	19.1		
			Farm laborers	48.6	Commerce	20.2						
			Production wrks.	21.9	Transport & communic.	21.2						
					Services	11.1						

Taiwan (1972)

Geographic location	Poor groups (%)	All groups (%)
Urban	14.5	30.0
Semi-urban	38.8	34.3
Rural	46.7	35.7

Thailand (1968/9)

Region	Incidence of pov. (%)
North	24.0
Centre & East	5.8
Northeast	39.9
South	22.3
Bangkok-Thonburi	1.5

% of total household income by source	Poor groups (%)	All groups (%)
Wages & salaries	16.0	18.6
Self-empl.	70.4	67.1
Property	8.3	9.8
Others	5.2	4.5

Pakistan (1969/70)

Employment status of household head	Relative incidence of pov.
Employer	0.2
Self-employed	1.2
Employee	0.9
Unpaid family wkr.	0.7

Of household head	Relative incidence of pov.
Prof. & tech.	0.6
Admin. & exec.	0.0
Clerical & sales	0.6
Farmers	0.9
Production process workers & related	1.2

153

Table 5.3, *part B.* (cont.)

Country/ date	Labor force status	Occupation	Sector of employment	Rural–urban			Regional data		Miscellaneous data	
				Annual disposable income (Rs.)	% of households Rural	Urban	Region (selected) 1963/4	% destitute	Land (in acres)	Average agric. income in cultivating households (Rs. per year)
India (1964/5)				Under 500	3.2	3.1	Assam	3.9	Under 1	544
				500–999	35.3	17.4	Bihar	23.4	1–2.9	1,060
				1,000–1,999	43.7	37.9	Gujarat	17.5	3–5.9	1,405
				2,000–4,999	10.6	30.5	Kerala	30.4	6–8.9	1,588
				5,000–9,999	2.0	7.1	Madras	20.8	9–10.9	1,740
				10,000 & up	0.2	3.0	Punjab	14.5	11–12.9	2,030
							U.P.	26.7	13–15.9	2,731
							West Bengal	13.2	16–30.9	3,888
									31+	8,868

Note: The following definitions of poverty are used:

Brazil: According to the 1960 Census, "The real minimum wage for 1960 in the Northeast, the poorest region, is taken as the lower limit of acceptable income for a family of 4.3 persons. For rural Brazil, the wage prevailing in the rural areas of the Northeast is taken; for the urban Northeast, the standard of the medium sized municipio is applied; and for all other urban residents, the Northeast level, incremented by 15% to allow for higher relative prices, is applied. The poverty line for different size families is defined with the aid of the elasticity of expenditure on food with respect to family size; because of economies of scale larger families need relatively less income, and conversely for smaller."

Malaysia: The 1970 Census Post-Enumeration Survey considers poor those households for which per capita monthly income falls below M $25 per month. This figure is rigorously derived from a nutritional needs base. The income concept is very broad and includes income in kind as well as imputable income.

Taiwan: The 1972 Survey of Family Income and Expenditure arbitrarily defines as poor those households with incomes below NT $10,000 per year.

Thailand: The 1968/9 Socio-Economic Survey arbitrarily includes as poor all those households for which the per person "total income" falls below 1,000 baht (= $50) per annum. "Total income" includes noncash income.

Pakistan: By the 1969/70 Household Income and Expenditure Survey, the bottom three income classes, constituting 35% of all households, are poor. The poverty line is defined at Rs. 150 per month.

India: In the 1964/5 Sample Survey, National Council of Applied Economic Research, and the 1963/4 National Sample Survey, the regional breakdowns use as the poverty line per capita expenditure below Rs. 13 per month for rural areas and below Rs. 18 per month for urban areas. No specific poverty line is used for the other entries in the table.

poverty line. Such a constant is precluded by differences across nations in income definition, poverty concept, and tabulation procedures, as well as by difficulties in settling on appropriate international exchange rates.[23] Hence the definition of poverty varies from country to country. In some cases it is possible to report results based on a rigorously defined poverty line (Brazil, India, Malaysia). In others, the best we can do is to use an arbitrary poverty line, one low enough to capture a suitable fraction of the population (Thailand). In the rest, the poverty group must be defined in practice as the bottom class or classes reported in the income-distribution tables (Pakistan, Taiwan). Although a standardized poverty line might be preferred, the use of country-specific definitions still produces valuable insights into the factors determining poverty status.

Poverty profiles for six less-developed countries are presented in Table 5.3. I shall now highlight some of the main results country by country and then look across countries for similarities and differences.[24]

Brazil. The salient features of Brazilian poverty appear to be the following:

1. Although poor families, like all other families, are predominantly male-headed, there are almost twice as many female-headed families among the poor (17%) as among the nonpoor (8%).

2. Poverty occurs predominantly among families headed by a prime-aged person. The age group 30–60 years includes 70% of the poor. In other words, the majority of the poor are not poor because of old age or very young age but because even when working at their prime they earn very little. This impression is reinforced by the employment status data: 83% of poor family heads are economically active, and 89% of poor families have at least one earner.

3. Poverty is clearly associated with education. Of the poor, 64% have no education, as compared with 35% of the nonpoor. On the other hand, 9% of the nonpoor have secondary or higher education, compared with 1% of the poor.

4. Poverty is associated with agriculture. Residence in the

rural areas and work in agricultural occupations raise the likelihood of poverty: 60% of the poor are located in predominantly rural areas, and 68% are in agricultural occupations. The incidence of poverty is about twice as high in rural as in urban areas.

5. Poverty is much more severe in some regions than in others; the incidence is about seven times as high in the Northeast as in the South.

6. Demographically, we find that poor families tend to have larger families, more small children, and fewer children in school than their nonpoor counterparts. They also tend to have somewhat fewer workers per family.

Malaysia. The principal features of Malaysia's poverty profile are as follows:

1. The highest incidence of poverty is among the Malays (51%, compared with an overall incidence of 37%). However, in the urban areas, because of the high concentration of Chinese, most of the poor are Chinese (though the incidence of poverty among the Chinese is much lower than among the Malays).

2. The relative incidence of poverty is greater among households where the head is an own-account worker (50%) than where he is unemployed (38%). This interesting finding suggests that the cause of poverty in Malaysia may be low earnings even when a person is fully employed, rather than lack of work. It also highlights the importance of secondary earners in determining a family's poverty status, an importance reinforced by the fact that families are less likely to be poor when there are more earners.

3. Poverty is disproportionately a rural phenomenon, the incidence being nearly three times as high in rural areas (45%) as in urban areas (16%). The highest incidence of poverty is among farmers and farm laborers and among workers in the agricultural sector of the economy.

4. Education and poverty incidence are inversely related, with a large drop in incidence of poverty occurring between primary and secondary school graduates.

5. The highest poverty rates are found among families with a middle-aged head (30-49), presumably because of

largeness of family. The incidence of poverty is higher among larger families, among families with more young children, and among female-headed families.

6. Poverty is found disproportionately in the smaller towns and in the less-urbanized regions and among farmers and agriculture sector workers.

Taiwan. From the data provided, the following seem to be important features of Taiwan's poverty:

1. Although the national average for illiteracy is only 12%, 81% of the poor are illiterate.

2. Whereas 7% of all families are headed by females, 49% of poor families have female heads. Thus poverty appears to be associated with the loss or absence of a male breadwinner.

3. There is a direct correlation between age and poverty. More than three-quarters of poor households have heads over 60 years of age, who are past the prime earning years. By contrast, none of the poor families in the sample had heads between 20 and 40 years of age, when earning power is at its peak. This suggests that able-bodied young men are not to be found in poverty. Hence poverty is Taiwan is not as much a problem of low earnings at full effort as of old age and social misfortune.

4. Of the poor, 47% are located in rural areas, compared with a national figure of 36%. At the other end, 15% of the poor are in urban areas, compared with a national average of 30%. Thus the incidence of poverty is considerably greater in the rural areas.

Thailand. Poverty in Thailand is associated with the following characteristics:

1. Of all households, 10% are in towns, but only 1% of the poor are to be found there; 99% of the poor are in the villages. Another way of seeing the rurality of poverty is this: 26% of all village households are poor, compared with 2% of town households. By region, less than 1% of the poor are to be found in the Bangkok–Thonburi region, the country's major urban center. In that region, the incidence of poverty is 1.5%, compared with incidences ranging from 6% to 40% elsewhere.

2. According to Table 5.3, Thailand has a lower incidence of poverty among female-headed families. The relative incidence of poverty in female-headed families is less than might have been thought, because of the Thai custom of providing supplementary earners (extended family members) when a male is absent.

3. Almost 99% of the poor have no education or less than middle secondary. The figure is almost as large for the nation as a whole (94%). The education breakdown in the available statistics is too gross to permit meaningful comparisons.

4. Of poor families, 63% are headed by prime-age workers (30-49). The incidence of poverty is highest in this age group. The high concentration of poverty among households headed by a prime-age worker might be due to any of several factors: larger family size for this age group, low earnings per working member even at prime working age, or low number of earners in this particular age group. The requisite tabulations needed to distinguish among the possible causes do not exist.

5. Poor families tend to be large and to have few earners. Of Thai poor, 50% had four or more children under the age of 15; 93% of poor families had one earner or none.

Pakistan. In Pakistan, we find:

1. Poor households are disproportionately small. Almost 65% of poor households have four or fewer members, as compared to 40% of all households. This suggests that a relatively larger dependency burden among the poor is unlikely to be an explanation for Pakistan's poverty.

2. The average number of earners is less for poor households than for the population as a whole. The great majority of poor families (95%) have one or two earners per household. The relative incidence of poverty appears to be highest for the one-earner households. This, together with the small household size, suggests that poverty in Pakistan results from a small number of earners coupled with low earnings per earner, though the effect is mitigated somewhat by the small number of members to feed and take care of.

3. In terms of occupation, the highest incidences of pov-

erty are found among farmers or fishermen and among production-process and related workers. The large majority of the poor (85%) are found in these categories.

4. The relative incidence of poverty is highest among the self-employed. The self-employed are also the largest group among the poor (62%). Employees and unpaid family helpers both have lower incidences of poverty. These categories are not entirely meaningful, because within them, the incidence of poverty is much higher for some groups (especially rural landless laborers and unpaid farm workers) than for others (urban factory workers and white-collar salaried employees). The precise magnitudes of these patterns cannot be pinpointed, owing to lack of appropriately disaggregated data.

5. A high proportion (86%) of the income of the poor comes from their employment. This reinforces the view that poverty is due to low earning capacity combined with lack of income from sources other than employment. Because most of the poor are self-employed, most of their total income (70%) comes from self-employment.

6. Demographic characteristics of the poor were not included in the survey reports. Supplementary information from other sources suggests that (*a*) because the literacy rate is very low, nearly all of the poor are illiterate; (*b*) reflecting the overall lack of education, schooling is more apt to determine nonpoverty (most of the schooled are not poor); (*c*) it is unlikely that many poor families are female-headed, because widows are taken into extended families; and (*d*) by all accounts, poverty in Pakistan appears to be a matter of low earning capacity concentrated among families headed by prime-age workers.

India. In India, most of the poverty literature has focused on the questions how best to measure poverty and how many are poor by various definitions.[25] Remarkably little work has gone into constructing a poverty profile. However, from the available sources, we may draw the following conclusions:

1. The poor are found disproportionately in rural areas. Bardhan (1974*b*) estimated that 45% of the rural population and 37% of the urban population were absolutely poor by his

definitions in 1964/5. Because of the ruralness of the Indian population (about 80%), poverty in India is largely a rural problem.[26]

2. The poor own disproportionately little land. DaCosta (1971) reported that 20% of the rural households were landless and another 25% had holdings of less than one acre. Incomes increase with size of landholding. Consequently, he concluded: "These vast multitudes of landless or near-landless people constitute the bulk of the utterly indigent and destitute people of India" (p. 50).

3. The severity of poverty varies substantially from region to region. The incidence was eight times as high in the highest-incidence state (Kerala) as in the lowest-incidence state (Assam).

4. Poverty varies inversely with education. College graduates' incomes are about five times higher than the incomes of illiterates.

International comparisons of poverty profiles. Poverty profiles have been presented for six less-developed countries.[27] From these data, we may make the following generalizations:

> *Education:* In each of the countries studied, the incidence of poverty decreases with educational attainment.
>
> *Age:* In three countries – Brazil, Malaysia, and Thailand – the highest incidence of poverty is found among families headed by prime-age workers. In Taiwan, in contrast, poverty hits hardest among the old.
>
> *Sex:* Except in Thailand, the incidence of poverty is greater among female-headed families.
>
> *Family size:* The probability of being in poverty rises with family size in Brazil, Malaysia, and Thailand. In Pakistan, however, lower frequencies of poverty are reported for large families. The reason Pakistan differs from the others is apparently definitional: It is the only one of these countries in which the poverty line is drawn according to *total* income rather than *per capita* income. In the Pakistani data, per capita income appears to decline with size, as in the other countries analyzed.
>
> *Number of earners:* As the number of earners increases, the rate of poverty declines.
>
> *Employment status:* In each country where employment status has been tabulated, the highest incidence of poverty is among the self-employed.

Sector: The highest incidence of poverty in each country is found in the agricultural sector.

Occupation: The highest incidence of poverty is among farmers and/or farm workers.

Location: Poverty rates are highest in rural areas or small villages.

Region: Pronounced regional disparities in poverty rates appear in each country examined.

Land ownership: The poor have disproportionately little or no land.

These results are largely in accordance with familiar perceptions of what characterizes the poor. Given the findings from regression and decomposition studies presented earlier in this volume, it comes as no surprise that poverty is concentrated among those with certain characteristics, such as poor education, large families, mediocre occupations, rural residence, and lack of land. The reader should remember, though, that these poverty profiles give us rates of poverty among individuals or families with particular characteristics and that no one characteristic is decisive in determining poverty or non-poverty. Or put another way, among those with a given attribute, many are poor and many others are not. This suggests that the targeting of development efforts and resources toward poverty groups must be done with rather fine instruments. Blunt approaches (e.g., concentrating exclusively on some regions or sectors of the economy) will automatically exclude many who need help while helping others who are outside the target group.

Before I close this section, two final points bear mention. One is that recent research has shown that absolute poverty is strongly associated with demographic factors. In a recent essay, Kuznets (1976) explored many aspects of these relationships. In empirical research, Musgrove (1977) has shown the great importance of family composition in explaining poverty in ten major Latin American cities in five countries. Additional literature on the relationship between demography and poverty in low-income countries is cited in surveys by Birdsall (1977), Boulier (1977), and Schultz (1979).

The other observation is that the central importance of land as a determinant of poverty (and of economic position more generally) has barely been touched upon here. Enormous amounts have been written on the subject. The evi-

dence shows that the majority of farm families in LDCs do
not own enough land to sustain themselves at even a basic
level. One such calculation for six Latin American countries
is presented in Table 5.4. The combined proportions of
"subfamily-sized farm operators" and "landless farm workers"
range from 54% in Chile to 88% in Guatemala. Land concentration is similarly high in other parts of the world. One
revealing calculation, by Minhas (1970), showed that even if
all the land in India were redistributed so that a household
could own no more than twenty acres and a noncultivating
household could own no more than half an acre, the proportion of landless farm labor households would be reduced by
just 20%; some 80-100 million people would remain landless.
Among the surveys of agriculture and development that
interested readers may find informative are those by Dorner
(1973), Reynolds (1975a), and Cline (1977).

The data given in this section only begin to hint at some
of the important relationships between demography and
poverty on the one hand and land and poverty on the other.
These are important subjects best left to another time and
place.

Economic growth, absolute income, and absolute poverty

We turn now to an important question in the study of economic development on which little hard evidence has been
gathered: To what extent do the incomes of the poor rise
with economic growth? It is a truism that growth in income
averaged among many does not necessarily reflect income
growth for all. Specific groups may or may not benefit from
particular types of growth. The absolute income and poverty
approach seeks to measure the extent to which the poor participate or are left behind. This section brings together some
of the available evidence on this vitally important issue.

In recent years, various national and international agencies
have compiled data on numerous social and economic indicators. As we shall now see, the evidence shows that in most
(but not all) countries absolute incomes for the poorest
groups have improved, and consequently absolute poverty
has diminished with economic growth.

Table 5.4. *Distribution of farm families by land ownership in six Latin American countries* (%)

	Argentina (1960)	Brazil (1950)	Chile (1950)	Colombia (1960)	Ecuador (1960)	Guatemala (1950)
Operators of large and medium-sized farms	5.2	14.6	9.5	5.0	2.4	1.6
Administrators of large and medium-sized farms	1.3	2.1	2.1	1.5	–	2.2
Owners of family-sized farms	16.4	12.0	14.8	17.9	8.0	6.6
Tenants with family-sized farms	16.2	2.9	2.9	5.4	1.5	1.2
"Communal farms"	–	–	16.6	–	1.3	–
Subfamily-sized farm operators	25.9	8.6	6.5	47.0	52.3	63.6
Landless farm workers	35.0	59.8	47.6	23.2	34.5	24.8
Total	100	100	100	100	100	100

Note: The following *definitions* are used: "subfamily" – farms large enough to provide employment for fewer than two people with the typical incomes, markets, and levels of technology and capital prevailing in each region; "family" – farms large enough to provide employment for two to four people on the assumption that most of the farm work is being carried out by family members; "multifamily medium" – farms large enough to provide employment for four to twelve people; "multifamily large" – farms large enough to provide employment for more than twelve people.
Source: Barraclough and Domike (1966).

Cross-section evidence

In the study of economic development, there is a long tradition of using evidence from an international cross section of countries at a single point in time to infer how development processes take place within countries over time. The available cross-sectional evidence on relative inequality and economic growth was reviewed in Chapter 4.

Some authors of cross-section studies have also examined the relationship between absolute incomes and poverty on the one hand and level of economic development (as measured by GNP per capita) on the other. A provocative and disturbing viewpoint was expressed in an important study by Adelman and Morris (1973). They contended that LDCs grow in a disequalizing manner, and as a consequence of unequal development, the rich get richer while the poor get poorer. Specifically, they assert that "development is accompanied by an absolute as well as a relative decline in the average income of the very poor" (p. 189). This conclusion has been echoed by others (e.g., Muller, 1973; and Foxley, 1976).

The cross-section evidence supporting the absolute impoverishment hypothesis has been thoroughly examined and found wanting. First, Adelman and Morris's statistical procedures were analyzed in detail by Cline (1975:n. 22).[28] Noting the "very indirect procedure" used by Adelman and Morris to derive their inference, Cline observed that their own regression results did *not* show a statistically significant decline in the absolute incomes of the poorest. Of course, neither does this observation establish the contrary: that the poor gain in the cross section. For evidence on that matter, we must turn to another study – that of Ahluwalia (1976b).

Ahluwalia performed two tests of the absolute impoverishment thesis. First he took regression equations in which the income shares received by the poorest 20%, 40%, and 60% were alternative dependent variables, and the independent variables were logarithm of per capita GNP (entered linearly and quadratically), share of agriculture in GDP, share of urban population in total population, literacy rate, secondary school enrollment rate, population growth rate, and a socialist/nonsocialist dummy variable. These predicted income shares

Table 5.5. *Average income levels of low-income groups, international cross section (Ahluwalia's first test)*

Per capita GNP (U.S. $)	Income level of poorest 60% ($)	Income level of poorest 40% ($)	Income level of poorest 20% ($)
75	45.5–51.6	37.8–42.0	27.7–32.6
100	55.4–63.2	42.0–50.2	31.7–38.3
200	89.0–103.8	63.7–77.3	44.9–56.3
300	118.2–140.3	84.6–101.2	57.5–70.8
400	145.5–175.2	106.4–124.0	71.1–84.1
500	171.8–209.4	129.6–146.7	86.3–96.8
600	197.6–243.4	154.4–169.6	103.1–109.4
700	223.1–277.4	180.7–193.0	121.6–122.1
800	248.5–311.6	209.1–217.0	135.0–141.6
900	273.9–346.0	238.9–241.6	148.1–163.3
1,000	299.4–380.7	266.9–270.2	161.8–186.5
1,500	560.0	403.6	235.7
3,000	1,158.9	909.1	519.1

Note: Numbers in the table are estimated income levels. The two figures in the ranges are estimated from the same regressions run on two different samples: countries at all stages of development and less-developed countries only.
Source: Ahluwalia (1976*b*:tab. 6).

were then combined with GNP information to estimate the per capita incomes of the poorest quintiles. Ahluwalia's other test consisted of using the actual income shares of the poorest quintiles rather than the predicted shares and proceeding in an otherwise analogous manner (that is, regressing the average absolute income of the quintile or quintiles on log per capita GNP, log per capita GNP squared, and the other variables mentioned).

By both tests, the incomes of the poor are found to rise systematically with level of economic development. Following Ahluwalia's first test, Table 5.5 shows the estimated average absolute incomes at various levels of GNP per capita. The absolute incomes of the poor rise monotonically with GNP. The evidence for Ahluwalia's second test appears in Table 5.6. If the absolute impoverishment hypothesis were correct (i.e., the absolute incomes of the poor decline as GNP increases), negative elasticities would be encountered. However, we find that all observed elasticities are positive, which

Table 5.6. *Estimated elasticities of absolute income of poorest with respect to per capita GNP, international cross section (Ahluwalia's second test)*

Per capita GNP (U.S. $)	Estimated elasticity		
	Income level of poorest 60%	Income level of poorest 40%	Income level of poorest 20%
100	.64	.45	.18
500	.73	.77	.65
750	.89	.85	.77

Source: Ahluwalia (1976*b*:333).

means that the poor gain in income in the cross section as GNP rises. Thus the notion that the absolute incomes of the poor decline in the early stages of economic development is disproven by Ahluwalia's evidence.

Note that the elasticities in Table 5.6 are appreciably below one. This means that relative inequality increases cross sectionally over these ranges, as we saw in Chapter 4. Although the poor lose out relatively, they do not lose out absolutely.

As recently as 1976, Ahluwalia could conclude: "A systematic treatment of the absolute impoverishment hypothesis obviously calls for an examination of the trends in per capita income in particular socio-economic groups in particular countries. It will be some time before reliable time series data suitable for such studies become available" (p. 335). This kind of data has started to become available already. The remainder of this section reports on the results obtained to date.

Intertemporal evidence: specially selected countries

Does economic growth reduce poverty? A heated debate is now raging. This section presents evidence from two studies that take almost diametrically opposed positions. What these studies have in common is their reliance on evidence drawn from the recent historical experiences of nonrandomly selected countries.

A progrowth position is taken by Walter Galenson (1977), who asks whether high growth reduces poverty. Galenson

selected for study those countries that achieved rapid economic growth over the 1960s (defined operationally as at
least a 7% annual growth rate of gross domestic product).
He then looked to see whether there had been increased consumption of a rather basic bundle of goods and services.
Increased consumption of such items would be taken as
presumptive (though admittedly indirect) evidence for the
position that poverty diminishes when growth takes place.

The evidence supports the progrowth view. Consumption
rose in nearly all high-growth countries for most of the items
for which data were available:

> Food: per capita food consumption, average calories per day, average
> protein supply
> Housing: average number of persons per room, percentage of dwell-
> ing units with running water, extent of electrification
> Medical care: population per physician, population per hospital bed
> Education: primary school enrollment rate, secondary school enroll-
> ment rate, adult literacy rate
> Other social indicators: radio receivers per thousand population,
> electric power consumption, newsprint consumption per capita

It should be noted that data on some of these measures were
not available for many countries.[29] On the other hand, data
were also available for slower-growing countries, and they give
a less clear picture.[30]

Galenson's own conclusion is that "rapid sustained growth
has had positive effects on the living standards of all economic groups of those countries that experienced it" (p. 21).
He continues: "Growth has not 'failed'; there has simply not
been enough of it in the great majority of less developed nations" (p. 22). LDCs as a whole grew by only 6% on the
average between 1965 and 1973; their per capita growth rates
averaged 3½%. Galenson puts it well:

> Growth rates of this magnitude are not likely to relieve poverty to any
> great extent, or to change anything else rapidly . . . If the point is that
> low growth rates are not an effective means of raising the living stan-
> dards of the poor, no one would be disposed to contest it.[31]

An opposing position is set forth by Keith Griffin (1977).
Drawing on a series of earlier studies, Griffin gives evidence of
persistent poverty for selected groups in particular countries,
even rapidly growing ones. The indicators of poverty differ

from country to country: proportion of the rural population below an absolute poverty line in several Asian countries; income share of the poorest 20% in the Philippines and poorest 80% in Bangladesh; incomes of smallholders and landless workers in Malaysia and Sri Lanka; average real income of cocoa producers in Ghana; incomes of informal sector workers and smallholder farmers in the poorest regions of Tanzania; "pure labor share" of national income in Colombia; and so on. In summary, Griffin writes:

> In the Third World as a whole the rate of growth in the last quarter century or so has been unprecedented. Never before have so many poor countries, containing such a large proportion of those who are inadequately fed, clothed and housed, enjoyed such a period of rapid and sustained expansion of output. Yet despite this growth of production the problems of widespread poverty seem to have remained as great as ever. The rise in aggregate production does not seem to have been matched by a corresponding rise in the income of the poor. [p. 1]

What are we to conclude from the works of Galenson and Griffin? The value of their work is to point out that economic growth alone is insufficient to guarantee decent standards of living for all. We now have documented instances where the poor have progressed and other instances where they have not. And as both authors correctly observe, we must understand the character of the underlying economic structures and growth processes before differences in various countries' positions can be satisfactorily explained.

Yet, Galenson and Griffin appear to differ fundamentally on the question whether economic growth improves the lot of the poor. Galenson says yes, Griffin no. They reach these conclusions following two distinct methodological approaches. In one kind of study, rapid-growth countries were examined and changes in the availability of food, education, medical care, and other basic goods and services tabulated. In the other kind of study, the experiences of particular groups in particular countries were singled out to show that growth leaves many of the poor behind. Put this way, it is not surprising that seemingly contradictory conclusions are reached. The opposing sides are asking different questions. Galenson is looking to see who benefited; Griffin is looking to see who did not.

The two authors' policy prescriptions also differ. They aim at different objectives. Galenson takes the long view; his basic policy question is, What policies will lead ultimately to a permanent lasting solution to the poverty problem? His answer – substantial expansion of highly productive employment through economic growth – can be the only correct one in the long term. Griffin, in contrast, is more concerned with the short run. He implies, by his continued attention to the situation of the poor in the year 2000, that he is willing to wait only a generation, if that. His policy prescription – redistribution of income and productive assets – is the only thing that might possibly help most of the world's poor today.

Galenson and Griffin differ in many ways. They ask different questions. They draw on different countries' experiences to support their claims. They have different time horizons in mind. And their policy prescriptions are aimed at somewhat different objectives.

Which is the better view? I personally am inclined toward the shorter-run view. It is little solace to those who are presently poor to be told that their continued economic misery is the price that must be paid to improve things materially for their great-great grandchildren. If a lasting solution requires a century or more to achieve under the existing international economic order, maybe it is time to question that order's legitimacy.

Let me not inflate my own importance or the importance of my profession. In all likelihood, what matters is not how we social scientists deal with the issues raised by Galenson and Griffin but rather how the poor in poor countries approach them. The course of world economic development, perhaps even the course of the world, may depend on how long the poor will work within the existing order before taking more drastic action.

Intertemporal evidence: all available countries

The studies by Galenson and Griffin reviewed in the preceding section have a common methodological approach: Both are based on a specially selected sample of countries. This methodological feature highlights a limitation they have in common: nonrepresentativeness. In Galenson's case, documenting that progress has taken place does not tell us how much progress. And in Griffin's case, identifying certain groups who remain poor does not tell us how many have progressed. What we need, and what this section seeks to provide, is an examination of progress or lack of progress toward alleviating poverty in a representatively chosen sample of countries.

Evidence on intertemporal change in absolute poverty has not to my knowledge been compiled in any central source. I have drawn together the available information for as many less-developed countries as I could. Countries for which income distribution data are published for two or more points in time are not included in the analysis here if reliability and comparability of the data sources were dubious or unconfirmed.

The resulting estimates of absolute income and poverty change in countries with available data are given in Table 5.7.[32] The principal poverty measure used is the proportion who are poor; it is supplemented when possible by other poverty measures. It would have been preferable to have compared Sen's poverty indexes, but this could not be done, owing to lack of requisite information (in particular, the absence of data on relative income inequality among the poor).

The best available absolute poverty measures for each of thirteen less-developed countries suggest that absolute poverty was alleviated in varying degrees in ten (Bangladesh, Brazil, Costa Rica, Pakistan, Puerto Rico, Singapore, Sri Lanka, Taiwan, Thailand, and Mexico) and that absolute poverty worsened in three (Argentina, India, and the Philippines).

We would expect that countries with moderate to rapid rates of aggregate economic growth would succeed in upgrading the economic condition of significant numbers of their people – this is the so-called trickle-down theory. The evidence is generally consistent with this view. In nine countries' experiences, growth led to demonstrable improvements in the economic position of the poor (Bangladesh, Brazil, Costa Rica, Pakistan, Puerto Rico, Singapore, Taiwan, Thailand, and Mexico), and in one country nongrowth did not (India). On the other hand, three countries' experiences run contrary to the predictions of the trickle-down theory: Argentina and the

Table 5.7. *Economic growth and changing poverty in less-developed countries*

Country/date	Poverty change		
Taiwan (1964–72; moderate growth)	Proportion of households with incomes below specified amount in specified year:		
	Amount (constant NT$)	1964 (%)	1972 (%)
	20,000	35	10
	30,000	55	20
	40,000	80	35
Brazil (1960–70; moderate growth)	Proportion in economically active population below minimum wage of Northeast Brazil, estimated (%):		
	1960	1970	
	37.0	35.5	
	Average income of those below minimum wage, estimated (constant NCr$):		
	1960	1970	
	800	1,300	

Argentina (1953–61; moderate growth)	Real personal income among persons in the remunerated population (excluding retirees):		
	Percentile group	Amount in constant m$n of 1960	Rate of growth (%)
		1953 1961	
	Poorest 10%	19,400 18,500	−4.2
	Next poorest 20%	36,500 38,400	+5.0
	Total, all recipients	90,100 102,200	+13.2
Puerto Rico (1953–63; rapid growth)	Rate of growth of real income by decile, families (%):		
	Poorest 10%	+28	
	Second 10%	+39	
	Third 10%	+49	
	Total, all families	+68	

Table 5.7. (cont.)

Country/date	Poverty change		
Pakistan (1963–69/70; moderate growth)	Proportion of persons with consumption below specified amount in specified year:		

Amount (constant Rs. per annum)	1963/4 (%)	1969/70 (%)
Rural population		
Below 300	60.5	59.7
Below 250	43.1	26.0
Urban population		
Below 375	70.0	58.7
Below 300	54.8	25.0

Singapore (1966–75; rapid growth)

Proportion of persons with incomes below S$200 per month (in 1975 prices) (%):

1966	1975
37	29

Thailand (1962/3–68/9; rapid growth)

Proportion of households with incomes below 1,500 baht (%):

1962/3	1968/9
63	49

Philippines (1961–71; rapid growth)

Average annual income per family by quintile group:

Quintile	1961	1971	Nominal* growth (%)
Poorest	383	687	+79
Second	712	1,532	+114
Third	1,090	2,470	+127
Fourth	1,738	3,924	+126
Richest	5,094	10,079	+98

*The consumer Price Index rose by 101.6% over that period.

Costa Rica (1961–71; rapid growth)

Proportion of families with real absolute incomes below:

Amount (constant colones)	1961 (%)	1971 (%)
250	20	10
500	65	30

Table 5.7. (cont.)

Country/date	Poverty change			
Sri Lanka (1953–73; slow growth)	Proportion of income recipients with incomes below:			
	Amount (constant 1963 Rs.)	1953 (%)	1963 (%)	1973 (%)
	Less than 100	63	59	41
	Less than 200	86	84	72
India (1960–68/9; virtually no growth)	Proportion of population with incomes below:			
	Amount	1960/1 (%)	1964/5 (%)	1968/9 (%)
	Rs. 15 constant per capita per month (rural)	38	45	54
	Rs. 18 constant per capita per month (urban)	32	37	41
	(Note: Other estimates are available; some give conflicting impression.)			
Mexico (1963–9; rapid growth)	Average annual income of poorest decile of families (in pesos, 1958 prices):			
		1963	1969	
		315	367	
Bangladesh (1963/4–73/4; moderate growth followed by severe disruption)	Proportion of population below "minimum acceptable consumption requirement" (%):			
	1963/4	1968/9		1973/4
	88	77		83
	Sen's poverty index:			
		1963/4	1968/9	1973/4
	Rural	.35	.22	.40
	Urban	.38	.19	.33

Sources: Poverty estimates for the countries covered in this table are based on data from the following: Taiwan-Kuo (1975) and Fei, Ranis, and Kuo (1979); Brazil-Fields (1977); Philippines-Mijares and Belarmino (1973); Costa Rica-Céspedes (1973); Sri Lanka-Karunatilake (1975); India-Bardhan (1974b); Argentina-Dieguez and Petrecolla (1976); Puerto Rico-Weisskoff (1970); Pakistan-Naseem (1973); Singapore-Rao and Ramakrishnan (1977); Thailand-Meesook (1975); Mexico-Gollás (1978); and Bangladesh-Alamgir (forthcoming).

173

Philippines, because they grew substantially but do not appear to have alleviated poverty during the years in question; and Sri Lanka, which grew slowly yet did substantially lessen poverty.

It is of great interest to know why these countries fared as they did. We will examine the experiences of six of them (Brazil, Costa Rica, India, the Philippines, Sri Lanka, and Taiwan) in Chapter 6. But before doing so, we consider the results of estimating absolute poverty change using two specific measures.

Intertemporal evidence: specialized measures

Ahluwalia–Chenery index. Chapter 2 presented the Ahluwalia–Chenery index as a special case of the absolute income approach. To recall, the Ahluwalia–Chenery index is a weighted index of income growth of particular population subgroups. If the subgroups are income quintiles (with 1 the poorest quintile and 5 the richest), weighted income growth is given by

$$G = w_1 g_1 + w_2 g_2 + w_3 g_3 + w_4 g_4 + w_5 g_5$$

where g_i is the rate of growth of quintile i's income and w_i is the associated welfare weight. GNP weights are represented by the special case where the w_i are simply the respective quintiles' income shares, which are monotonically increasing. An alternative welfare judgment, which would give the same weight to a 1% increase for each income class, is the case $w_1 = w_2 = w_3 = w_4 = w_5 = .2$. Poverty weights would go even further and give *higher* weight to a given percentage increase for the poorer classes, in which case $w_1 > w_2 > w_3 > w_4 > w_5$.

Table 5.8 presents Ahluwalia and Chenery's calculations of weighted growth for thirteen less-developed countries.[33] By their estimates, it appears that:

1. Four countries did more poorly by the Ahluwalia–Chenery index than would be indicated by their GNP experiences alone: Panama, Brazil, Mexico, and Venezuela.
2. Four countries did better by the Ahluwalia–Chenery index than would be indicated by their GNP experiences alone: Colombia, El Salvador, Sri Lanka, and Taiwan.
3. Five countries' experiences were largely unaffected by the Ahlu-

Table 5.8. *Income distribution and growth: the Ahluwalia-Chenery index*

Country/date	Income growth			Annual increase in welfare		
	Poorest 40%	Middle 40%	Richest 20%	GNP weights	Equal weights	Poverty weights
Korea (1964–70)	9.3	7.8	10.6	9.3	9.0	9.0
Panama (1960–9)	3.2	9.2	8.8	8.2	6.7	5.6
Brazil (1960–70)	5.2	4.8	8.4	6.9	5.7	5.4
Mexico (1963–9)	6.6	7.0	8.0	7.6	7.0	6.9
Taiwan (1953–61)	12.1	9.1	4.5	6.8	9.4	10.4
Venezuela (1962–70)	3.7	4.1	7.9	6.4	4.7	4.2
Colombia (1964–70)	7.0	7.3	5.6	6.2	6.8	7.0
El Salvador (1961–9)	5.3	10.5	4.1	6.2	7.1	6.7
Philippines (1961–71)	5.0	6.4	4.9	5.4	5.5	5.4
Peru (1961–71)	3.2	7.5	4.7	5.4	5.2	4.6
Sri Lanka (1963–70)	8.3	6.2	3.1	5.0	6.4	7.2
Yugoslavia (1963–8)	4.3	5.0	4.9	4.8	4.7	4.6
India (1954–64)	3.9	3.9	5.1	4.5	4.1	4.0

Note: The weights pertain to the poorest 40%, middle 40%, and richest 20% respectively. "GNP weights" use each group's income shares as weights. "Equal weights" use each group's population share, i.e., $w_1 = .4$, $w_2 = .4$, $w_3 = .2$. "Poverty weights" are arbitrary; the authors use $w_1 = .6$, $w_2 = .3$, $w_3 = .1$.
Source: Ahluwalia and Chenery (1974).

walia-Chenery weighting scheme: Korea, the Philippines, Yugoslavia, Peru, and India.[34]

The Ahluwalia-Chenery index has received considerable attention as a means of combining growth and distribution in a single index. It has both the advantage and the disadvantage of relying on obviously arbitrary weights assigned to income growth of different quintiles. This is advantageous insofar as it makes welfare judgments explicit, and it is certainly a great improvement over a simple GNP approach for evaluating economic growth. However, as with all explicitly arbitrary measures (for instance, that suggested by Atkinson, 1970), we do not yet have a firm theoretical basis for arriving at the specific weights to be used.

But perhaps a more serious difficulty with the Ahluwalia-Chenery index is a conceptual one. In relying on comparisons of growth rates of income of particular income quintiles, the index conceptualizes the groups in *ex ante* ordering; that is, what was the rate of growth of income of those who originally were in the poorest quintile, second quintile, and so on? To answer this question, longitudinal data are needed charting the same individuals over time. In practice, however, national census data or sample surveys in less-developed countries do not chart the same people over time. At best, we have two comparable cross sections, and we therefore can look only at the *ex post* quintiles. The data presented in Table 5.8 are based on *ex post* and not *ex ante* quintiles.

What difference does it make to use comparable cross sections rather than longitudinal data? The models developed in Chapter 3 provide a useful analytical framework. There, I distinguished among three kinds of simple dualistic development:

> Traditional sector enrichment growth: Incomes in the traditional sector are assumed to rise, incomes in the modern sector remain the same, and the allocation of the labor force between the two sectors also remains the same.
>
> Modern sector enrichment growth: Incomes in the modern sector are assumed to rise, incomes in the traditional sector remain the same, and the allocation of the labor force between the two sectors also remains the same.
>
> Modern sector enlargement growth: The fraction of the labor force in the modern sector is assumed to increase; incomes among those working in both sectors are unchanged.

After a little consideration, it should be apparent that the Ahluwalia–Chenery index works well for the two enrichment growth types. In modern sector enrichment growth, all income growth is received by "the rich." In traditional sector enrichment growth, all income gains accrue to "the poor." The Ahluwalia–Chenery index is sensitive to these differences. What about modern sector enlargement growth? The results are disappointing, as the following example indicates. In a simple five-person economy, suppose four families have incomes of $1 and one family has an income of $2. After modern sector enlargement growth, one of the $1 families has its income upgraded to $2. Then the distributions are

$$Y_{\text{original}} = (1, 1, 1, 1, 2)$$

and

$$Y_{\text{final}} = (1, 1, 1, 2, 2)$$

Development progress and growth strategies:
case studies

We come now to the motivating question of this book: Who
benefits how much from economic growth and why? We saw
in earlier chapters that the development performances of
some countries far exceeded those of others. In some cases,
the poor benefited substantially from economic growth;
in other cases, they did not. Inequality rose in half the
countries studied and fell in the other half. Why? What
accounts for differences among countries in poverty, inequality, and development? This chapter takes a first step toward
clarifying these crucial issues.

Analyzed here are the development experiences of six
countries—Costa Rica, Sri Lanka, India, Brazil, the Philippines,
and Taiwan. Although each country study is necessarily
brief, I have tried in each instance to highlight the available
information on poverty, inequality, and development strategy.
Accordingly, the country studies have four methodological
themes in common.

One unifying theme is a concern with the overall distribution of income. Many accounts of development experiences
select particular groups for attention. Some, particularly the
studies of national planning departments and international
development agencies, single out the beneficiaries: the small
farmers whose lands become irrigated, the newly electrified
urban neighborhood, the peasants' children studying abroad,
and so on. Other observers, especially radical academicians
and opposition political parties, single out other instances:
poor farmers hurt by depressed prices for their produce
brought about by the introduction of high-yielding varieties
in other parts of their country, villages that remain untouched
by macroeconomic development and therefore stagnate, the
still illiterate masses, and so on. An optimist viewing these

particularistic kinds of studies might conclude that progress has been made and that many ch llenges lie ahead. To a pessimist, these same findings suggest that no matter how much is done, the poor will always be with us.

The mere identification of groups that are uplifted from poverty by economic growth and of groups that remain poor cannot tell us how many are in each category. We require a more comprehensive overview of development progress. We must know by how much poverty and inequality are being alleviated (if at all) in the course of economic development and how much poverty and inequality remain. Such a comprehensive picture accords with a basic principle of statistical inference: that *all* data points must be considered, not just those consistent with a given view. Accordingly, the analyses in this chapter are based on holistic measures and not on specially chosen instances.

A second methodological similarity among the country studies is an emphasis on absolute incomes and absolute poverty. As I showed in Chapters 2 and 3, the choice of a relative inequality or absolute poverty measure may make an important difference in assessing whether economic development is benefiting the poor. My own main concern-and, as I perceive it, the concern of the international development community-is with the alleviation of absolute economic misery. Given this judgment, it does not seem desirable to use relative inequality indexes to measure changing income distribution. Rather, it is more appropriate to use absolute income and poverty measures, such as the position of the absolute income distribution, the number of individuals or families with incomes below a constant real poverty line, or the average gap between the incomes of the poor and the poverty line. Most of the discussion in the present chapter is therefore in terms of absolute incomes and absolute poverty; relative inequality comparisons, when they are made, receive less weight in the overall conclusions.

Thirdly, in each country study, I construct absolute income and absolute poverty distributions for each point in time for which we have data. The poverty lines are not the same between one country and another for two reasons: difficulties in establishing appropriate intercountry exchange rates and problems of making reliable intracountry data imputations. The poverty lines are, however, consistent within each country, holding real incomes constant by adjusting for price changes. To avoid arbitrariness, results are presented using alternative poverty lines wherever possible.[1]

The last common theme in each of the country studies is an examination of changing employment conditions, in particular, changing occupational and industrial structure and changing wage structure. The poor may share in a country's economic growth either by being drawn into better-paying jobs ("job" being defined broadly to encompass all work, including self-employment and work in family enterprises) or by being paid more in the same activity. As with the absolute poverty and relative inequality data, the specific ways of dealing with changes in wages and employment differ somewhat, owing to lack of standardized international data.

A useful framework for analyzing these changes is that of dualistic economic development, the welfare economics of which were analyzed in Chapter 3. To measure the various components of dualistic economic development, it would seem at first that we could simply look at the rates of growth of real income in the modern and traditional sectors. Unfortunately, that way of measuring the participation of various groups in economic growth will *not* work. Here is the reason: Suppose we knew that income produced in a country's modern sector grew by 10% and its traditional sector registered no growth in value of product. One possibility is that those who were already in the modern sector experienced income gains of 10% and those still in the traditional sector experienced no income gains whatever; if this were the case, the growth would have been highly uneven and the poor traditional sector workers would not have shared in it at all. But another possibility consistent with the same sectoral growth rates–10% in the modern sector, 0% in the traditional sector–is that average incomes in the modern sector might have *fallen* by 10% on the average, 20% *more* people might have found relatively high-paying jobs in that sector and so left the traditional sector, and average traditional sector incomes might have *risen* for the remaining population; in this second case, the growth would have been highly favorable to the poor. The important point is that from just the data on rates of growth of output in modern and traditional sector activities, we cannot determine whether the poor are sharing in economic development or not.

Another way that the participation of the poor is sometimes measured is by looking at the growth rates of income among particular decile groups, in comparable cross sections. The problem with this method is that it gives a mistaken impression for a particularly important kind of economic growth, which Chapter 3 termed modern sector enlargement growth. Consider a simple ten-person economy with the following distribution of incomes: (1.0, 1.1, 1.2, 1.3, 1.4, 1.5, 1.6, 1.7, 1.8, 5.0). Assume that modern sector growth led to an additional high-paying job for which the median poor person was hired. The new distribution would be (1.0, 1.1, 1.2, 1.3, 1.5, 1.6, 1.7, 1.8, 5.0, 5.0), and we would record the decile growth rates as (0, 0, 0, 0, -7%, -6%, -6%, -5%, +177%, 0). In this case it would appear that the middle class had lost while the rich gained, when actually the sole income change was that a poor person became better off. Clearly, decile income growth rates will *not* work as a measure of the poor's participation in economic growth of this type.

A preferred method of analyzing dualistic economic development, and one that I try to implement here, is to distinguish the enlargement and enrichment components of each sector's growth, where enlargement refers to an increasing number of people in that sector and enrichment refers to the average real income gain among them. In several cases, the available wage and employment data give useful insights into the importance of enlargement and enrichment in major economic sectors.

Before we proceed, a word should be mentioned about the data. The six countries studied here were selected according to the availability of data on income distribution for at least two points in time at least a decade apart. To some extent, our perceptions about whether the poor shared in economic development may depend on the particular base and terminal years for which data were available. I have made a serious effort to assure comparability between various censuses or surveys in each country. On this basis (lack of comparability over time), some seemingly good data countries were rejected.[2]

The countries analyzed are Costa Rica, Sri Lanka, India, Brazil, the Philippines, and Taiwan.

Costa Rica

Costa Rica is a small open economy. Consequently, events and policies in the foreign sector play an important role in determining the country's development course.

Our period of analysis is from the early 1960s to the early 1970s. Over that time, Costa Rica reversed its trade orientation, switching from emphasis on import substitution to greater reliance on export promotion. The main exports stimulated, both by encouraging expansion and by diversification, were agricultural products. This emphasis on agricultural exports helped spread the benefits of growth throughout the country. In addition, Costa Rica gave high priority to investments in economic infrastructure, including agricultural extension. Other factors of note in the 1960s were high and rising levels of education (by 1971, the school attendance ratio exceeded 90% for 6–12-year-olds), early family planning efforts, good public health conditions, and a land distribution that was relatively even by Latin American standards. In short, the policy orientation in Costa Rica during our period of study was one of decentralized development.

Let us begin our examination of Costa Rica's development experience by reviewing the record of aggregate growth. Between 1960 and 1971, gross domestic product doubled in real terms–a particularly good performance; of the countries covered in this chapter, only Taiwan grew faster. By 1971, per capita GDP was U.S. $586, which implies that Costa Rica ranks in Latin America's "upper middle class."[3] Growth slowed in the 1970s, and the economy suffered from serious inflationary pressures and balance-of-payments difficulties.

Income inequality in Costa Rica is moderate; the Gini coefficient of family income in 1971 was .45, which is about at the midpoint for less-developed countries as a whole but relatively low by Latin American standards.

The growth in the Costa Rican economy seems not to have

Table 6.1. *Costa Rica: distribution of national income by industry*

Industrial classification	% of gross domestic product		
	1960	1965	1970
Agriculture	26	24	23
Industry	15	18	20
Construction	4	5	4
Wholesale and retail trade	21	20	21
Transportation	4	4	4
Other	28	29	28
Total	100	100	100

Source: Costa Rica, *National Accounts Statistics* (1975: vol. 3, tab. 3).

engendered any major change in the composition of national income. The share of industry has risen and the share of agriculture fallen somewhat, but not drastically; see Table 6.1.

The general growth of production and the small reduction in agriculture's share of GDP reflect the growth of export-oriented commercial agriculture. Trade is very important to the Costa Rican economy. The ratio of imports to gross domestic product is about .31, which is very high by international standards.[4] Exports increased in value from $95 million in 1963 to $344 million in 1973 for reasons that include Costa Rica's incorporation into the Central American Common Market, favorable changes in world prices for exports, expansionary monetary and fiscal policies, and the influx of foreign capital. About 70% of exports are accounted for by coffee, bananas, meat, sugar, and cocoa.

Income distribution data for Costa Rica are available from specially conducted household surveys in 1961 and 1971. Data on the labor force, employment, wages, and other aspects of the Costa Rican economy are derived from the population censuses of 1963 and 1973. In recognition of the two-year gap between the data sources, I shall refer to these dates as the "early sixties" and "early seventies" respectively.

The source for the income distribution data in the early seventies is the report by Céspedes (1973). For the early sixties, the source is an unpublished estimate derived from a

Survey of Family Income and Expenditures conducted by the Central Agency for Statistics and Censuses in Costa Rica. Although this source is widely cited in subsequent work by the Economic Commission for Latin America, the World Bank, and others, details of the survey are extremely sketchy.

On the assumption that the income distributions for the early sixties and early seventies are derived in similar fashion, we may compare absolute incomes and relative inequality at the two points in time. The basic data are presented in Table 6.2.

Our concern in this chapter is with measuring how much of the economic growth is received by households at different points in the income distribution. The way this is usually done in economic development studies is by drawing a Lorenz curve and then computing one or more relative inequality measures. The Lorenz curves are shown in Figure 6.1. When Lorenz curves cross, as in the figure, one inequality index may increase while another declines. If we use the Gini coefficient, we can see in the figure and in the table that inequality declined by a substantial amount between the early sixties and the early seventies. Many would interpret this as evidence that the lower classes did at least as well as the middle and upper classes.

There is a growing awareness among development economists that relative inequality measures like the Gini coefficient provide only indirect information about changing economic positions of the poorest segments in society. For this reason, overall inequality measures are being supplemented by less aggregative analyses of the income shares of particular population groups. Such calculations are presented in Table 6.2 for the various income deciles in Costa Rica.

We observe a small decline in the share received by the lowest deciles, a very large decline in the share of the richest, and gains for the other seven deciles. This pattern–falling shares at the top and bottom of the income distribution and rising shares in the middle–would be seen by many as evidence that the middle class gained at the expense of the rich and poor.[5] Research would be directed toward finding out how the middle class mobilized itself to bring about so substantial a redistribution. Concerned scholars evaluating the Costa

Poverty, inequality, and development

Table 6.2. *Costa Rica: income-distribution change, early 1960s to early 1970s*

	Income share		Absolute income (1971 colones)		Change in absolute income	% change in absolute income
	Early 1960s[a]	Early 1970s[b]	Early 1960s[c]	Early 1970s		
Income decile						
Poorest	2.6%	2.1%	195	248	+53	+27
Second	3.4	3.3	255	384	+131	+51
Third	3.8	4.2	285	490	+205	+72
Fourth	4.0	5.1	300	603	+303	+101
Fifth	4.4	6.2	330	730	+400	+121
Sixth	5.4	7.5	405	883	+478	+118
Seventh	7.1	9.3	535	1,085	+550	+103
Eighth	9.3	11.7	700	1,378	+678	+97
Ninth	14.0	16.2	1,050	1,895	+845	+80
Richest	46.0	34.4	3,445	4,104	+659	+19
Total	100.0%	100.0%				
Average			745	1,175	+430	+58
Richest 5%	35.0%	22.8%				
Richest 1%	16.0%	8.5%				
Gini co-efficient[d]	.521	.445				
Real GDP growth						+102
GDP per capita (constant colones)			2,430	3,840	1,410	+58

[a] ECLA (1969).
[b] Céspedes (1973).
[c] Estimated.
[d] Jain (1975).

Rican experience would also note that the smallest gains (in both absolute and relative terms) were received by the lowest deciles–those who presumably have the greatest needs. Costa Rica would be cited as yet another instance of "growth without development."[6]

These inferences from decile income changes, I submit, are largely fallacious. The reasons are simple. One is that

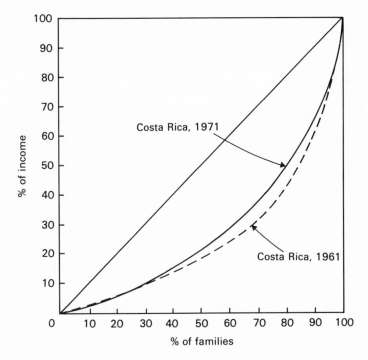

Figure 6.1. Lorenz curves for Costa Rica, 1961 and 1971. *Source*: Céspedes (1973: 62).

absolute poverty calculations give a quite different picture. The proportion of families below an absolute poverty line of 250 constant colones fell from about 20% to 10% from the early sixties to the early seventies. If the poverty line is instead drawn at 500 constant colones, the decline is even more marked-from approximately 65% to 30%. Thus absolute poverty was alleviated and alleviated rapidly.

Another difficulty with inferences from decile income changes is that the poor may benefit from economic growth by becoming employed in higher-income activities in the modern sector. However, for a variety of reasons-which might include lack of resources, entrepreneurial capacity, or political will-the modern sectors in poor countries may not grow fast enough to create sufficient advancement opportunities for everyone. In modern sector enlargement growth, some of the poor experience income gains, but the growth

Table 6.3. *Costa Rica: employment and income by occupation, industry, and education, early 1960s and early 1970s*

Occupation	Early 1960s[a]		Early 1970s[b]		% change in employment	Approximate median income, early 1970s (colones)[c]
	Number employed (thousands)	% employed	Number employed (thousands)	% employed		
Professional and technical workers	21	5	47	8	+126	2,600
Managers	5	1	10	2	+88	1,800
Office workers	21	5	34	6	+62	1,600
Storekeepers and vendors	30	8	46	8	+52	1,200
Farmers, cattlemen, etc.	187	47	208	35	+11	–
Other	131	34	240	41	+83	700
Total	395	100	585	100	+48	

Industry	Early 1960s[d]		Early 1970s[e]		% change in employment	Mean income (colones)[f]
	Number employed (thousands)	% employed	Number employed (thousands)	% employed		

Industry	Early 1960s Number economically active (thousands)	% economically active	Early 1970s Number economically active (thousands)	% economically active		
Agriculture, forestry, hunting, and fishing	194	49	213	36	+10	793
Mining, electricity, gas, and water	5	1	7	1	+40	1,372
Manufacturing	45	11	70	12	+54	1,213
Construction	23	6	39	7	+68	1,203
Commerce	39	10	68	12	+75	1,539
Services	68	17	119	20	+75	1,624
Other	21	6	69	12	+228	1,134
Total	395	100	585	100	+48	

Worker categories	Early 1960s[g] Number economically active (thousands)	% economically active	Early 1970s[g] Number economically active (thousands)	% economically active
Wage earners	261	66	430	74
Employers and self-employed	82	21	100	17
Nonremunerated family workers	41	10	35	6
New entrants	11	3	20	3
Total	395	100	585	100

Table 6.3. (cont.)

Education and literacy	Early 1960s[h]			Early 1970s[i]			% change in employment	Mean income (colones)[j]
	Number employed (thousands)	% employed		Number employed (thousands)	% employed			
No education	134	15		131	10		−2 ⎫	637
Primary, grades 1–3	323	37		335	26		+4 ⎬	971
Primary, grades 4–6	312	37		587	45		+88 ⎭	
Secondary	80	9		213	16		+166	⎧ 1,695
University	20	2		57	4		+185	⎨ 2,823[k]
								⎩ 5,255[l]
Total, age 10 and over	870	100		1,323	101		+52	
Literate	745	86		1,188	90		+59	—
Illiterate	124	14		135	10		+9	—
Total, age 10 and over	869	100		1,324	100		+52	

[a] Censo de Población (1963:76).
[b] Censo de Población (1973:61).
[c] Céspedes (1973:113).
[d] Censo de Población (1963:261).
[e] Censo de Población, (1973:67).
[f] Céspedes (1973:114).
[g] Calvo (1978:228).
[h] Censo de Población, 1963:474, 520–1).
[i] Censo de Población (1973:309, 333).
[j] Céspedes (1973:111).
[k] Incomplete university.
[l] Complete university.

will be recorded in the higher deciles rather than the lowest (as illustrated by the example in the introduction to this chapter). This statistical anomaly may well be a large part of the explanation of the changing patterns in Costa Rica.

Evidence of considerable modern sector enlargement may be gleaned from several pieces of information, presented in Table 6.3. Consider first the occupational distribution of the labor force. A disproportionate share of the low-income population is in agriculture. The data show that whereas the labor force grew by 48%, the number of farmers and cattlemen grew by only 11%. All other occupational groups showed above-average gains in employment. Because these are the better-paying occupations, this provides one piece of evidence that the Costa Rican economy grew by expanding the share of modern sector workers in total employment—the essence of modern sector enlargement growth. The industrial data show a similar pattern. The fast-growing sectors in employment were those associated indirectly with the modern sector (construction, commerce, transportation); manufacturing itself increased at a more moderate rate. In other words, there was a relative shift from agriculture to commerce and services. The share of wage earners in total employment increased with declines in the proportions of nonremunerated family workers and employers and self-employed. Educational data support the supply side of the picture. Despite the rapid growth of population, we find that the number with no education declined absolutely and the number who completed only the first three years of primary education rose by just 4%. In contrast, the number with four to six years of education increased by 88%, the number of secondary school graduates by 166%, and the number of university graduates by 185%. In short, the Costa Rican economy grew, creating more modern sector job opportunities and educating the skilled labor force needed.

Is there also evidence of income gains among those already in the modern sector and of enrichment (or impoverishment) of those left behind? To answer these questions, we require occupation- or industry-specific wage or income data. This type of data is not available for Costa Rica.

Let us now turn to the case of Sri Lanka, where the patterns are rather different.

Sri Lanka

The period of analysis in Sri Lanka is the twenty years extending from 1953 to 1973. Income-distribution data are available from large-scale national household income and consumption surveys for the three years 1953, 1963, and 1973 and from the census of 1971. It happens that the early 1960s mark a turning point in economic and social policy: Sri Lanka moved from an open to a closed economy and then approached welfare statism.

Sri Lanka is a poor, slow-growing country. It is, however, firmly committed to the alleviation of poverty and has been so committed since independence in 1948. It has made impressive progress. The poor are gaining absolutely and relatively; the reverse is true of the rich. Unlike Taiwan, in which we shall see that poverty alleviation and inequality reduction are due to *growth*, in Sri Lanka declining poverty and inequality are due to *redistribution*. Let us now examine the record.

In the late 1940s and early 1950s, Sri Lanka followed an export-oriented course. The overall development strategy was to stimulate the modern export sector and use the surpluses generated to fund investment elsewhere in the economy. Following several crises, this strategy broke down completely around 1960, owing to the inability of the export sector to generate enough foreign exchange to pay for needed imports. Consequently, the economy turned inward. Severe import restrictions and nearly prohibitive tariffs were instituted in the hopes of improving the balance of payments. Underlying these moves was the perceived insufficiency of domestic savings and capital inflow. Shortages of capital and intermediate goods appeared, living standards were reduced for many, and aggregate economic growth ground nearly to a halt. By 1963 (the second year for which we have income distribution data), Sri Lanka had closed its economy and redirected production toward locally produced goods for domestic consumption, and was devoting an unusually large share of the national product to social welfare expenditures and consumer goods.[7]

The inward-looking development policies of the early and mid sixties also ran into difficulties. In part, this was because of a precipitous decline in world prices for Sri Lanka's major exports–tea, rubber, and coconuts, which together account for 90% or more of export earnings. Also, the strategy of industrialization via import substitution had a number of negative features: price distortions, overvalued exchange rates, and low interest rates. The balance-of-payments situation worsened in the 1960s, and economic growth was seriously impeded. Those difficulties persist up to the present.[8]

For three decades, the Sri Lankan government has emphasized income distribution and sought to lessen inequality. According to one expert:

> Economic planners in Sri Lanka have the view that the increase in Gross National Product alone is not a sufficient indicator of economic progress because even with a relatively high annual growth rate, the Gross National Product could be unequally distributed resulting in serious income disparities. In view of this, there has been a great deal of emphasis on redistributing existing income and wealth in Sri Lanka because the addition to income, due to the relatively low rate of economic growth, has been inadequate to make an appreciable impact on the incomes of those in the lowest income brackets. [Karunatilake, 1975:702]

A major redistributionist push has come since 1970. The measures adopted include both rural development policies (price guarantees for rice growers, land reform, rural credit, irrigation, and legislation to protect tenant farmers) and more general measures (a free rice ration; ceilings on income, wealth, and assets; more progressive taxation; subsidized transport; free education and health services). Some say that Sri Lanka is living far beyond her means.[9] Yet these welfare policies are part of a deliberate attempt to alleviate poverty through redistribution, and the data show that Sri Lanka has been succeeding.

The income distribution data for Sri Lanka come to us from Consumer Finance Surveys and from a recent census. The surveys have been conducted by the Central Bank at ten-year intervals. Although the sampling frames are not entirely equivalent (see Karunatilake, 1975:705–7), they appear close enough for intertemporal comparisons to be warranted.[10]

The Consumer Finance Surveys indicate modest economic growth: approximately 15% gains in real mean per capita

Table 6.4. *Sri Lanka: income and income distribution, 1953-1973*

	1953	1963	1973
GNP per capita, current Rs., National Accounts[a]	605	390	1120
GNP per capita, constant Rs., National Accounts[a,b]	665	690	735
Mean per capita income, monthly, current Rs., Consumer Finance Surveys[c]	107	134	228
Mean per capita income, monthly, constant Rs., Consumer Finance Surveys[c]	117	134	150
% of total income received by decile groups of spending units[c]			
Poorest	1.9	1.5	2.8
Second	3.3	3.0	4.4
Third	4.1	4.0	5.6
Fourth	5.2	5.2	6.5
Fifth	6.4	6.3	7.5
Sixth	6.9	7.5	8.8
Seventh	8.3	9.0	9.9
Eighth	10.1	11.2	11.7
Ninth	13.2	15.5	14.9
Richest	40.6	36.8	28.0
Gini coefficient among spending units[c]	.46	.45	.35
Distribution of absolute incomes among income recipients (constant 1963 Rs.)[c,d]			
Less than 100	63	59	41
100-200	23	25	31
200-400	6	12	25
Over 400	8	4	3
Total	100%	100%	100%

[a]Jain (1975:tab. 6).
[b]Deflated by price index for Colombo.
[c]Karunatilake (1975:712-15).
[d]Approximate.

income from 1953 to 1963 and from 1963 to 1973 (see Table 6.4). These rates are higher than real per capita GNP figures. The difference is thought to be due to a changing functional distribution in favor of the household sector.

By all accounts and measures, income inequality declined over the period of study. The Lorenz curve among spending units clearly shifted inward (see Figure 6.2), the Gini coeffi-

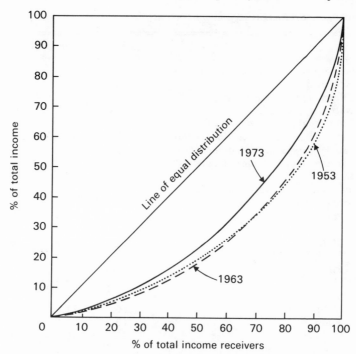

Figure 6.2. Lorenz curve showing distribution of income for Sri Lanka, 1953, 1963, and 1973. *Source*: Karunatilake (1975: 722).

cient of inequality declined from .46 to .35, the income share of the richest decile fell from 41% to 28%, and the income share of the poorest decile increased from 1.9% to 2.8%. As is clear from the data, most of the inequality reduction took place in the decade 1963–73.

We also find substantial reductions in absolute poverty.[11] The percentage of income recipients with incomes below a poverty line of Rs. 100 (in constant 1963 prices) fell from 63 in 1953 to 59 in 1963 and 41 in 1973. Using a higher poverty line (Rs. 200), the corresponding figures are 86%, 84%, and 72%.

What accounts for Sri Lanka's success in alleviating absolute poverty and relative inequality despite unimpressive aggregate growth? Among the factors that may be examined are education, demographic change, urbanization, changing employment structure, and social welfare policies.

Table 6.5. *Sri Lanka: education data, 1963 and 1973*

Proportion literate, by sex (%)[a]			
	1953	1963	1971
Male	80.7	85.6	85.2
Female	55.5	67.3	70.7
Total	69.0	76.9	78.1

Proportion of population by educational level (%)[b]			
	1953	1963	1973
No schooling	41.6	36.6	23.6
Primary	46.8	39.3	42.7
Secondary	9.8	19.6	23.8
Passed GCE/SSC	.9	3.4	8.8
Higher and technical	.9	1.1	1.1
Total	100.0	100.0	100.0

Median income, current Rs., by educational level[c]

	1963			1973		
Educational level	Median income (Rs.)	As % of median for primary	As % of median for higher	Median income (Rs.)	As % of median for primary	As % of median for higher
No schooling, illiterates	106	63	19	197	57	27
No schooling, literates	153	92	27	300	87	41
Primary	167	100	30	344	100	46
Secondary	257	154	46	450	131	61
Passed GCE/ SSC	475	284	84	617	179	83
Higher	563	337	100	740	215	100

[a] *Statistical Pocket Book of Sri Lanka (Ceylon)* (1975:tab. 11).
[b] Central Bank of Ceylon (1963:tab. 12); Karunatilake (1975:tab. 9).
[c] Karunatilake (1975:tab. 10).

Some aspects of educational change are seen in Table 6.5. Illiteracy was reduced from 31% to 23% between 1953 and 1963 and remained at about the same level between 1963 and 1971. The proportion without schooling has exhibited a steady decline (42% in 1953, 37% in 1963, and 24% in 1973), and the proportion with secondary education a steady

Table 6.6. *Sri Lanka: locational aspects of economic activity, 1953, 1963, and 1973*

Population by location (millions)[a]

	1953	1963	1972
Urban	1.2	1.9	2.3
Rural	6.1	7.6	9.2
Estate[b]	.9	1.2	1.4
Total	8.3	10.6	13.0

Mean income by location (current Rs.)[c]

	1963	1973	% change, 1963–73
Urban	441	601	+26
Rural	248	458	+84
Estate[b]	126	227	+80
All Sri Lanka	253	442	+75

Location of economic activity (thousands of current Rs.)[d]

	1963	1973	% change, 1963–73	% of total change, 1963–73
Urban	508	772	+52	21
Rural	1,266	2,171	+72	71
Estate[b]	193	294	+53	8
All Sri Lanka	1,966	3,237	+65	100

[a] Karunatilake (1975:728).
[b] "Estate" refers to agricultural plantations. Most of these are small villages, but some are so large as to constitute their own towns.
[c] Karunatilake (1975:734).
[d] Computed from population and mean income.

increase (from 10% in 1953 to 24% in 1973). At the same time, and perhaps because of the greater supply of relatively well-educated workers, educational differentials narrowed, especially from literacy through secondary level.

Another aspect is demographic change. Young workers became less numerous in proportional terms between 1963 and 1973.[12] Because young workers earn less than others,[13] this compositional effect would tend to reduce inequality among income recipients, although not necessarily among families.

Interestingly, urbanization does *not* appear to be a major component of economic development in Sri Lanka. To the contrary, rural development is the key. Some data on locational aspects of economic activity are given in Table 6.6. Most of the population growth (between 65% and 75%) took place in rural areas. In addition, in a pattern unlike that of most other countries, urban incomes grew more slowly than rural incomes. Consequently, the bulk of the gain in economic activity (about 70%) was concentrated in rural areas. Agricultural development is due in part to the Green Revolution and in part to the public policies cited. An assessment of the relative importance of the various parts of the rural development program has not yet appeared.

We may also look into the distribution of employment by industry or occupation. In some countries, these distributions are found to shift decidedly in favor of the higher-paying industries and occupations, reflecting the creation of new income opportunities. In Sri Lanka, however, the data reveal only vague tendencies in this direction (see Table 6.7). The industry distribution changed only a little over our period of analysis, not enough to make much difference. The occupational distribution changed but in no clear direction. As would be expected, employment in agriculture grew at a below-average rate, its share therefore declining. Where the relative gains occurred is unclear. Middle-level occupations show a mixed pattern: Clerical, sales, and transport occupations grew at rates well above average, but service employment declined. At the upper end of the distribution, professional and technical employment increased at an above-average rate, but administrative and managerial employment exhibited an absolute decrease. From this lack of a pronounced overall tendency, it might be suspected that Sri Lanka's economic development benefited the poor *within* occupational groups (i.e., by traditional sector enrichment) rather than by transferring the poor *across* occupational groups (i.e., by modern sector enlargement). Unfortunately, the requisite cross-tabulations needed to test this speculation do not seem to have been produced.

Finally, there is the impact of the government's social welfare policies. Taken together, the free rice ration, free education and health services, and subsidized food and trans-

Table 6.7. *Sri Lanka: distribution of employment by industry and occupation, 1953, 1963, and 1971*

Employment distribution by industry	1953 (%)[a]	1963 (%)[a]	1971 (%)[b]
Agriculture, mining, and related	53.4	53.2	50.8
Manufacturing	10.1	9.8	9.6
Services (public)	16.1	15.5	13.5
Commerce, transport, and communication	11.7	13.2	13.8
Other	8.7	8.3	12.3
Total gainfully employed	100.0	100.0	100.0

Employment distribution by occupation	1963 (thousands)[c]	1971 (thousands)[d]	Change, 1963–71 (thousands)	% change, 1963–71
Professional, technical, and related workers	143	176	+33	+23
Administrative and managerial workers	33	12	−21	−64
Clerical and related workers	118	189	+71	+60
Sales workers	212	277	+65	+31
Agricultural and related workers	1,654	1,791	+138	+8
Mining and related workers	5			
Transport and communication workers	101	892	+158	+22
Craftsmen and production workers	633			
Service workers	259	196	−63	−24
Not elsewhere classified	41	88	+47	+146
Total gainfully employed	3,199	3,621	+423	+13

[a] *Statistical Pocket Book of Ceylon* (1968:tab. 18).
[b] *Statistical Pocket Book of Sri Lanka* (1975:tab. 18).
[c] *Statistical Pocket Book of Ceylon* (1968:tab. 19).
[d] *Statistical Pocket Book of Sri Lanka* (1975:tab. 19).

Table 6.8. *Sri Lanka: estimated effects of social benefits on income distribution, 1963*

| | % of income in spending unit | |
Deciles	Unadjusted for social benefits	Adjusted for social benefits[a]
Poorest	1.5	2.0
Second	3.0	3.8
Third	4.0	2.7
Fourth	5.2	7.5
Fifth	6.3	6.8
Sixth	7.5	7.6
Seventh	9.0	9.5
Eighth	11.2	11.1
Ninth	15.5	15.0
Richest	36.8	34.0
Gini coefficient	.45	.40

[a]These consist of a subsidy on rice, losses incurred by public transport, free education, and health services.
Source: Jayawardena (1974).

port add up to half the government budget. These expenditures are directed toward the poor. One study (Jayawardena, 1974) estimates that these public goods and services raise the incomes of the poor by about one-third while lowering the incomes of the richest by a corresponding amount (though, of course, by a lesser percentage); see Table 6.8. But note too that the adjustments for social welfare policies are not sufficient to account for the changes in income distribution between 1953 and 1973; that is, much of the change was due to a changing distribution of *earned* income and not just to the impact of socially oriented public expenditures.

Some observers of the Sri Lankan economy question the appropriateness of early attention to social welfare, taking the view that aggregate growth might have been faster had social expenditures been less. This may be so, but confirmation of this view requires detailed modeling of a sort not yet undertaken. In any case, even if the speculation were correct, it is not at all clear whether poverty alleviation would have been greater or less had a poverty-oriented strategy not been followed. All we can go by is the record of poverty alleviation. On that score, Sri Lanka comes out looking quite successful.

India

India is a miserably poor country. Per capita yearly income is under $100. Of the Indian people, 45% receive incomes below U.S. $50 per year and 90% below U.S. $150. Of the total number of absolutely poor in the world (according to the AID data in Table 1.1), more than half are Indian. During the 1960s, per capita private consumer expenditure grew by less than $\frac{1}{2}$% per annum. India's poverty problem is so acute and her resources so limited that it is debatable whether any internal policy change short of a major administrative overhaul and radical redirection of effort might be expected to improve things substantially.[14]

India offers abundant data on the distribution of income and consumption dating back to the 1950s. Given the richness of the data in so poor a country with so large a research establishment, it is not surprising that we find a multitude of income-distribution studies. Some of the findings from some of the more important of these are reported in Table 6.9.

The data in Table 6.9 differ with respect to the concept of income or consumption employed, the procedures by which the figures were derived, and the years for which the distributions were estimated. The remarkable feature about the relative inequality data is that no clear pattern of change emerges. More specifically:

1. Overall, as measured by the nationwide Gini coefficient and the income shares of the bottom 20% and the top 20%, relative income inequality shows no pronounced trend, but the indications are toward diminished inequality. Because Lorenz curves crossed, other relative inequality measures would probably have yielded similarly mixed results.
2. The Gini coefficient within the urban sector may have risen somewhat, suggesting greater inequality, but the evidence is mixed.
3. The Gini coefficient within the rural sector seems to have declined, suggesting lesser inequality, but the changes are not large. Because the large majority of the population is rural, this suggests that nationwide inequality also diminished somewhat.

Table 6.9. *India: estimates of relative income inequality, various years and studies*

Study by Bhatty (1974) (data from NCAER[a])				
Income distribution measure	1961/2	1964/5	1967/8	1968/9
Gini coefficient of household income distribution, rural India	.41	.35	.46	.43

Study by Ojha and Bhatt (1974)(data from NSS[b] and National Accounts)		
Income distribution measure	1953/5	1963/5
Share in personal disposable income	7%	7%
Poorest 20%	50%	48%
Gini coefficient		
National	.371	.375
Urban	.392	.448
Rural	.341	.319

Study by Ranadive (1973)(data from NSS[b] and National Accounts)		
Income distribution measure	1953/4	1961/2
Share of total personal disposable income		
Poorest 20%– estimate A	7.50%	7.80%
Poorest 20%– estimate B	7.20%	7.60%
Richest 20%– estimate A	44.34%	45.47%
Richest 20%– estimate B	45.89%	46.70%
Gini coefficient		
Rural	.340	.317
Urban	.453	.487

Table 6.9. (*cont.*)

Study by Ahmed and Bhattacharya (1972) (data from NSS[b] and National Accounts) Income distribution measure	1956/7	1963/4		
Share of pretax personal income				
Poorest 20%	6.9%	7.6%		
Richest 20%	49.4%	45.6%		
Gini coefficient	.418	.372		

Study by Bardhan (1974b) (data from NSS[b]) Income distribution measure	1958/9	1960/1	1963/4	1967/8	1968/9
Gini coefficient of expenditure					
Rural	.340	.321	.297	.293	.310
Urban	.348	.350	.360	.345	.350

Study by Minhas (1970) (data from NSS,[b] rural India) Income distribution measure	1956/7	1960/1	1964/5	1967/8
Consumption share, rural				
Poorest 5%	1.36%	1.46%	1.47%	1.48%
Richest 5%	15.76%	16.82%	13.33%	13.24%
Gini coefficient, rural	.32	.31	.29	.29

[a] NCAER = National Council of Applied Economic Research.
[b] NSS = National Sample Survey.

In summary, given the contradictory indications of whether inequality increased or decreased and the small magnitudes of the changes as compared with probable errors in sampling and measurement, it appears warranted to conclude that the pattern of relative inequality in India changed little, but what change did occur was probably in the direction of lesser inequality.

A leading Indian economist, P. K. Bardhan, takes issue with relative inequality measurements of income distribution. He contends: "For a desperately poor country like India, there are many who believe that no measure of inequality which is in terms of relative distribution and is independent of some absolute poverty standard can be entirely satisfactory" (1974*b*:119). Accordingly, he has calculated estimates of the percentage of the population below a constant absolute poverty line: Rs. 15 per capita per month at 1960/1 prices in the rural sector, Rs. 18 in the urban sector.[15] His results, shown in part A of Table 6.10, are striking: He estimates that *absolute poverty worsened greatly in India over the 1960s even though relative inequality did not.*[16] Note particularly the comparison with his own relative inequality estimates in Table 6.9 under Bardhan (1974*b*).

Several other studies have also estimated absolute poverty changes in rural India. Bardhan's conclusion that absolute poverty increased in India during the 1960s was sustained in a paper by Ojha (1970) published contemporaneously with Bardhan's original work (1970). Defining poverty according to consumption of food grains rather than in rupees, Ojha found that the incidence of absolute rural poverty increased considerably between 1960/1 and 1967/8 (see part B of Table 6.10). Further corroborating evidence may be found in a study by Vaidyanathan (1974), who estimated that real per capita consumption declined for each fractile group in the rural population, and the proportion below a constant absolute poverty line increased (see part C of Table 6.10).

Before accepting the conclusion that absolute poverty worsened in India in the 1960s, we should also take note of contradictory evidence presented by another eminent Indian economist, B. S. Minhas. In a 1970 study, Minhas reported a *decline* in absolute rural poverty (see part D of Table 6.10).

After looking into the conflicting data at some length, I would side with Bardhan and others who conclude that Indian poverty *increased* during the 1960s. Among the possible sources of divergence are the following:

1. Bardhan uses a poverty line set at Rs. 15 per month (at 1960/1 prices). Minhas presents poverty data alternately for two figures, Rs. 200 and Rs. 240 per year. Minhas therefore shows more poverty, but how these figures on levels of poverty influence computations of changes in poverty is not immediately apparent.

2. Although Bardhan and Minhas both worked with con-

Table 6.10. *India: estimates of absolute poverty in the 1960s*

A. Study by Bardhan (1974b)	1960/1	1964/5	1968/9
Rural, % below Rs. 15 per capita per month[a]	38	45	54
Urban, % below Rs. 18 per capita per month[a]	32	37	41

B. Study by Ojha (1970)	1960/1	1967/8	
Rural, % whose consumption of food grains was below nutritional norms	52	70	

C. Study by Vaidyanathan (1974)	1960/1	1964/5	1967/8
Rural per capita expenditure (monthly) by fractile group (%)[a]			
0-5	Rs. 6.3	9.0	7.0
5-10	8.4	10.6	8.7
10-20	10.3	10.6	8.7
20-30	12.5	12.4	10.6
30-40	14.5	13.3	12.4
40-50	16.4	15.1	14.3
50-60	18.8	17.5	16.4
60-70	21.4	22.2	19.1
70-80	25.1	23.8	22.4
80-90	31.8	30.2	27.7
90-95	40.9	35.8	34.6
95-100	72.2	65.7	51.0
All groups	21.5	20.3	18.0
Rural population, % with per capita consumption below Rs. 20 per month, NSS[b] data[a]	60	60	68

D. Study by Minhas (1970)	1960/1	1964/5	1967/8
Rural, % below Rs. 20 per month	46	39	37

[a] In 1960/1 prices.
[b] NSS = National Sample Survey.

sumption data from the National Sample Surveys, they did so in different ways. Bardhan used the rural and urban distributions separately. Minhas, however, appears to have constructed an overall income distribution for all India and then estimated rural and urban distributions by applying the ratio of rural to urban consumption to the overall distribution. For this procedure to be correct, it must be assumed that the shapes of the rural and urban distributions are the same, though at different levels. But it is well known that the shapes are not the same, the rural distribution being more equal than the urban. It follows, therefore, that Minhas *overstates* the incomes of the rural poor and *understates* the number below an agreed-upon rural poverty line. It is not clear what Minhas's methodology implies for estimates of changing income distribution over time. But there is little doubt that his estimates are less accurate than those of Bardhan.

3. Another important difference between the studies is in the adjustment for inflation. Bardhan used the government's Agricultural Labor Price Index, which doubled between 1960/1 and 1967/8. Minhas, on the other hand, used the implicit National Income Deflator, which showed a much smaller increase (+70%). For this reason, Bardhan tends to show more poverty in the latter 1960s than does Minhas. The qualitative issue is resolved, though, when Minhas's estimated distribution is deflated by the Agricultural Labor Price Index rather than by the National Income Deflator. The use of these different price adjustments accounts for about half the difference between the two estimates of poverty in 1967/8; see Table 6.11.

It seems to me that the rural farm laborers' price index is the appropriate one in India, where 80% of the population is rural. When this index is used, even Minhas's distribution estimate indicates *increasing* absolute poverty. When Bardhan's distribution estimates are used, the increase in rural poverty is even greater.

In summary, evidence on whether absolute poverty and relative inequality were alleviated or exacerbated in the 1960s in India is conflicting. For our purposes, the most important finding is that relative inequality measures are found to sug-

Table 6.11. *India: % of rural population below Rs. 200 per annum at 1960/1 prices*

Estimate	1960/1	1967/8
Minhas's distribution estimate	46.0	37.1
Minhas's distribution estimate deflated by Agricultural Labor Price Index rather than by National Income Deflator	46.0	49.2
Bardhan's distribution estimate deflated by Agricultural Labor Price Index	46.0	63.1

Source: Bardhan (1971:tab. 1).

gest one set of conclusions about changing income distribution, whereas absolute poverty comparisons suggest another. Relative income inequality may have declined a little. Some observers have inferred from this that, although India did not grow very fast, it at least held the line on income distribution. When the figures are reexamined from an absolute poverty perspective, we see that India did not hold the line at all. Rather, absolute poverty appears by most accounts to have increased considerably.

Brazil

We will begin our study of Brazil at 1960, the date when the first comprehensive overview of income distribution became available. At the time, the Brazilian economy was in chaos. Growth was low, inflation rampant, the economic future uncertain, and political instability imminent. Following the military takeover of 1964, one of the first priorities of the new regime was economic stabilization. Whether the policies of the new government were responsible for the subsequent improvement, or whether things would have improved anyhow, is a matter of some discussion, because the government both continued old policies (encouraging savings and investment, promoting exports, supporting industrialization) and introduced new ones (indexing, flexible and realistic exchange rates, tax reform). In any event, 1964–7 was a period of marked reduction in inflation, creation of a favorable market environment, and encouragement of investment from all sources, including foreign capital and multilateral lending. The years 1967–74 marked the so-called Brazilian economic miracle. Real GNP doubled over that period, reflecting an average growth rate of 10% per year. In the mid 1970s economic growth slowed because of a combination of factors, including the higher cost of imported petroleum after 1974; the frost of 1975, which destroyed nearly all of that year's coffee crop; and serious balance-of-payments difficulties that caused the government to tighten monetary and fiscal policies. Throughout, Brazil has followed a more capitalistic, market-oriented development strategy than nearly any other developing country.

National population censuses were conducted in 1960 and 1970. These provide bench-mark data on income distribution, even though they do not conform to turning points in the growth cycle. During the 1960s, income grew by 79%, income per capita by 32%. The income distribution for 1970 was absolutely superior to the 1960 distribution; that is, a smaller fraction of the population was below any given income level, and conversely, any given population group had a larger average income than before.

If a poverty line appropriate to Brazilian standards is drawn at 2,100 cruzeiros (NCr.), and if we examine the distributions above and below the line, the following findings emerge:

1. The entire income distribution shifted in real terms, benefiting every income class.
2. There was a small decline in the fraction of the economically active population classified as below the poverty line (according to my estimates, from 37% to $35\frac{1}{2}$%), but those who remained "poor" experienced a marked percentage increase in real income (from one-third to as much as two-thirds higher).
3. The percentage increase for those below the poverty line was greater than the increase for those not in poverty and may well have been twice as high or more.
4. The relative income gap between "poor" and "nonpoor" persons narrowed in terms of ratios, although the absolute gap widened.
5. The bulk of the income growth over the decade accrued to persons above the poverty line. A similar pattern is observed for the United States, an allegedly more egalitarian society.
6. The poverty gap in Brazil was reduced by 41% between 1960 and 1970; see Figure 6.3. The United States reduced its poverty gap by exactly the same percentage over the same decade.[17]

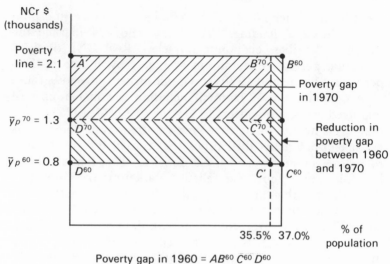

Figure 6.3. Poverty gap in Brazil, 1960 and 1970.   *Source*: Fields (1977: 576).

Although absolute incomes were growing and absolute poverty was being alleviated, relative income disparities were widening. Overall measures of relative inequality showed an increase. The Gini coefficient rose–from .59 to .63 in the economically active population, from .49 to .56 among income recipients. The rich got relatively richer, the income share of the top 3.2% rising from 27% to 33%. Inequality also increased in a number of other dimensions. Skill differentials widened; whereas incomes of university graduates rose by 52%, incomes of those with primary school educations rose by only 14%. Occupationally, incomes of nonagricultural employers and the self-employed increased by 50%, incomes of nonagricultural employees by 25%, and incomes of landless laborers not at all. Average income rose by 32%, but the real minimum wage fell (by 25% between 1964 and 1970). Geographically, growth was concentrated disproportionately in urban areas, industrial output growing by 96%

over the decade, as opposed to 53% in agriculture. Regionally, some areas (particularly São Paulo) advanced rapidly, whereas others (especially the Northeast) barely progressed at all; one result was an interregional per capita income gap of more than four to one. Across all these dimensions, then, inequalities grew as the economy grew.

Brazil's uneven economic growth is manifested in a changing employment structure (see Table 6.12). The occupations that grew were relatively high-level ones. Employment in primary occupations (defined as agricultural activities, mining, forestry, and fishing) increased by just 2%; secondary activities (mineral extraction, industrial production and services, and construction) grew by 96%; and tertiary employment (in the professions, selling of services, merchandising, transport and communication, and civil service) increased by 107%. The urban labor force grew six times as fast as the rural labor force, owing to substantial rural–urban migration. The number of college graduates in the labor force increased by 79%, as compared with a population growth rate of 33% overall. Enrollments expanded at all levels; between 1960 and 1972, the number enrolled in primary schools increased by 100%, in secondary schools by 250%, and in higher education by 350%. For the most part public education is now free.

In recognizing these improvements, we should not forget the severe economic conditions that remain. Of the Brazilian population, 20% received incomes below $75 per capita in 1970. More than 40% of the economically active population continue to be engaged in primary activities. Of those children who enter first grade, no more than 10% finish fourth grade.

In short, the Brazilian economy presents a mixed picture. Aggregate measures of growth and absolute income change look good, but relative inequality measures do not. During the period under study the favored sectors grew larger, absorbing more and more people. Those who were drawn into the enlarging modern sectors or who moved up within them benefited handsomely. On the other hand, whole sectors of the economy made little economic progress; consequently, tens of millions of people experienced at best minor economic gains. As compared with other countries, the Brazilian economy followed a highly uneven growth path.

Table 6.12. *Brazil: some aspects of economic growth during the 1960s*

Income source, 1970[a]

Wage earners as % of income recipients	74
Income received by wage-earners as % of total	71

Median earned income by rural–urban breakdown, 1960 (approximate) (Cr$)[b]

Urban and suburban households	1,250

Median earned income by economic sector, 1970 (approximate) (NCr$)[c]

Industrial	195
Agriculture	110
All sectors	165

	1960	1970	Growth(%)
Population (millions)[d]			
Total	70.1	93.2	33
Urban	32.5	52.1	60
Rural	37.6	41.1	9
Real output by sector (1949 = 100)[e]			
Industrial	261.4	511.8	96
Agriculture	156.1	239.5	53
Total real product	205.7	368.5	79
Employment by sector (millions)[f]			
Industrial	3.0	5.8	77
Agriculture	12.2	13.1	9
Total economically active population	22.6	29.5	30
Employment by occupational type (thousands)[g]			
Primary: agricultural activities, mining, forestry, fishing	12,271	12,533	2
Secondary: mineral extraction, industrial production and services, construction	2,791	5,476	96
Tertiary: professions, selling of services (including repair and domestic work, merchandising, transport and communications, and civil service (including police and army)	5,341	11,082	107

Table 6.12. (*cont.*)

	1960	1969
Rate of employment as % of population in each age-sex group[h]		
Men		
15-19	72.4	68.2
20-24	92.3	89.3
25-34	97.2	96.0
35-44	96.9	95.8
45-54	94.0	92.5
55-64	83.2	81.5
65+	59.1	51.4
Men 15 and over	88.6	84.8
Women		
15-19	23.4	37.4
20-24	22.5	41.7
25-34	17.8	36.3
35-44	17.1	34.2
45-54	15.6	31.0
55-64	12.6	22.7
65+	8.5	10.0
Women 15 and over	18.4	33.6

	1960	1968-70	% change
Employment/output ratio by sector[i]			
Agriculture	2.27	2.50	+10
Industry	.52	.63	+20
Services	.49	.68	+38

	August 1960	First quarter 1970	% change
Mean monthly incomes (1960 NCr $)[j]			
Agricultural employees	2.6	2.5	-4
Nonagricultural employees	8.0	10.5	+31
All employees	6.6	9.4	+43
Nonagricultural employers and self-employed	14.0	19.5	+39

Table 6.12. (*cont.*)

	% change of labor force in that educational group	% change of relative incomes in that educational group
Changes in relationship between education and the labor market, 1960–70[k]		
Primary	+5	−17
Secondary	+96	−7
University	+79	+11

[a]Comisión Económica para América Latina (1974:22).
[b]Brasil (1960:tab. 6).
[c]Brasil (1970:tab. 8).
[d]Brasil (1960:tab. 1); Brasil (1970:tab. 1).
[e]Fundaçao Getúlio Vargas (1973:tab. 2).
[f]Brasil (1970:tab. 5).
[g]Singer (1971:tabs. 2.5, 2.6).
[h]Singer (1971:tab. 1.1).
[i]Wogart (1974:tab. 6).
[j]Fishlow (1973b:91).
[k]Malan and Wells (1973:1110).

Why did economic conditions in Brazil change as they did? Why the unevenness? Experts on the Brazilian economy disagree strenuously and often bitterly on a number of dimensions:

1. Government industrialization and stabilization policy: The Brazilian government instituted a number of fiscal and other incentives to encourage industrialization and stabilize the economy while pursuing an avowedly capitalistic course. Whether these policies act as stimulants to growth of employment and incomes for the poor or as a way of satisfying the demands of the rich for consumer durables produced by multinational corporations is a key point of debate. Government economists generally take the former position, known in some quarters as the trickle-down position: see, for example, *Brazilian Trends* (1973). The consumer-demand argument has a number of adherents, among the most prominent of whom are Furtado (1970) and Singer (1977). A third view is that government policy is directed toward a few while

disregarding the many; see, for example, the writings of Fishlow (1973*a* and *b*).

2. International trade policies: A second issue is the impact of public policy toward international trade. During the 1960s, Brazil shifted toward an export-promotion development strategy and away from a policy of import substitution. In Brazil as in many other less-developed countries, it is generally thought that import substitution was accompanied by factor price distortions that hindered employment growth by favoring capital-intensive techniques in manufacturing.[18] The export-promotion phase, beginning in 1964, raised capital costs by means of monetary correction and lowered labor costs via wage controls. The expected results–more labor-intensive production–indeed took place. Whether these are cause and effect is open to interpretation.

3. Government wage policy: We have observed that the Brazilian wage structure clearly widened during the 1960s, both because wages in the relatively high-paying sectors and occupations rose and because the real minimum wage fell. Some researchers see this as cause and/or effect of rapid economic growth.[19] Others with a less favorable perspective hold that constant wages at the bottom of the income distribution and rising wages elsewhere are part of a more general governmental strategy aimed at minimizing expressions of discontent by highly educated and skilled workers in order to maintain the existing economic order (see Mericle, 1976).

4. Educational policy: Langoni (1972 and 1975) contends that much of the increase in growth and employment can be explained by increased numbers of highly educated workers receiving higher wages because of their higher productivity. He attributes growing relative income inequality in Brazil in large part to the realization of quasi rents by persons possessing scarce human capital. Because he sees education as the cause of growth, Langoni's main message is that "the simple workings of the development process would, in the Brazilian situation, lead to an increase in income inequality." Furthermore, Langoni sees this situation as only temporary and anticipates a reduction in inequality once the educational system and the labor market have had time to respond to the sudden surge of growth. This interpretation

has been challenged by Fishlow (1973*a* and *b*), Malan and Wells (1973), and Wells (1974) for a number of reasons, including the following: (*a*) Income differentials between university graduates and secondary school graduates widened considerably over the decade (from 105% to 150%); (*b*) average social rates of return are found to be highest at the lowest educational levels, yet Brazilian policy favors educational investment at the upper levels; and (*c*) education's importance in explaining income distribution change is considerably diminished once occupational adjustments are made.

Could more have been done to ameliorate present-day poverty? Undoubtedly. Why was more not done? The answer varies. Some students of Brazilian political economy see the growth strategy adopted as being in the direct interests of the ruling class. Adherents of this view see the concentrated structure of ownership of the means of production as determining the structure of goods produced (largely consumer durables) and the growth effort as aimed at creating a demand for those goods among the middle and upper classes. Others see the Brazilian growth strategy as the result of a callous but apparently defensible decision to augment future productive capacity through current savings and investment at the expense of antipoverty efforts in this generation. Still others point not to a preplanned strategy but to circumstances that arose more or less independently, such as the availability of foreign loans for factories and industrial equipment but not for potable water and health clinics. On this view, the incentives were to grow unevenly or not at all, and uneven growth was the outcome.

Which view is right? All have elements of truth. The key, in my view, is that Brazilian policy was characterized by inattention to the short-run poverty problem. Call it benign neglect or heartless exploitation according to your emotive valuation. Deliberate unevenness is the central feature of Brazilian growth.

The Philippines

The Philippines[20] ranks in the middle of the income scale of the developing countries: In 1969 its per capita GDP was about U.S. $250. However, its overall growth performance is well above average. Real GNP more than tripled between 1950 and 1973, the date of the most recent distribution statistics. This implies a growth rate of 6% per year (compounded) in real output and 3% per year in real output per capita. The average annual real growth rate (by percent) breaks down by subperiods as follows:

Years	Gross domestic product	GDP per capita
1950–60	6.4	3.2
1960–5	5.1	2.1
1965–73	5.8	2.7

Few countries in the world-and only Taiwan and Costa Rica among the countries studied here-have done better.[21]

Before trying to discover who benefited from the Philippines' growth, we should note the apparent dualism of the Philippine economy. Postwar economic growth followed quite different courses in the two major economic divisions. In the rural sector, where 70% of the people are located, little has changed. Although the agricultural sector has grown slowly (about 3% per year in real terms) but steadily. Nonetheless, food is still produced using methods similar to those of previous generations, although high-yielding rice varieties have become quite important in some regions. Nonagricultural rural activities (e.g., cottage industries, small-scale commerce) have not surfaced to any appreciable extent, nor are they likely to do so in the foreseeable future. In contrast to the rural situation, the urban economy developed more rapidly but less evenly. Organized manufacturing in particular grew quickly at first (more than 10% real growth per annum in the 1950s). Growth slowed in the last decade, but real manufacturing production still grew at a 6% annual rate from 1965 to 1973.

These overall growth figures conceal great diversity of experience. The report of the ILO Mission to the Philippines (ILO, 1974:4-5) goes so far as to say: "The Philippine economy provides a striking example of the inadequacy of conventional aggregate criteria of economic growth both to judge past development performance and to appreciate future prospects." More disaggregated income-distribution data are available, and they exhibit a deeply disturbing pattern: Despite a tripling of the national product and a doubling of national product per capita, mean family incomes grew by less than 1% per year. We see in Table 6.13 that mean income evaluated at constant prices went from an index value of 100 in 1956 to a high of 126 in 1965 and then down to 117 in 1971.[22] Evidence like this led the ILO Mission to characterize the postwar period as one of "narrow participation and unbalanced growth" and other authors to regard Philippine development as a "crisis of ambiguity" (Averch et al., 1971).

Other social indicators also suggest little success in distributing the benefits of growth in the Philippines. A good example is nutrition. The World Bank reports that just after World War II the Philippines was comparable in nutritional status to Malaysia, Japan, and Taiwan. Various studies estimate that there are now serious nutritional deficiencies for about 40%–45% of the population, though some estimates are even higher (Cheetham and Hawkins, 1976:chap. 11). Clearly, the Philippines has lagged behind her neighbors in providing basic needs for her people.

Let us look at relative inequality. Data on nominal incomes by quintile group are presented in Table 6.14. We see that the three middle quintiles gained relatively, compared with the richest and poorest quintiles. This means that the Lorenz curves for the past two years necessarily cross, and summary measures of relative inequality will not always agree; for example, the Gini coefficient of inequality showed a small *decline* between 1961 and 1971, whereas another index of inequality, the ratio of income of the top quintile to the bottom quintile, was found to *increase* over the same time.

What about absolute poverty? The data in Table 6.14 are based on nominal incomes, unadjusted for inflation. Using the change in the Consumer Price Index (+101.6%) as an approximation to the inflation experienced by the poor, it follows that the average real incomes of the poorest quintile groups *fell* by more than 10%. Average absolute income among the poorest 40% remained unchanged in real terms.

Is the falling real income in the lowest quintile evidence of

Table 6.13. The Philippines: income-distribution data, 1956–71

Indicator	1956			1961			1965			1971		
	Total	Rural	Urban	Total	Rural	Urban	Total	Rural	Urban	Total	Rural	Urban
Quintile of families (% of total family income)												
Poorest	4.5	7.0	4.5	4.2	5.9	3.8	3.5	5.0	3.8	3.8	4.4	4.6
Second	8.1	11.1	8.0	7.9	11.8	7.5	8.0	9.5	8.0	8.1	8.9	9.4
Third	12.4	14.7	12.2	12.1	13.5	12.5	12.8	15.3	12.0	13.2	13.9	13.4
Fourth	19.8	21.1	20.0	19.3	21.9	19.5	20.2	23.0	18.7	21.1	21.8	21.9
Richest	55.1	46.1	55.3	56.4	46.9	57.1	55.4	47.2	57.5	53.9	51.0	50.7
Top 10%	39.4	30.1	39.6	41.0	31.1	40.9	40.0	30.0	41.7	36.9	34.4	33.4
Top 5%	27.7	—	—	29.0	—	—	28.7	—	—	24.3	22.6	22.6
Index of quintile inequality	0.44	0.34	0.44	0.46	0.36	0.46	0.45	0.38	0.47	0.40	0.41	0.41
Gini coefficient	0.48	0.38	0.49	0.50	0.40	0.52	0.51	0.42	0.53	0.49	0.46	0.45
Mean income (current pesos)	1,471	989	2,427	1,804	1,203	2,970	2,541	1,755	4,405	3,736	2,818	5,867
Index, current price	100	100	100	123	123	123	173	178	182	254	285	242
Index, constant price	100	100	100	111	110	111	126	130	133	117	132	111
Mean urban income/mean rural income	2.45			2.47			2.51			2.08		

Source: ILO (1974:tab. 3).

Table 6.14. *The Philippines: average income per family in current pesos, 1961 and 1971*

Mean in current pesos			Nominal growth [a]
Quintile group	1961	1971	
Poorest	383	687	+ 79%
Second	712	1,523	+114%
Third	1,090	2,470	+127%
Fourth	1,738	3,924	+126%
Richest	5,094	10,079	+ 98%

[a]The Consumer Price Index rose by 101.6% over that period.
Source: Mijares and Belarmino (1973).

absolute impoverishment in the Philippines? Before drawing that conclusion from decile data alone, we ought to examine occupation or industry-specific wages or incomes. In the case of the Philippines, the data show that incomes in constant pesos declined for many groups: salaried employees, wage earners, and skilled and unskilled industrial laborers (see Table 6.15). In agriculture the picture looks little better: Real agricultural wages seem not to have risen in the postwar period, but real earnings of households headed by farm laborers were about 20% higher in 1971 than in 1965 (ILO, 1974: 11, 60). Thus, for major groups of the poor, the improvements in economic position are at best modest. This reinforces the bleak picture conveyed by the overall income distribution data presented in Table 6.14.

There is one other possible way the poor might have been made better off. As Morley and Williamson (1974) argued for Brazil, falling wages might have induced employers to hire more workers. Either these persons would have been unemployed and receiving no income at all or they would have been attracted from even lower-paying activities. Thus the poor might have shared in economic development by becoming employed in large numbers in expanding modern sector jobs that offer relatively advantageous conditions, for example, in skilled occupations, in high-paying industries, or in wage and salary jobs more generally. Data on the changing industrial and occupational composition of the Philippine labor force are given in Tables 6.16 and 6.17. The signs are

Table 6.15. *The Philippines: average incomes for select groups*

	1957	1961	1965	1971	1975
Index of average monthly earnings, nominal pesos (1965 = 100)[a]					
Salaried employees	76.2	90.8	100.00	132.3	190.2
Wage earners	78.9	88.1	100.00	142.1	215.3
Index of average monthly earnings, constant pesos (1965 = 100)[a, b]					
Salaried employees	105.8	113.8	100.00	82.6	65.1
Wage earners	109.6	110.4	100.00	88.7	73.7
Index of wage rates for laborers in industrial establishments in Manila and suburbs, constant pesos	(1965 = 100)[c]				
Skilled laborers	117.5	115.7	100.00	91.3	62.5
Unskilled laborers	110.2	104.8	100.00	101.3	69.6

[a] Central Bank of the Philippines (1975:tab. 140).
[b] Central Bank of the Philippines (1975:tab. 138).
[c] Central Bank of the Philippines (1975:tab. 141).

not encouraging. Total employment expanded by 4.9 million between 1956 and 1972. Nearly half the growth took place in agriculture (2.3 million). Of the rest, the occupational breakdown reveals large gains in sales and clerical jobs (1 million) and in professional employment (400,000). By industry grouping, employment gains were large in commerce and in domestic and personal services (1.1 million). Manufacturing employment, in contrast, expanded by only 400,000. It seems fair to conclude from this evidence that a small percentage of the poor benefited by being drawn into an enlarged modern sector, but that these movements did not produce widespread opportunity for upward mobility.

We have encountered a lower average absolute income in the poorest quintile, falling or stagnant wages and incomes for major occupational groups, and small increases in employment in job categories likely to benefit low-income persons. The apparent conclusion is that the poor in the Philippines did *not* participate much in economic growth; rather, they are *absolutely poorer*. This is a disturbing result whenever it

Table 6.16. *The Philippines: employed persons by major industry group, selected years (thousands)*

	October 1956[a]	October 1961[a]	October 1965[a]	November 1972[b]
Agriculture, forestry, hunting, and fishing	4,548	5,514	5,725	6,863
	(59.0%)	(60.6%)	(56.7%)	(54.5%)
Mining and quarrying	31	31	24	36
	(.4%)	(.3%)	(.2%)	(.3%)
Construction	198	230	295	432
	(2.6%)	(2.5%)	(2.9%)	(3.4%)
Manufacturing	962	1,026	1,101	1,323
	(12.5%)	(11.3%)	(10.9%)	(10.5%)
Electricity, gas, water, and sanitary services	26	19	22	44
	(.3%)	(.2%)	(.2%)	(.3%)
Commerce	803	873	1,114	1,478
	(10.4%)	(9.6%)	(11.0%)	(11.7%)
Transport, storage, and communication	228	278	339	467
	(3.0%)	(3.1%)	(3.4%)	(3.7%)
Government, community, business, and recreational services	392	538	708	1,071
	(5.1%)	(5.9%)	(7.0%)	(8.5%)
Domestic services	332	368	500	617
	(4.3%)	(4.0%)	(5.0%)	(4.9%)
Personal services other than domestic	135	179	227	246
	(1.8%)	(2.0%)	(2.2%)	(2.0%)
Industry not reported	47	39	47	4
	(.6%)	(.4%)	(.5%)	(.03%)
Total employment	7,702	9,095	10,101	12,582
	(100%)	(100%)	(100%)	(100%)

[a] *Statistical Handbook of the Philippines* (1971:tab. 3.4).
[b] *Statistical Handbook of the Philippines* (1976:tab. 61).

is encountered. When impoverishment is found in a rapidly growing economy, it is all the more distressing.

What development strategies and policies led the Philippines to alleviate poverty so little while growing so much? The obvious answer is a political one: Successive regimes in the Philippines did not take direct measures to spread the benefits of growth. They seem to have hoped that the benefits would filter down to the poor through multiplier effects, forward and backward linkages, and changing internal terms of trade. The Philippine economy is a clear example of how trickle-down growth strategies can go awry when accompanied by disequalizing policies that favor a select few.

The Philippines has rightly been classified as a labor-abundant economy. In such an economy, we would expect that the encouragement of labor-intensive production methods would both enhance growth and increase the economic participation of the poor. But this was not the course followed. Instead, the macroeconomic policy measures in force since the early 1950s (overvalued exchange rates, artificially low interest rates, investment subsidies) created incentives for excessive capital intensity in production and for imports of consumer goods and raw materials. The manufacturing sector fell behind the rest of the economy, in both employment and output. This placed increasing burdens on the agricultural sector to support economic growth, which it was unable to do. Rural inequality increased steadily. Although the Philippines extended the acreage under cultivation and introduced high-yielding varieties of rice, participation in these improvements was limited. The barriers to full participation have included the unavailability of credit for small farmers, lack of access to modern inputs, an underdeveloped transport and marketing network, and limited irrigation facilities. Even in the rural areas, public investment projects tend to be large and to favor those individuals already in advantageous positions.

Public policy clearly favors urban concentration. Some 80% of industrial activity in the Philippines is located in Manila. Industries benefit from favorable energy distribution and rates and other fiscal incentives, provided they relocate in Manila. In marked contrast to, say, Taiwan, in the Philippines rural industrialization receives little public support.

One other indication of the narrowness of development strategy in the Philippines is the change in the functional distribution of income. Because of a substantial increase in the share of undistributed corporate profits (from 10% of national income in 1961 to 16% in 1971), the functional

Table 6.17. *The Philippines: employed persons by major occupation group, selected years (thousands)*

	October 1956[a]	October 1961[a]	October 1965[a]	November 1972[b]
Professional, technical, and related workers	216 (2.8%)	309 (3.4%)	375 (3.7%)	595 (4.7%)
Proprietors, managers, administrators, and officials	352 (4.6%)	340 (3.7%)	432 (4.3%)	136 (1.1%)
Clerical, office, and related workers	153 (2.0%)	273 (3.0%)	352 (3.5%)	457 (3.6%)
Salesmen and related workers	456 (5.9%)	537 (5.9%)	675 (6.7%)	1,314 (10.4%)
Farmers, farm laborers, fishermen, hunters, lumbermen, and related workers	4,525 (58.8%)	5,501 (60.5%)	5,677 (56.2%)	6,829 (54.3%)
Workers in mine, quarry, and related occupations	30 (.4%)	23 (.2%)	14 (.1%)	20 (.2%)
Workers in operating transport occupations	145 (1.9%)	184 (2.0%)	272 (2.7%)	507 (4.0%)
Craftsmen, factory operatives, and workers in related occupations	1,071 (13.9%)	1,100 (12.1%)	1,270 (12.6%)	1,471 (11.7%)

Manual workers and laborers, not elsewhere classified	171 (2.2%)	168 (1.8%)	151 (1.5%)	226 (1.8%)
Service and related workers	541 (7.0%)	636 (7.0%)	840 (8.3%)	1,019 (8.1%)
Occupation not reported	41 (.5%)	29 (.3%)	42 (.4%)	7 (.06%)
Total employment	7,702 (100%)	9,095 (100%)	10,101 (100%)	12,582 (100%)

a Statistical Handbook of the Philippines (1971:tab. 3.5).
b Statistical Handbook of the Philippines (1976:tab. 62).

Table 6.18. *The Philippines: percentage distribution of families by main source of income, 1971*

Agriculture	
Wages and salaries	10.7%
Farming	34.4
Fishing, forestry, and hunting	4.3
Total	49.4%
Nonagriculture	
Wages and salaries	32.3%
Entrepreneurial activities	12.3
Total	44.6%
Other	6.0%
Total	100.0%

Source: ILO (1974:tab. 117).

distribution shifted away from the household sector. This implies a gain for the relatively well-to-do, because nonemployment incomes are concentrated in few hands (see Table 6.18).

The lesson from the Philippines is a clear one. The ILO report (1974:14) puts it well: "Not every type of growth, regardless of its rapidity, is sufficient in itself to ensure a matching of over-all supply and demand." It is, rather, the *kind* of economic growth that may prove decisive in determining the extent to which the poor participate in economic development. This is a matter of policy, not nature. Certainly, shortages of natural resources may seriously constrain the range of possibilities. But whatever the resource endowments may be, the lesson from the Philippines is that political will may well be decisive for the fate of the poor.

Taiwan

Taiwan is in the admirable position of combining rapid economic growth, sharply reduced inequality, and widespread alleviation of poverty. As such, it is both the only country in our sample and one of the very few low-income countries in the world to be developing so rapidly.

We begin our study of Taiwan in the early 1950s, shortly after the political separation from the mainland. During the 1950s, real gross national product per capita grew by around 3% per year despite rapid population growth. The first income-distribution data were published for 1953 and the second for 1961. These data give the impression of declining inequality, but these estimates ought not to be taken seriously, because the 1953 data were based on fitted rather than actual incomes and were constructed from a sample of only three hundred households selected non-randomly. The first reliable income distribution data for Taiwan became available only in the 1960s, and the accuracy of the data from the early 1960s is subject to doubt.

Since 1964, Surveys of Family Income and Expenditure have been conducted regularly. To date, the surveys through 1972 have been published and analyzed; data from them are shown in Table 6.19.

Part A of this table indicates that per household income nearly doubled in real terms between 1964 and 1972. This remarkable growth performance is well known. The distributional aspects of that growth are reported in parts B-F. We see in parts B and C that two measures of relative inequality – the Gini coefficient and the ratio of incomes of the top decile to the bottom decile – both declined, the latter more than the former.[23]   This reflects a Lorenz improvement, the 1972 curve lying everywhere inside the 1964 curve; see Figure 6.4. Parts D and E of Table 6.19 present the absolute real incomes of various decile groups. We see that the income share of the poorest decile increased, which in a rapidly growing economy implies even more rapidly growing incomes among the very poorest. A comparison of the rates of growth of real incomes by decile grouping (part E) shows a clear pattern: highest rates of income growth at the lowest end of the income distribution. These decile shares are translated into absolute poverty data in part F. The record of achievement is extraordinary: In just eight years, Taiwan alleviated absolute poverty among the majority of its poor. As far as I know, no other country in the world has accomplished that.

How do we account for the decline in inequality and poverty in Taiwan? Let us first consider proximate causes.

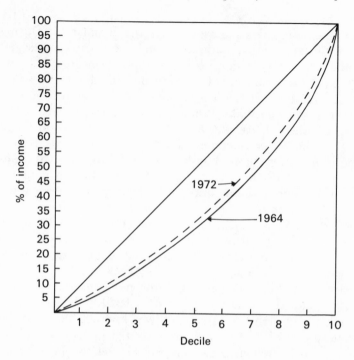

Figure 6.4. Lorenz curves for Taiwan, 1964 and 1972.

Data on functional income distribution reveal a clear shift
in favor of labor income and an almost equal reduction in the
importance of agricultural income (see Table 6.20). This
shift has two important implications. One is that because
wage income is distributed more evenly than is agricultural
income, the rising importance of labor income is likely to
reduce inequality in the economy as a whole. Second, because
wages are higher on the average than agricultural incomes, if
the wage income share increased and the agricultural income
share declined while inequality was falling, it must be because
the population shifted from agriculture to the wage sector.
Indeed, the data in Table 6.21 show just that: a large decline
in the share of labor force employed in agriculture, a corresponding gain in the share in industry, and virtual constancy
of service's share. Taiwan's ability to create sufficient industrial jobs for the workers released from agriculture con-

Table 6.19. *Taiwan: household income distribution, 1964 and 1972*

	1964	1972	Rate of increase, 1964–72 (%)
A. Mean income per household at constant 1972 prices (thousands of NT$)	32.5	61.0	+88
B. Gini coefficient	0.328	0.301	−9
C. Ratio of income share of richest 10% to poorest 10%	8.6	6.8	−21
D. Income share by decile group, cumulative			
Poorest	3.0	3.6	
Second	7.7	8.9	
Third	13.5	15.3	
Fourth	20.3	22.5	
Fifth	28.1	30.7	
Sixth	36.9	39.9	
Seventh	47.0	50.4	
Eighth	58.9	62.6	
Ninth	73.9	77.3	
Richest	99.9	100.0	
E. Mean income at 1972 constant prices (thousands of NT$)			
Poorest	9.9	20.6	+109
Second	15.2	30.2	+98
Third	18.9	36.1	+91
Fourth	22.0	41.1	+87
Fifth	25.3	46.2	+83
Sixth	28.5	52.1	+83
Seventh	32.9	59.6	+81
Eighth	38.7	69.0	+78
Ninth	48.8	83.4	+71
Richest	84.5	128.8	+53
F. Proportion of households with incomes below specified amount (thousands of constant NT$) in specified year			
20	35%	10%	
30	55%	20%	
40	80%	35%	

Sources: Kuo (1975:tabs. 5, 6; Fei, Ranis, and Kuo (1978:diagram 1).

Table 6.20. *Taiwan: functional income distribution*

Functional income grouping	Functional share, 1964	Functional share, 1972
Wage income	.432	.590
Agricultural income	.275	.103
Property income	.240	.258
Other income	.053	.049
Total	1.000	1.000

Source: Fei, Ranis, and Kuo (1978:diagram 1).

trasts with the experience in most LDCs of growing under-employment in low-level jobs, especially in the cities, in areas like commerce and services.

Another indication of labor-force upgrading in Taiwan is the distribution of the labor force by occupational position. Let us divide the economically active population into three groups–wage employees, own-account workers, and unpaid family workers; see Table 6.22. We find that the proportion of paid employees rose from 40% to 60% in thirteen years, the fraction of unpaid family workers fell nearly in half, and the proportion of own-account workers fell also. This means that commercialization and industrialization were proceeding rapidly enough to draw more and more of the work force into modern sectors.

The upgrading of employment in favor of higher-income jobs is shown in occupational data; see Table 6.23, columns 1 and 2. The fraction of workers employed as managers and professionals increased from 2.3% of the labor force in 1964 to 11.1% in 1972–a fivefold increase. Salaried workers and owners of small firms also became relatively more numerous. The occupational groups that diminished in importance were the lowest-paying ones, farmers and laborers. This shift in the occupational distribution toward the upper end is evidence of substantial modern sector enlargement.

Where Taiwan differs from other countries is in the pattern of income change by occupation; see columns 3–5 of Table 6.23. Incomes in the lowest occupational categories grew

Table 6.21. *Taiwan: sectoral distribution of employment, various years*

Pre-1966 classification system	Agriculture, forestry, fishing		Mining, manufacturing, transport, communications		All other industries	
	Number (thousands)	%	Number (thousands)	%	Number (thousands)	%
1953	1,812	61.3	339	11.5	803	27.2
1958	1,813	57.0	435	13.7	930	29.3
1964	2,010	54.2	556	15.0	1,144	30.8
1966	2,050	53.0	604	15.6	1,216	31.4

Post-1966 classification system	Agriculture		Industry		Services	
	Number (thousands)	%	Number (thousands)	%	Number (thousands)	%
1966	1,617	43.5	1,050	28.2	1,055	28.3
1972	1,632	33.0	1,847	37.3	1,469	29.7
1975	1,652	29.9	2,276	41.2	1,593	28.9

Source: Galenson (1979).

considerably: Farmers' incomes rose by 53% in eight years and laborers' incomes by 123%. Thus those who remained in low-level occupations shared in economic growth, their combined incomes rising at a faster rate than the combined incomes of managers and professionals. This is evidence of substantial traditional sector enrichment, both absolutely and relatively, on a scale unequaled in any of the other countries studied.

In summary:

All these indicators point to the conclusion that rapid economic growth has led to a marked improvement in Taiwan's employment situation [since the 1950s and 1960s] without any radical redistribution of income or wealth. This is not to say that full employment has been achieved in Taiwan, any more than it has in the industrial market economies. But Taiwan has clearly left the stage of gross unemployment that still characterizes most of the developing world. [Galenson, 1979]

What sorts of structural changes in Taiwan's economy accompanied these shifts? We may identify the following

Table 6.22. *Taiwan: occupational position of the labor force,
various years (%)*

	1964	1968	1972	1975
Paid employees	41.7	50.6	57.8	59.8
Own account workers	29.8	26.9	25.4	24.3
Unpaid family workers	28.5	22.5	16.8	15.9
Total	100.0	100.0	100.0	100.0

Source: Galenson (1979).

factors in Taiwan's growth since the early 1950s: gains in
agricultural labor productivity of nearly 250%, which financed
rapid growth, industrialization, and reallocation of the labor
force out of agriculture; growing external orientation of the
economy, with industrial exports increasing fourteenfold;
changing export composition, shifting from primarily agricultural goods to over 90% industrial; investment in labor-
intensive industries including electrical machinery, chemicals,
and textiles; the end of the labor surplus around 1968,
followed by rising wage shares in national income; and high
and growing rural industrialization. For further analysis of
Taiwan's growth experience, see Fei and Ranis (1975) and
Galenson, ed. (1979).

What kinds of economic development policies and strategies
produced these outcomes? There are four key elements
(Ranis, 1978):

1. Strategy of decentralized development: Taiwan inherited
from colonial days the start of a network of roads, railways,
irrigation systems, and industrial estates. Farmers' organizations and agricultural extension services were also in place.
After independence, Taiwan not only maintained these
decentralized systems but also continued their development
and added new ones (e.g., rural electrification). As one
indicator of the extent of decentralized development, we
have the fact that in the fifties and sixties there were more
new rural than urban business establishments in Taiwan.
Another is the fact that the majority of Taiwan's industrial
workers are in rural areas, with the proportion increasing
steadily. Taiwan's strategy of early attention to backward

Table 6.23. *Taiwan: income and employment by occupational group, 1964 and 1972*

	(1)		(2)	(3)		(4)		(5)
Occupation	Share of employment (%)		% change in employment share,	Average income per family (thousands of constant NT$)		Average income in that occupation relative to the mean		Growth rate of average income in occupation (%),
	1964	1972	1964–72	1964	1972	1964	1972	1964–72
Managers	1.4	3.8	+171	87	116	2.69	1.92	+33
Professionals	0.9	7.3	+711	48	83	1.46	1.40	+74
Owner of small firms	11.1	12.8	+15	39	67	1.20	1.10	+69
Salaried workers	17.9	21.0	+17	38	66	1.25	1.10	+74
Farmers	39.6	25.9	−35	32	49	.99	.81	+53
Laborers	27.3	22.8	−17	24	54	.74	.88	+123
Workers in other industries	1.8	6.4	+255	20	41	.61	.68	+110
Whole economy	100.0	100.0		32	61			+87

Source: Kuo (1975:tab. 15).

areas contrasts with most other countries' emphasis on urban growth: developing industrial complexes, building housing, and supplying physical and social services in the major cities. One consequence of decentralized development was the unusually low rate of rural–urban migration experienced in Taiwan.[24]

2. Balanced rural development strategy: The development of rural Taiwan combined the standard concern with agriculture with unusually heavy attention to nonagricultural activities. In most less-developed countries, 90% or more of the economically active rural population is employed in agriculture; in Taiwan, the percentage is more like 50. This attention to nonagricultural rural activities is seen as providing the goods and services needed to make rural growth viable and preventing the rapid urbanization via rural–urban migration that is found in most other low-income countries. It should be recognized that this did not come about through

happenstance. Taiwan made major efforts toward agricultural development, with land reform a key ingredient. Between 1949 and 1953, Taiwan compelled the sale of land by landlords, sold public lands for cultivation, and imposed rent controls. Institutional structures were reorganized in support of land reform, and such measures as agricultural research and extension programs, farmers' cooperatives for purchasing and marketing, and credit to small farmers were instituted. Roads and other physical infrastructures were maintained and expanded.

3. Industrial and trade strategies: Around 1960, Taiwan made a major change in its policies toward industrialization and trade. Before then, heavy reliance had been placed on import substitution, by means of policies including high tariffs to protect domestic industries, overvalued exchange rates, artificially low domestic interest rates, and other measures aimed at increasing production at home of goods that once were imported. Such policies can be in effect only so long before the domestic market is satisfied. A country must then choose whether to export the additional goods for sale in world markets ("export promotion") or to produce at home more of the raw materials and intermediate goods that are presently imported (known as "secondary import substitution"). Around 1960, Taiwan chose the first option. Exchange rates were made more realistic, interest rates were reformed, and barriers to trade were reduced. In short, the policy was to rely on market prices, lessening distortions of relative prices and technologies and avoiding premature capital intensity. The outcome, it is argued, is "the embodiment of labor service in export to the world market . . . conducive to both rapid growth and full employment" and to the alleviation of poverty and reduction in inequality, owing to the absorption of the poor in new activities.[25]

4. Human resource development: For a country at its stage of development, Taiwan has invested exceptionally large sums from her own resources in education. At the upper levels, enrollments in higher education increased sixfold from 44,000 in 1962 to 282,000 in 1974. The increased supply of highly educated workers may well have permitted the growth of employment in high-level occupations. At the

Table. 6.24. *Taiwan: educational composition of the labor force*

Educational level	Number (thousands)	%
Illiterate	581	11
Self-educated	228	4
Primary school	2,613	48
Secondary	1,683	31
Higher	369	7
Total	5,475	101

Source: Galenson (forthcoming: tab. 10).

lower levels, six grades of primary education have been com-
pulsory and free for a decade and a half. School attendance
ratios are approaching 100% among children 6–12 years of
age. At the intermediate level, three additional years of free
education have been available since 1968. The educational
composition of the labor force at present is as shown in Table
6.24. This is a particularly well-educated populace for a
country as poor as Taiwan. Many would regard Taiwan's
investments in education and the consequent high skill
level of the labor force as important factors contributing
to both the modern sector enlargement and the traditional
sector enrichment components of the country's rapid economic growth.

Are Taiwan's policies and strategies applicable to other
countries? Taiwan's economic gains are sometimes thought
to be something of a special case because of particular
advantages: uniform geography and culture, rich human
resources, a rural orientation during colonial development
in the past, or a special relationship with the United States
until very recently. But as Ranis (1978) reminds us, Taiwan
also has had some particular disadvantages: poor natural
resource endowment, scarcity of land, political upheavals
at time of national birth, quota restrictions on a key export
(textiles), and the drain of high military spending. How these
advantages and disadvantages balance in comparison with the
"typical" developing country is not easy to discern.

Taiwan's development success – and indeed it is a success in terms of alleviation of poverty, reduction of inequality, and promotion of overall economic growth – offers an important lesson. There can be little doubt that Taiwan's development strategy had the effect of benefiting *all* her people, more or less. It is unclear whether the people who were determining policy ever thought of development planning in that way.[26] Still, they took some tough decisions – in particular, land reform and reliance on market prices, both of which were opposed by powerful and vocal special interests. Most countries concentrate on expanding a small modern sector with the intention of redistributing some of the proceeds after the fact. It may take a century until everyone is raised above a basic poverty level. Taiwan, in contrast, developed all major sectors (agriculture and rural industry as well as the urban economy) gradually and evenly. This strategy of broad-based economic growth led to economic well-being of the masses within a single generation. Such a strategy may hold considerable promise for other less-developed countries, especially where diminishing returns in leading sectors may have set in.

Development progress and growth strategies: conclusions

This book has explored distributional aspects of economic development in poor countries. At issue are two fundamental questions: Which countries upgraded the economic positions of their poor most quickly? What combinations of circumstances and policies led to differential performance? The main results are as follows.

1. Absolute poverty was alleviated in some countries but not in others. Absolute poverty and absolute incomes were the subject of Chapter 5. Information was compiled for thirteen countries in Table 5.7. Those data showed ten countries (Bangladesh, Brazil, Costa Rica, Pakistan, Puerto Rico, Singapore, Sri Lanka, Taiwan, Thailand, and Mexico) in which poverty had diminished to varying degrees. Absolute poverty was not ameliorated in the other countries (Argentina, India, and the Philippines); poverty increased noticeably in all three.

2. Relative inequality increased in some countries and declined in others. Chapter 4 addressed relative inequality. Data on economic growth and changing inequality in thirteen LDCs were presented in Table 4.6. (Several other countries were excluded because of questions about the quality of the data.) For this group of countries, the evidence shows that inequality rose in seven (Argentina, Bangladesh, Brazil, El Salvador, Mexico, the Philippines, and Puerto Rico); fell in five (Costa Rica, Pakistan, Singapore, Sri Lanka, and Taiwan); and is mixed but leaning toward a slight decline for one country (India).

3. The absolute poverty and relative inequality measures agree in some cases and disagree in others. Qualitative agreement (i.e., with respect to direction of change) appears in seven countries. In five of these (Costa Rica, Pakistan,

Singapore, Sri Lanka, and Taiwan), both poverty and inequality declined; in two others (Argentina and the Philippines), both poverty and inequality increased. In five cases, however, the absolute poverty and relative inequality measures are in conflict. In Bangladesh, Brazil, Mexico, and Puerto Rico, although relative inequality increased, absolute poverty was alleviated. A reverse pattern is found in India. There relative inequality showed a slight decline, yet absolute poverty rose substantially. These results suggest that the choice of an absolute poverty or relative inequality measure is important *empirically* as well as theoretically in assessing the participation of the poor in economic development. Economists and others evaluating development performances must choose between absolute poverty and relative inequality measures in accordance with the value judgments they wish to make. Perhaps the measurement issues posed in Chapter 2 and the welfare economic analysis of Chapter 3 will aid in this choice.

4. A high aggregate growth rate is neither necessary nor sufficient for reducing absolute poverty. Chapter 6 examined development progress and growth strategies in six countries. Included in the sample were both fast- and slow-growing countries. Their poverty performances are given in Table 7.1.

Two deviant cases stand out – the Philippines and Sri Lanka. The Philippines grew rapidly, yet incomes of the poor were not demonstrably raised. On the other hand, Sri Lanka grew very slowly, yet absolute poverty was substantially reduced. We have no readily calculable index of these countries' commitment to helping the poor toward a better life. Nonetheless, it can fairly be said that in both countries the outcome is clearly linked to public policy – welfare statism as part of a large-scale antipoverty campaign in Sri Lanka, virtual inattention to the poverty problem in the Philippines over the period of analysis.

5. A high aggregate growth rate is neither necessary nor sufficient for reducing relative inequality, as is shown in Table 7.2.

The two fastest-growing countries – Taiwan and Costa Rica – experienced declining inequality, as did the two slowest-growing – Sri Lanka and India. These four countries pursued development strategies in which rural development figured

Table 7.1. *Six countries: growth and poverty change*

Poverty	Growth	
	High	Low
Increasing	Philippines	India
Decreasing	Taiwan	Sri Lanka
	Costa Rica	
	Brazil	

heavily. Inequality increased in the two countries with high but not spectacular growth rates – the Philippines and Brazil. Both these countries followed uneven development strategies aimed at modern industrial enclaves, which engage relatively few.

These data suggest a pattern that may not be entirely accidental. It is arguable, though far from proven, that a distributionally oriented development program that integrates the poor into the mainstream of the economy may *cause* a higher growth rate, other things being equal. Obversely, a development strategy aimed at a limited segment of the economy may result in a lower growth rate than could be achieved given that country's resource endowment. In the present state of our knowledge, we do not understand the economic, political, or sociological dynamics of growth well enough to evaluate the merits of this argument. Research on the matter merits highest priority among development economists and planners.

6. Commitment to helping the poor does not necessarily result in progress; progress may take place even in the absence of such commitment. India, according to its rhetoric, was committed to improving conditions for the poor (though the actuality may have been otherwise); despite its seeming commitment, India did not succeed. Taiwan did not appear to be particularly committed, judging from public pronouncements; but its actions suggest that it may well have done many of the right things for the purpose of helping the poor majority. Sri Lanka was committed and did succeed. Brazil and the Philippines showed little commitment to spreading

Table 7.2. *Six countries: growth and inequality change*

Inequality	Growth	
	High	Low
Increasing	Philippines Brazil	
Decreasing	Costa Rica Taiwan	Sri Lanka India

the benefits of growth widely; and in both, the gains were highly concentrated.

These country studies lead me to advance a general rule as a working hypothesis: In the absence of a firm commitment to developing for the poor and the courage to act on that commitment, it seems only natural that economic systems will perpetuate the flow of resources to the haves with at best some trickle-down to the have-nots. More may trickle down to the poor in some cases than in others. Commitment to developing to help the poor does not guarantee progress, but it helps a great deal.

We should bear in mind that any commitment, no matter how resolute, or any strategy, no matter how well conceived in its broad outlines, will be doomed to failure if specific policy changes are made in the wrong direction or at the wrong time. Consider Taiwan's changed trade strategy and emphasis on rural development. The lesson is *not* that export promotion is always better and that import-substituting countries can never succeed, nor that rural development will always work. Rather, we should conclude that the shift from import substitution to export promotion is an example of the right policy being pursued at the right time in response to changing conditions (generated in this case internally); the same conclusion holds for the attention paid to rural industry and infrastructure. No one policy is right once and for all; the circumstances must be carefully examined. Perhaps, under present conditions, broad-based rural development may be the most appropriate antipoverty strategy for a developing country to follow, but it goes without saying that

Table 7.3. *Six countries: enlargement and enrichment components of changing labor market conditions*

Country	Modern sector enlargement	Traditional sector enrichment	Modern sector enrichment
Costa Rica	High	Yes	Yes
Sri Lanka	Low	Yes	No
India	Low, if any	Negative	No
Brazil	Low	Yes & no	Yes
Philippines	Low	Negative	Yes
Taiwan	High	Yes	Yes

Source: Derived from Chapter 6.

one rural development strategy is not the same as another. Expert opinion is needed to plan an appropriate policy package in light of the circumstances that led to success or failure elsewhere.

7. Progress in alleviating poverty is mirrored in changing labor market conditions.[1] The poor may benefit from economic growth because of modern sector enlargement or traditional sector enrichment. Modern sector enlargement has been defined as an expansion in the number of relatively high-paying jobs so as to employ a larger percentage of the economically active population. Traditional sector enrichment is the increase in wages or incomes in the major occupational groups in which the poor are found. Qualitative data on the enlargement and enrichment components of development in the six countries are displayed in Table 7.3. In two countries with both high rates of modern sector enlargement and indications of traditional sector enrichment (Taiwan and Costa Rica), poverty was alleviated rapidly. The two countries with modern sector enlargement or traditional sector enrichment but not both (Sri Lanka and Brazil) also alleviated poverty. In the two countries with neither modern sector enlargement nor traditional sector enrichment (the Philippines and India), absolute poverty worsened. This pattern implies that research into determinants of employment and growth structures in less-developed country labor markets would be of much value in helping to determine the

causes of poverty and its amelioration or exacerbation in the process of economic growth.

The data needed for such an analysis are conceptually straightforward. What is required is information on employment distributions and wage structures singly and in cross tabulations, by occupation and/or industry. With these data in hand, it would be simple to look at changing numbers of persons in each occupation/industry group (that sector's "enlargement effect") and at changing wages and incomes within those groups (the "enrichment effects"). More formal procedures are also available. When better data become available, the contribution of the various enlargement and enrichment effects to total economic growth can be quantified by the procedures given in Chapter 3.

A key research question of considerable interest is how these various components differ in fast- and slow-growing countries and between countries that are pursuing different development strategies. Research aimed at understanding the causes of changing employment and wage structures in the labor markets of less-developed countries is likely to have a major payoff. I believe it will provide the missing link among development economists between the old concerns with aggregate growth and the new concerns with income distribution. But that is another whole study yet to be done.

Notes

Chapter 1. Introduction

1 Also, there may be growth without development (of institutions, infrastructure, etc.), but that observation gets into an entirely different area of inquiry, one not pursued here.
2 Meier (1976:vii). These same concerns with poverty, unemployment, and inequality had been articulated earlier (e.g., Seers, 1969; Haq, 1971), but they did not gain currency until recently.

Chapter 2. Approaches to income distribution

1 Examples are the Social Science Research Council's *Social Indicators*, the Overseas Development Council's *Physical Quality of Life Index*, the World Bank's *World Tables*, the U.S. Agency for International Development's *Socio-Economic Performance Criteria for Development*, and the United Nations' *Social and Demographic Statistics*.
2 For references on the indicators mentioned in n.1 to this chapter, see, respectively, Social Science Research Council (periodical), Overseas Development Council (1979), World Bank (1977), AID (1977), and United Nations (1976).
3 Nutrition is often suggested as a useful alternative indicator, perhaps even preferred to income. However, most nutritional estimates I have seen are derived under such heroic assumptions that I regard them as too imprecise for measuring changes in economic position of the poor over time. For more information on food supplies and nutrition, see D'Silva and Tracy (1978), Morawetz (1977), Reutlinger and Selowsky (1976), and the references cited therein.
4 For certain statistical purposes, however, access to the raw data is essential.
5 This book presumes familiarity with the basic tools of income distribution measurement. Readers who are unfamiliar with the terminology just used are referred to more basic sources on income distribution. Among the clearer ones are Reynolds (1978:chap. 13), Atkinson (1975:chap. 2, 3), and Bronfenbrenner (1971:chap. 3).
6 Indeed, this judgment is the raison d'être for the field of development economics.

7 Probably his most widely known writings in this field are Kuznets (1955, 1963, and 1966).

8 Absolute income studies of less-developed countries are the exception rather than the rule. Economists at the Institute of Development Studies, University of Sussex, have been taking an absolute income approach for some time; see ILO (1970). More recently, the World Bank has begun to shift its focus as well; see Ahluwalia (1974). These studies are noteworthy precisely because they do differ from the usual approach.

9 Four thoughtful essays on definitions of poverty in less developed countries are those of Altimir (1978), Sen (1978), Szal (1977), and Srinivasan (1978).

10 This third judgment is not always made, often because of inability to measure it with existing income tabulations. For an example, consider two societies of equal size. Suppose they have the same number of poor people, and suppose further that the average income of the poor in both countries is $50. Let all the poor in country *A* have incomes of $50; in *B*, half the poor have incomes of $25, the other half $75. By (3), *B* has more poverty.

11 A shorter paper presenting the highlights of his analysis is Rawls (1973).

12 By the Pareto criterion, social welfare increases if somebody is made better off and nobody else is made worse off.

13 The choice of poorest 40% is purely arbitrary. What matters in this approach is the constancy of population share, along with income variability within that share.

14 Whether inequality really worsened, even in relative terms, is not entirely obvious when one looks at the absolute figures presented in Table 2.2.

15 Note that the difficulties with the relative poverty measure arise in cross-sectional data, where we look at those who are the poorest 40% *ex post* at different times. If we had longitudinal data and were able to trace the progress of those individuals who were the poorest 40% *ex ante*, the problem would not arise. This is because their average income would be higher as the rate of growth of higher-paying employment increased. Unfortunately, to my knowledge longitudinal data are not available for a representative sample of the population in *any* less-developed country.

16 For a particularly interesting discussion of poor people's perceptions of the progress of others and the implications for economic development strategies, see Hirschman and Rothschild (1973).

Chapter 3. Growth and distribution

1 This is not to downplay the importance of capital and other sources of income and wealth in determining economic position. Rather, because most people in less-developed countries receive most or all of their income from the work they do, and because variation in

labor income is the most important source of overall income inequality, a high-wage sector–low-wage sector dichotomy would appear more relevant than any other dualistic classification.

2 The assumption of identical wages for all workers within a given sector is simply for algebraic and diagrammatic convenience and is not necessary for any of the results. Intrasectoral wage diversity is allowed for in an unpublished annex to Chapter 3, which is available from the author upon request.

3 Consider statements of the form "Income of the richest $X\%$ grew by $A\%$, but income of the poorest $Y\%$ grew by only $B\%$ (less than A); therefore, income growth was disproportionately concentrated in the upper income groups." This interpretation is correct if average income among those who were originally the richest $X\%$ of the people rose much faster than among those who were originally the poorest $Y\%$. However, the interpretation is incorrect if what mainly happened was that the high-income sector expanded to include more people. From data on income growth of the richest $X\%$ and poorest $Y\%$, we cannot tell which is the case.

4 This statement applies only to studies based on data from comparable cross sections, such as are available for many countries. It does not apply to longitudinal data, which as of now are rare.

5 The formula for the Gini coefficient in our dualistic model is

$$G = 1 - \frac{[W^t + (W^m - W^t)(f^m)^2]}{[W^t + (W^m - W^t)f^m]}$$

This is a quadratic function. By inspection, $G = 0$ when $f^m = 0$ and $f^m = 1$, and $G > 0$ if $0 < f^m < 1$. Thus the Gini coefficient follows an inverted-U path. To determine the location of the maximum, find

$$\frac{\partial G}{\partial f^m} = \left\{ \frac{[W^m - W^t]}{[W^t + (W^m - W^t)f^m]^2} \right\} \left\{ \frac{-2f^m W^t + W^t}{-(f^m)^2 (W^m - W^t)} \right\}$$

and equate the result to zero. Because the first term in brackets is strictly positive, we need only work with the second term. Setting it equal to zero and applying the quadratic formula to solve for f^m, we find

$$(f^m)_C = \frac{-W^t \pm (W^m W^t)^{1/2}}{W^m - W^t}$$

It is evident that one of the roots, $(f^m)_C = [-W^t - (W^m W^t)^{1/2}]/(W^m - W^t)$, is negative, so must be rejected. Considering now the other root, $(f^m)_C = [(W^m W^t)^{1/2} - W^t]/(W^m - W^t)$, the fact that $W^m > W^t$ implies that both numerator and denominator are positive, and therefore $(f^m)_C > 0$. Likewise, $W^m > W^t$ implies $(W^m W^t)^{1/2} < W^m$, and therefore $(f^m)_C < 1$. Thus, G achieves an economically meaningful critical value at $f^m = (W^m W^t)^{1/2} - W^t / W^m - W^t$, and that root is strictly between zero and one.

6 In his original study, Kuznets (1955) produced a number of numerical examples consistent with the inverted-U pattern in modern
   sector enlargement growth, using as his measure of relative inequality the difference in percentage shares between the first and fifth
   quintiles. He did not, however, establish its inevitability (under the
   same maintained assumptions as those employed here). After the
   first draft of this chapter was completed, I learned that the result
   in proposition 3(d) had been proven earlier by Swamy (1967),
   using the coefficient of variation. The result has since been reconfirmed independently by Robinson (1976), using the log variance;
   by Knight (1976) using the Gini coefficient; and by Lydall (1977),
   with extensive examples based on the Gini coefficient and income
   shares of specified groups.

Chapter 4. Inequality and development

1 Kravis's measures of inequality were quintile shares, the Gini coefficient, coefficient of variation, and standard deviation of the logarithms of income.
2 Income inequality is measured alternatively by the income shares
   of the poorest 60%, richest 5%, and middle 20%.
3 It is interesting to note that an earlier version of Adelman and
   Morris's study found a contrary conclusion. In a 1971 report, they
   stated that six factors had been found to be important in explaining variations in relative inequality, but the level of economic
   development was not one of them. The reason for this discrepancy
   is unclear.
4 Besides the Gini coefficient, he used various quintile shares and the
   maximum equalization percentage.
5 Their measures are the income shares of the highest 20% and lowest
   40%.
6 This characterization is attributable to Ahluwalia (1976a:128).
7 Kuznets's early work was of this sort. Later, this mode of analysis
   was carried on by Chenery and others in a series of studies on patterns of economic growth. Some of the best known of these works
   are Chenery (1960), Chenery and Taylor (1968), and Chenery and
   Syrquin (1975).
8 The inverted-U hypothesis may be tested by regressing the inequality measure on GNP per capita and GNP per capita squared. If the
   relationship is in fact of the inverted-U form, GNP per capita would
   have a positive coefficient and GNP per capita squared a negative
   coefficient.
9 See Lal (1976) for a particularly penetrating critique.
10 The specific mathematical equation is

$$\text{Var}(lnY) = k^2 [N'^2 \text{Var}(r) + r'^2 \text{Var}(N) + \text{Var}(N)\text{Var}(r)]$$

   where Y is individual earnings, k is the rate of human capital investment, N' is the average number of years of training in the population, and r' is the average rate of return to investment in training.

11 Chiswick's measures of inequality are $P(5)$, $P(10)$, $P(75)$, where $P(i) = 100p_i/p_{50}$, p_i is earnings at the ith percentile from the upper end of the distribution, and p_{50} is the median.

12 Intertemporal comparability of these data is a real question mark. Weisskoff acknowledges the data limitations. See also the critique by Cline (1972).

13 See Sen (1973), Champernowne (1974), Szal and Robinson (1977), and Fields and Fei (1978) for more on this.

14 In reporting these patterns, I am not necessarily endorsing the reliability of these figures for the purposes at hand. Ahluwalia himself recognizes that individual observations are subject to substantial error.

15 I have exercised considerable discretion in the selection of countries. For each one, I went back behind the compilations of data to the original studies. I included countries if I could verify that the basic censuses or surveys were conducted in reasonably comparable fashions in the base and terminal years and if researchers expressed confidence in the quality of the data. To give an example of why a country was excluded, consider the case of Korea. Although Korea appears in many international comparisons (e.g., Figure 4.4), Adelman and Robinson (1978:48) have stated flatly: "There are no acceptable data for the size distribution of income in Korea . . . We reconstructed two size distributions . . . for 1964 and 1970." However, since the Adelman–Robinson book appeared, and after this chapter was written, unpublished studies by Skolka and Garzuel (1978), Choo (1978), and Perkins (1979) have appeared. In private communication, Robinson has expressed satisfaction with these new estimates and has indicated that they supersede his 1978 statement. Because of the publisher's deadline, I have been unable to include the findings of these new studies of Korea in this book.

16 A good example of this position is Harbison (1973).

17 See, for example, Bowles (1972). This question is examined in some detail for Colombia in Fields (1976).

18 The phrase and the idea behind it are attributable to Carnoy (1974).

19 But for conflicting evidence on the distribution of costs and benefits of higher education in Kenya and Colombia, see Fields (1975) and Jallade (1974), respectively.

20 Most other studies cover changes over a decade or less.

21 The decomposition studies in LDCs include works by Altimir and Piñera (1977), Ayub (1977), Chiswick (1976), Fei and Ranis (1974), Fei, Ranis, and Kuo (1978), Fields (1979), Fields and Schultz (forthcoming), Fishlow (1972, and 1973a), Langoni (1972 and 1975), Mangahas (1975), Mehran (1974), Pyatt (1976), Theil (1967 and 1972), Uribe (1976), and van Ginneken (1975).

22 The existing literature is too extensive to catalog. Some of it is reviewed in Chapter 5.

23 More formal comparisons of decomposition procedures for the various inequality measures are made in Szal and Robinson (1977) and Das and Parikh (1977).

24 The term pseudo-Gini comes from Fei and Ranis. This is exactly the same as what Rao (1969) had referred to as the concentration ratio.

25 Atkinson derives his measure on the assumption that utility is a function only of the individual's own income; yet the reason many observers are interested in inequality is the belief that utility functions also depend on one's income relative to others'.

26 See Fields and Fei (1978) for an axiomatic development of social welfare judgments concerning inequality comparisons.

27 From equation (1), for an exact Gini decomposition, we must calculate the Gini coefficient of the residual errors ϵ_i in the linear model $Y_i = a_i + \Sigma_j \beta_j X_{ij} + \epsilon_i$. But roughly half the ϵ_i are negative and the sum of the ϵ_i is zero. The Gini coefficient of such a variate is undefined.

28 There is also the practical matter of the availability of ANOVA programs in many standard statistical packages.

29 See Fields and Schultz (forthcoming) for a direct comparison of ANOVA and regression results.

30 A Theil decomposition would tell only that rural residence is associated with income, not in which direction or by what magnitude income is affected.

31 There is also some literature examining changes over time in one or more of these problems (e.g., Fei, Ranis, and Kuo, 1978; Ayub, 1977), but that work lies outside the purview of this book.

32 Mixed income includes agricultural income, business income, and similar mixtures of returns to capital and labor.

33 This method introduces certain inaccuracies, but the findings are interesting nonetheless.

34 Intuitively, an income type that is a very small part of total income would not contribute much to overall income inequality.

35 For example, if transfer incomes were highest for the poor, the correlations would be negative, and the decomposition formula would then show transfers as contributing to equality, not inequality.

36 Ayub used the same kind of aggregated data that Fei and Ranis used, whereas my computations were carried out on the individual household data.

37 In Pakistan, nonlabor income refers to income from property. In Colombia, income from capital and income from transfers are distinguished, capital income including an imputation for the value of owner-occupied housing.

38 Self-employment income in Pakistan accounted for 65% of total income in 1971/2, and an additional 19% was provided by wages and salaries. In urban Colombia, they were 35% each in 1967/8.

39 Factor inequality weights were not computed for Pakistan. For urban Colombia, they were labor income, 69%; capital income (including imputed rent), 27%; and transfer income, 4%.

40 Typically, the regional variables explain 5%–15% of overall inequality, with an average contribution of about 10%. Thus about 90% of overall inequality is within regions, not between them.

41 Apparently unaware of these decomposition results, Hansen (1975: 168) wrote: "The present levels of inequality in average per capita incomes *between* rich and poor countries is [sic] greater than that *within* the vast majority of countries, developed or developing" (emphasis in original). The statistical basis for this claim is unclear.

42 An additional finding emerges from a study of Malaysia by Anand (1977): Only about 10% of overall income inequality is due to differences in income between racial groups. He continues: "Thus a *doubling* of all Malay incomes to bring them on a par with the Chinese will reduce national inequality by only about 10%. It is misleading, therefore to quote income disparity ratios between the races in attempting to explain economic inequality in the country although this is often done in public debate" (n. 4). Anand's work does not appear in Table 4.9, because race was the only factor considered.

Chapter 5. Absolute income, absolute poverty, and development

1 When earnings cannot be distinguished from other forms of income, earnings functions are referred to as income-generating functions. The terminology "earnings function" will be used here to emphasize the fact that most income-distribution theories deal with labor earnings, not total income. Human capital theory, for example, does not try to explain the distribution of inherited wealth or income from capital.

2 There is an enormous literature emphasizing the supply side of the labor market. The human capital tradition relates income diversity to education, training, parental time inputs, and other forms of human investment. Schultz (1960), Becker (1964), and Mincer (1974) cover the theoretical aspects of these relationships. Harbison (1973) and Blaug (1973) discuss the issues and present empirical evidence relevant to LDCs. An extensive bibliography has been compiled by Blaug (1976).

3 This problem has been analyzed with considerable skill by Stiglitz (1974 and 1976).

4 Among the well-known works in this area are the studies of Berg (1969) and Reynolds (1969). A more recent paper emphasizing institutional determinants of wages in LDCs is that of Gregory (1976). The predictions of market theories and institutional theories are compared and contrasted by Heady (1976).

5 Recognition of the importance of compensating differentials dates back to Adam Smith (1776). Modern theoretical arguments and empirical evidence for the United States have been compiled by Robert Smith (1979).

6 My own work has appeared in a series of papers on Colombia, including Fields (1978).

7 Of interest in this regard is Rosenzweig's (1977) integration of farm households' labor supply decisions with off-farm labor demand conditions.

8 Several of these studies are available as working papers from the Employment and Rural Development Division of the World Bank.

9 This section is condensed and modified from a paper presented at the 1978 meeting of the International Union for the Scientific Study of Population.

10 In the U.S. literature, some of the studies that make this error are cited by Cain (1976). LDC examples are the studies of urban Colombia by Kugler (1977) and of Brazil by Langoni (1975).

11 This error has been made in studies of the United States (Osterman, 1975), Malaysia (Mazumdar and Ahmed, 1977), and Brazil (Merrick, 1976), among others.

12 An example is Harrison (1972).

13 Credit for pioneering this approach in India is often given to the late Pitambar Pant (1962; reprint ed., 1974). Recent refinements include the work of the Indian economists P. K. Bardhan (1974*b*), T. N. Srinivasan (n.d.), and Amartya Sen (1976*a*).

14 These figures are reported in Bardhan (1974*b*:119–23), which also contains the specifics of the nutritional factors and price indexes entering into the calculations.

15 The extent of absolute poverty is highly sensitive to this choice of methodology. Webb (1976) reports a calculation by Selowsky (1976) for Colombia using the price comparisons suggested by Kravis et al. (1975). Selowsky's findings indicate that 20.8% of the urban families in Colombia have per capita incomes below U.S. $100 when the official exchange rate is used, but only 5.3% when the Kravis rate is used.

16 Papers oriented specifically toward less-developed countries include those of Kuznets (1976), Sen (1978), and Srinivasan (n.d.). Two good summaries of these issues in the context of developed countries are the works of Bowman (1973) and Atkinson (1975).

17 The "additional worker effect" refers to the entry into the labor force of an additional family member because of low income of the principal breadwinner. Standard labor economics textbooks in the United States (e.g., Reynolds, 1978, or Fleisher, 1970) present substantial evidence for the importance of these effects. Similar evidence is reported in studies of less-developed countries (e.g., Urrutia, 1968; Rosenzweig (1977).

18 Attempts have been made to document the extent of nutritional and caloric deprivation in the poor countries of the world. One such study, by Reutlinger and Selowsky (1976), estimated a world calorie deficit of 350–500 billion calories on a daily basis. This translates into a per capita daily deficit in the afflicted population of approximately 350 calories. These numbers are mind-boggling, even if the assumptions made to derive them are enormously heroic.

19 Recent research studies suggest that many more poor families

possess the income to purchase a nutritionally adequate diet than in fact do so, and that the intrafamily distribution of consumption is frequently far from equal.

20 For example, those who say: "It's impossible for a quarter of a billion people in India to have annual incomes below $50, when we all know that nobody whose income is so low can stay alive. You bleeding-hearts lie with statistics to drum up support for your cause."

21 Sen (1978:20) contends: "The 'direct method' and the 'income method' are, in fact, *not* two alternative ways of measuring the same thing, but represent two alternative conceptions of poverty. The direct method identifies those whose actual consumption fails to meet the accepted conventions of minimum needs, while the income method is after spotting those who do not have the ability to meet these needs within the behavioural constraints typical in that community" (emphasis added).

22 Note that this argument is made for the specific purpose of intra-country time-series comparisons. For other purposes, such as international cross-section comparisons, the biases and limitations are more serious in some places than in others, rendering international comparisons more tenuous.

23 Perhaps the most careful examination of the exchange rate question is Kravis et al. (1975).

24 Some of the information in the text is drawn from other country information not reproduced in Table 5.3.

25 The important contribution of Indian economists is illustrated by the prominence with which their work is presented elsewhere in this section.

26 Anyone who has set foot in Calcutta or other major urban centers, however, would emphasize the qualifier "largely."

27 In addition to the cited country studies, other sources give support to similar patterns. One detailed piece of work, which is excluded from Table 5.3 because the data are not national in coverage, is Musgrove (1978*a*). Using data for ten Latin American cities (Bogotá, Barranquilla, Cali, and Medellin in Colombia; Santiago, Chile; Quito and Guayaquil, Ecuador; Lima, Peru; and Caracas and Maracaibo, Venezuela), Musgrove found that the incidence of poverty (defined according to total family income) falls with the following variables: education, age, household size, and occupation (where the highest category is professional, technical, and managerial and the lowest is mining, agricultural, and services).

28 Other critics include Lal (1976), Little (1976), and Papanek (1975). Little's criticism is particularly acid: "I believe that the Adelman–Morris conclusions are derived from far-fetched fantasy, and there is a danger that they will damage the prospects of the mass of the people in developing countries by contributing to the fashionable populist economic doctrine of immiserizing growth." See also the reply to Cline by Adelman and Morris (1975).

29 Galenson is forthright in acknowledging the limitations of the data

and of the available measures. I think he is unjustified, however, in dismissing income-distribution data out of hand while using these other, less conceptually appealing measures.

30 In regressions for sixteen such basic needs variables, growth in per capita GNP was a significant determinant of improvement for only five indicators – three nutrition measures, infant mortality, and access to electricity. See Morawetz (1977:54–8).

31 P. 3. Here he is reacting to an earlier statement by Ahluwalia (1974:3) that "economic growth by itself may not solve or even alleviate the problem" of poverty in low-income countries.

32 Table 5.7 includes only those studies that are national in coverage. Some excellent research limited to a particular city is not presented (e.g., Musgrove (1978*b*), on Caracas, Venezuela).

33 After this chapter was completed, I learned that an intertemporal analysis of absolute poverty had been carried out independently by Loehr (1978). Loehr sustains the general result – that growth usually (but not always) results in poverty alleviation, and nongrowth does not – but used different countries.

34 I report these data for illustrative purposes only, because income-distribution data in several of these countries are too crude to yield precise estimates of who benefited from growth.

35 Throughout this book, results cited for Brazil have used data on individuals reported by Fishlow (1972). The family data give results that differ from the results for individual data in some important respects.

36 The inconsistency is this. On the one hand, Fishlow claims that the average income shortfall $(\bar{I})$ rose over time. On the other hand, he also reports that the average incomes of the poor increased slightly. These two statements are mutually incompatible.

Chapter 6. Development progress and growth strategies

1 See Chapter 5 for further discussion of procedures for establishing a poverty line in a particular country.

2 In Colombia, for example, we have income-distribution estimates constructed by Berry (1974) and others dating back to the 1930s.

3 By comparison, GDP per capita was $493 for Brazil, $336 for Colombia, $332 for Peru, $206 for Bolivia, and $97 for Haiti.

4 The countries of the Central America Common Market have an average ratio of imports to GDP of .28. Other countries at a similar stage of development range from .27 (Kenya) to .09 (several South American countries) (UNCTAD, 1976:tabs. 1.2, 6.1A).

5 For example, we have a 1975 speech by the minister of planning: "In the last ten years, however, the relative position of the poorest 40% of the population has not improved. In effect, between 1958 and 1971, the average annual growth of GNP was in the neighborhood of 8%, while the growth in income of the lowest 40% of the population was approximately 5%, which indicates that their rela-

tive position worsened. In other words, there was a concentration of income, which was fundamentally in favor of the middle class" (Arias, 1975:11). Also, San Jose data are interpreted as follows: "In other words, the absolute gap in incomes is increasing not only between the poor and middle income groups, but between the middle groups and the rich. The very poor (0–10 percentiles) face not only a widening gap in absolute terms and a loss of relative share, but a stagnation in the absolute level of income itself" (OFIPLAN, 1977:60).

6 The terminology is from Seers (1969).

7 For an in-depth discussion of economic policy at the time, see Snodgrass (1966).

8 For recent economic developments, see the Central Bank's *Review of the Economy* for various years.

9 For instance, this characterization was voiced by the ILO Employment Mission (ILO, 1971) and by the Marga Research Institute (1974).

10 For Sri Lanka there also exists a study of changing income distribution by Rasaputram (1972), which uses the Consumer Finance Surveys for 1953 and 1963. However, for 1969/70, data were drawn from a Socio-economic Survey. The Socio-economic and Consumer Finance Surveys are not comparable, even in the definition of income. Therefore, Rasaputram's evidence will receive no further mention.

11 The poverty measure used is the percentage of income recipients below a given amount. Other measures, such as the average income received by the poor or the Sen index of poverty, could not be computed from the available data.

12 In 1963, 5.5% of income recipients were below age 18 and 20.0% below age twenty-five. The corresponding percentages in 1973 were 3.7% and 18.9%.

13 Mean two-month income in 1973 was Rs. 133 for those under age 14 and Rs. 169 for 14–18-year-olds, as compared with Rs. 455 for all income recipients.

14 Experts on India are divided on whether the problem was one of pursuing the wrong policies, not effectively pursuing any policies, or being overwhelmed by uncontrollable events. Lal (1973), for example, stresses the inappropriateness of the policies pursued. He sees past development efforts as being too highly concentrated; he favors instead small-scale rural development, encouragement of small business units with a minimum of bureaucratic controls, and more appropriate pricing policies, both internal and external. Others, such as Bardhan (1974a) and Mellor (1976), see the problem as a gap between rhetoric and execution. In Bardhan's words: "In sum, the problems of poverty in India remain intractable, not because redistributive objectives were inadequately considered in the planning models . . . But the major constraint is rooted in the power realities of a political system dominated by a complex constellation

of forces representing rich farmers, big business, and the so-called petite bourgeoisie, including the unionized workers of the organized sector" (p. 261). In addition, there is a widely held view that the continued population growth is a major impediment to Indian development. Finally, the vagaries of the Indian climate pose severe difficulties for a poor agriculturally oriented economy.

15 In Bardhan (1974*b*:119-24), he describes how these poverty lines are computed. The minimally adequate diet for a moderately active adult as recommended by the Central Government Employees' Pay Commission consists of 15 oz. of cereals, 3 oz. of groundnut, and 6 oz. of vegetables per day, totaling 2,100 calories and 55 grams of protein. To figure the family income required to achieve this diet, Bardhan works out the cost per adult, adjusts for family makeup by the adult-equivalent ratio, expands to a requisite family income figure using the ratio of food to nonfood expenditures, divides by family size to obtain a per capita amount, and finally deflates by the official Agricultural Labour Consumer Price Index for the appropriate year for the rural poor and by the official Working Class Consumer Price Index for the urban poor.

16 Bardhan (1974*b*:131) notes: "The *direction* of change in the estimates of poverty is the same if one takes the various alternative minimum standards for the poverty line suggested in the literature" (emphasis in the original).

17 These findings are taken from Fields (1977). Challenges to them, based on new evidence, and my reply are to be published in a forthcoming issue of the *American Economic Review*.

18 But for a contrasting view of the labor-absorption experience during the import-substitution phase, see Morley and Williamson (1974).

19 Morley and Williamson (1975) argue that stability in the minimum wage had the beneficial effect of stimulating employment of the unskilled; thus growth is stimulated by a widening wage structure. Turning to the effects of growth on wage dispersion, they state: "We have two conflicting forces at work. Rapid growth employs the reserve army of the unskilled thus fostering equality. Rapid growth also implies an unbalanced output growth which favors sectors requiring heavy doses of human and physical capital, thus fostering 'wage stretching' and inequality among the employed. Which dominates?" (p. 19). Their empirical estimates for Brazil lead them to conclude that "the 'bulk' of the widening pay differentials among the employed is attributable to conventional market forces stemming from unbalanced output growth favoring those sectors which are intensive in skills and machines rather than nonmarket wage control" (p. 25).

20 Many studies of Philippine economic development have been undertaken. Among the most useful are those by the ILO (1974), Cheetham and Hawkins (1976), and Averch et al. (1971).

21 Brazil did better in the late sixties and early seventies but not over the decade of the 1960s.

22 Presumably the figure is even lower today, owing to recent economic difficulties and the consequent negative rates of growth.
23 Fei, Ranis, and Kuo (1978) note that most of the change took place after 1968, which marked the end of labor surplus conditions in Taiwan.
24 I have emphasized the decentralization of economic resources. Others (e.g., Morawetz, 1977) also give weight to the decentralization of decision making and entrepreneurship.
25 The quotation is from Fei and Ranis (1975:52). The more general theme is developed in Fei, Ranis, and Kuo (1979:chap. 2).
26 Experts on Taiwan's recent economic history disagree. See Ranis (1974 and 1978), Grant (1976), and Galenson, ed. (1979).

Chapter 7. Development progress and growth strategies

1 For a similar conclusion reached in a quite different way, see Lal (1976:737): "Efficient growth which raises the demand for labor is probably the single most important means available for alleviating poverty in the Third World." See also Galenson (1977) for yet another approach to the same result. This result was foretold a decade ago in a prescient paper by Ranis (1971).

Bibliography

Adelman, Irma and Cynthia Taft Morris, 1973. *Economic Growth and Social Equity in Developing Countries.* Stanford, Calif.: Stanford University Press.

    1975. "Distribution and Development: A Comment." *Journal of Development Economics* 1 (1975):401–2.

Adelman, Irma and Sherman Robinson, 1978. *Income Distribution Policy in Developing Countries: A Case Study of Korea.* New York: Oxford University Press.

Ahluwalia, Montek, 1974. "Dimensions of the Problem," in Hollis B. Chenery et al. (eds.), *Redistribution with Growth*, pp. 3–37. New York: Oxford University Press.

    1976a. "Income Distribution and Development: Some Stylized Facts." *American Economic Review*, May, pp. 128–35.

    1976b. "Inequality, Poverty and Development." *Journal of Development Economics* 3:307–42.

Ahluwalia, Montek and Hollis Chenery, 1974. "The Economic Framework," in Hollis B. Chenery et al. (eds.), *Redistribution with Growth*, Chap. 2. New York: Oxford University Press.

Ahmed, M. and N. Bhattacharya, 1972. "Size Distribution of Per Capita Personal Income in India." *Economic and Political Weekly*, special no. Reprinted in T. N. Srinivasan and P. K. Bardhan (eds.), *Poverty and Income Distribution in India*, pp. 167–82. Calcutta: Statistical Publishing Society, 1974.

AID (Agency for International Development), 1975. "Implementation of 'New Directions' in Development Assistance." Committee on International Relations, 94th Cong., 1st sess., July 22.

    1977. *Socio-Economic Performance Criteria for Development.* Washington, D.C.: Government Printing Office.

Alamgir, Mohiuddin, 1975. "Poverty, Inequality and Social Welfare: Measurement, Evidence and Policies." *Bangladesh Development Studies* 3, no. 2 (April):153–80.

    Forthcoming. *Bangladesh: A Case of Below Poverty Level Equilibrium Trap.* Dacca: Bangladesh Institute of Development Studies.

Altimir, Oscar, 1978. "La Dimensión de La Pobreza en América Latina," Naciones Unidas, Consejo Económico y Social, doc. no. E/CEPAL/L.180, September.

Altimir, Oscar and Sebastían Piñera, 1977. "Decomposition Analysis of the Inequality of Earnings in Latin American Countries." E nomic Commission for Latin America and World Bank, mim August.

Anand, Sudhir, 1977. "Aspects of Poverty in Malaysia." *Review of Income and Wealth,* March, pp. 1–16.

Arias, O. S., 1975. *Caracteristicas del Desarrollo Pasado en Costa Rica y Perspectivas para el Futuro.* San José, Costa Rica: Government pamphlet.

Atkinson, A. B., 1970. "On the Measurement of Inequality." *Journal of Economic Theory* 2:244–63.

   1975. *The Economics of Inequality.* Oxford: Oxford University Press.

Averch, H. et al., 1971. *The Matrix of Policy in the Phillippines.* Princeton, N.J.: Princeton University Press.

Ayub, M., 1977. "Income Inequality in a Growth-Theoretic Context: The Case of Pakistan." Unpublished doctoral dissertation, Yale University.

Bacha, Edmar L., 1976. "On Some Contributions to the Brazilian Income Distribution Debate–I." Harvard Institute for International Development, discussion paper no. 11, February.

Bardhan, P. K., 1970. "On the Minimum Level of Living and the Rural Poor." *Indian Economic Review* 5, no. 1 (April):129–36.

   1971. "On the Minimum Level of Living and the Rural Poor: A Further Note." *Indian Economic Review* 6, no. 1 (April):78–87.

   1974*a*. "India," in Hollis B. Chenery et al. (eds.), *Redistribution with Growth,* pp. 255–62. New York: Oxford University Press.

   1974*b*. "The Pattern of Income Distribution in India: A Review," in T. N. Srinivasan and P. K. Bardhan (eds.), *Poverty and Income Distribution in India,* pp. 103–37. Calcutta: Statistical Publishing Society.

Barraclough, Solon and Arthur L. Domike, 1966. "Agrarian Structure in Seven Latin American Countries." *Land Economics* 42, no. 4 (November): 41–94.

Becker, Gary S., 1964. *Human Capital.* New York: Columbia University Press.

Berg, Elliot, 1969. "Wage Structures in Less Developed Countries," in A. D. Smith (eds.), *Wage Policy Issues in Economic Development,* pp. 294–337. London: Macmillan.

Berry, R. A., 1974. "Changing Income Distribution under Development: Colombia." *Review of Income and Wealth,* no. 3, (September):289–316.

Bhagwati, Jagdish, 1978. *Foreign Trade Regimes and Economic Growth: Liberalization Attempts and Consequences.* New York: Ballinger, for the National Bureau of Economic Research.

Bhatty, I. Z., 1974. "Inequality and Poverty in Rural India," in T. N. Srinivasan and P. K. Bardhan (eds.), *Poverty and Income Distribution in India,* pp. 291–336. Calcutta: Statistical Publishing Society.

Birdsall, Nancy, 1977. "Analytical Approaches to the Relationship of

Population Growth and Development." *Population and Development Review* 3, nos. 1 and 2 (March/June):63–102.

Blaug, M., 1973. *Education and the Employment Problem in Developing Countries.* Geneva: International Labor Organization.

1976. "Human Capital Theory: A Slightly Jaundiced Survey." *Journal of Economic Literature* 14, no. 3 (September):827–55.

Blitzer, C. R., P. Clark, and L. Taylor, 1975. *Economy-Wide Models and Development Planning.* New York: Oxford University Press.

Boulier, Bryan L., 1977. "Population Policy and Income Distribution," in Charles R. Frank, Jr., and Richard C. Webb (eds.), *Income Distribution and Growth in the Less-Developed Countries,* pp. 159–213. Washington, D.C.: Brookings Institution.

Bowles, Samuel, 1972. "Schooling and Inequality from Generation to Generation." *Journal of Political Economy,* pt. 2, May/June, pp. 219–51.

Bowman, Mary Jean, 1973. "Poverty in an Affluent Society," in Neil W. Chamberlain (ed.), *Contemporary Economic Issues,* pp. 51–113. Homewood, Ill.: Irwin.

Brasil, 1960. *Censo Demografico: Resultados Preliminares.* Rio de Janeiro: Brazilian Government.

1970. *Tabulacoes Avancadas do Censo Demografico.* Rio de Janeiro: Brazilian Government.

Brazilian Trends, 1973. São Paulo: Editora Abril.

Bronfenbrenner, Martin, 1971. *Income Distribution Theory.* Chicago: Aldine.

Bruton, Henry, 1977. "Industrialization Policy and Income Distribution," in Charles R. Frank, Jr., and Richard C. Webb (eds.), *Income Distribution and Growth in the Less-Developed Countries,* pp. 79–125. Washington, D.C.: Brookings Institution.

Cain, Glen, 1976. "The Challenge of Segmented Labor Market Theories to Orthodox Theory: A Survey." *Journal of Economic Literature* 14, no. 4 (December):1215–57.

Calvo, Ml. Felipe, 1978. "Costa Rica: Evolución y Características de la Mano de Obra," in Juan J. Buttari (ed.), *El Problema Ocupacional en América Latina,* pp. 187–246. Buenos Aires: Ediciones Siap.

Carnoy, Martin, 1974. *Education as Cultural Imperialism.* New York: McKay.

Central Bank of Ceylon, 1963. Survey of Ceylon's Consumer Finances. Colombo.

Central Bank of the Philippines, 1975. *Statistical Bulletin 27* (December).

Céspedes, V. H., 1973. *Costa Rica: La Distribución del Ingreso y el Consumo de Algunas Alimentos.* San José, Costa Rica: Universidad de Costa Rica.

Champernowne, D. G., 1974. "A Comparison of Measures of Inequality of Income Distribution." *Economic Journal,* December, pp. 787–816.

Cheetham, R. and E. Hawkins, 1976. *The Philippines: Priorities and Prospects for Development.* Washington, D.C.: World Bank.

Chenery, Hollis, 1960. "Patterns of Industrial Growth." *American Economic Review*, September, pp. 624–54.

Chenery, Hollis B. et al (eds.), 1974. *Redistribution with Growth*. New York: Oxford University Press.

Chenery, Hollis and Moises Syrquin, 1975. *Patterns of Development, 1950–1970*. New York: Oxford University Press.

Chenery, Hollis and Lance B. Taylor, 1968. "Development Patterns among Countries and over Time." *Review of Economics and Statistics*, November, pp. 391–416.

Chiswick, Barry, 1971. "Earnings Inequality and Economic Development." *Quarterly Journal of Economics*, February, pp. 21–39.

Chiswick, Carmel U., 1976. "Application of the Theil Index to Income Inequality." International Bank for Reconstruction and Development Working Paper ser. B-2, July.

Choo, Hakchung, 1978. "Economic Growth and Income Distribution in Korea." Korean Development Institute, Working Paper no. 7810, September.

Cline, William R., 1972. *Potential Effects of Income Redistribution on Economic Growth: Latin American Cases*. New York: Praeger.

1975. "Distribution and Development: A Survey of the Literature." *Journal of Development Economics*, 1:359–400.

1977. "Policy Instruments for Rural Income Distribution," in Charles R. Frank, Jr., and Richard C. Webb (eds.), *Income Distribution and Growth in the Less-Developed Countries*, pp. 281–336. Washington, D.C.: Brookings Institution.

Comisión Económica para América Latina, 1974. *Proyecto Sobre Medición y Análisis de la Distribución del Ingreso en Paises de América Latina, Tabulados de Trabajo, Brasil*. Doc. no. E/CEPAL/L. 115/8, November.

Costa Rica, *National Accounts Statistics*, 1975.

DaCosta, E. P. W., 1971. "A Portrait of Indian Poverty," in A. J. Fonseca (ed.), *Challenge of Poverty in India*, pp. 48–59. Delhi: Vikas Publications, 1971.

Dalton, H., 1920. "The Measurement of the Inequality of Incomes." *Economic Journal*, September, pp. 348–61.

Dandekar, V. M. and Nilakantha Rath, 1971. "Poverty in India: Dimensions and Trends." *Economic and Political Weekly*, January 2 and 9, pp. 25–146.

Das, T. and A. Parikh, 1977. "Decomposition of Inequality Measures and a Comparative Analysis." School of Social Studies, University of East Anglia, Discussion Paper no. 44, May.

Dieguez, Hector L. and Alberto Petrecolla, 1976. "Crecimiento, Distribución y Bienestar: Una Nota Sobre el Caso Argentino." *Desarrollo Económico* 16, no. 61 (April–June):101–22.

Doeringer, Peter and Michael Piore, 1970. *Internal Labor Markets and Manpower Analysis*. Lexington, Mass.: Heath, Lexington Books.

Dorner, Peter, 1973. *Land Reform and Economic Development*. Baltimore: Penguin.

D'Silva, Emmanuel H. and Ruth M. Tracy, 1978. *Annotated Bibliogra-*

phy Relating to World Food Issues. Program in International Agriculture, Cornell University, August.

ECLA (Economic Commission for Latin America), 1969. *Economic Survey of Latin America, 1968.* New York.

ECLA (Economic Commission for Latin America), 1971. *Economic Survey of Latin America, 1970.* New York.

Edwards, Richard, Michael Reich, and David Gordon, 1975. *Labor Market Segmentation.* Lexington, Mass.: Heath, Lexington Books.

Fei, J. C. H. and G. Ranis, 1964. *Development of the Labor Surplus Economy.* Homewood, Ill.: Irwin.

——— 1974. "Income Inequality by Additive Factor Components." Economic Growth Center, Yale University, Center Discussion Paper no. 207, June.

——— 1975. "A Model of Growth and Employment in the Open Dualistic Economy: The Cases of Korea and Taiwan." *Journal of Development Studies* 11, no. 2 (January):32-63.

Fei, John C. H., Gustav Ranis, and S. W. Y. Kuo, 1978. "Growth and the Family Distribution of Income by Factor Components." *Quarterly Journal of Economics,* February, pp. 17-53.

——— 1979. *Growth with Equity: The Taiwan Case.* Oxford: Oxford University Press.

Felix, David, 1977. "Income Inequality in Mexico." *Current History,* March, pp. 111-14.

Fields, Gary S., 1975. "Higher Education and Income Distribution in a Less Developed Country." *Oxford Economic Papers,* July, pp. 245-59.

——— 1976. "Education and Economic Mobility in a Less Developed Country." Economic Growth Center, Yale University, Center Discussion Paper no. 237, rev. version, June. To be published in Spanish in Maria Cristina de Ferro (ed.), *Economics of Education.* Bogotá: CEDE, Universidad de Los Andes.

——— 1977. "Who Benefits from Economic Development?–A Reexamination of Brazilian Growth in the 1960's. *American Economic Review,* September, pp. 570-82.

——— 1978. "Analyzing Colombian Wage Structure." World Bank, Studies in Employment and Rural Development no. 46, May.

——— 1979. "Income Inequality in Urban Colombia: A Decomposition Analysis." *Review of Income and Wealth.* In press.

Fields, Gary S. and John C. H. Fei, 1978. "On Inequality Comparisons." *Econometrica,* March, pp. 303-16.

Fields, Gary S. and T. Paul Schultz, forthcoming. "Regional Inequality and Other Sources of Income Variation in Colombia." *Economic Development and Cultural Change.* In press.

Fishlow, Albert, 1972. "Brazilian Size Distribution of Income." *American Economic Review,* May, pp. 391-402.

——— 1973*a*. "Distribuicao da Renda no Brasil: Um Novo Exame." *Dados,* no. 11, pp. 10-80.

——— 1973*b*. "Some Reflections on Post 1964 Brazilian Economic Policy," in A. Stepan, ed., *Authoritarian Brazil*, pp. 69-118. New Haven: Yale University Press.

forthcoming. "The Fallacies of Decomposition: A Comment on Fields' Reexamination of Brazilian Income Distribution in the 1960's." *American Economic Review.*

Flanagan, Robert, 1973. "Segmented Market Theories and Racial Discrimination." *Industrial Relations*, October, pp. 253-73.

Fleisher, Belton, 1970. *Labor Economics: Theory and Evidence.* Englewood Cliffs, N.J.: Prentice-Hall.

Foxley, Alejandro, 1976. *Income Distribution in Latin America.* Cambridge: Cambridge University Press.

Freedman, Marcia, 1976. *Labor Markets: Segments and Shelters.* New York: Allenheld, Osmun/Universe.

Friedman, Milton, 1957. *A Theory of the Consumption Function.* Princeton, N.J.: Princeton University Press.

Fuchs, Victor, 1967. "Redefining Poverty and Redistributing Income." *Public Interest,* Summer, pp. 88-95.

Fundação Getúlio Vargas, 1973. *Atualizacao Parcial do Sistema da Cantas Nacionais 1971-1972.* São Paulo: Fundação Getúlio Vargas.

Furtado, C., 1970. *Economic Development of Latin America.* Cambridge, Cambridge University Press.

Galenson, Walter, 1977. "Economic Growth, Income, and Employment." Paper presented at the Conference on Poverty and Development in Latin America, Yale University, April.

1979. "The Labor Force, Wages and Living Standards in Taiwan," in Walter Galenson (ed.), *The Economic Development of Taiwan, 1945-1975: The Experience of the Republic of China.* Ithaca, N.Y.: Cornell University Press.

Galenson, Walter (ed.), 1979. *The Economic Development of Taiwan, 1945-1975: The Experience of the Republic of China.* Ithaca, N.Y.: Cornell University Press.

Gollás, Manuel, 1978. "El Desempleo en México: Soluciones Posibles," *Ciencia y Desarrollo,* no. 20, May-June, pp. 73-86.

Gordon, David, 1972. *Theories of Poverty and Underemployment.* Lexington, Mass.: Heath, Lexington Books.

Grant, James P., 1976. "The International Economic Order and the World's Poorest Billion: A Fresh Approach?" Paper prepared for delivery at the Washington Center of Foreign Policy Research, Washington, D.C., November 4.

Gregory, Peter, 1975. "The Impact of Institutional Factors on Urban Labor Markets." Paper prepared for the Workshop on Urban Poverty, International Bank for Reconstruction and Development, April. Rev. 1976.

Green, Reginald H., 1974. "Tanzania," in Hollis B. Chenery et al. (eds.), *Redistribution with Growth*, pp. 268-73. New York: Oxford University Press.

Griffin, K., 1977. "Increasing Poverty and Changing Ideas about Developing Strategies." Paper presented at the Conference on Distribution, Poverty, and Development, Bogotá, June.

Hansen, Roger D., 1975. "The Emerging Challenge: Global Distribution of Income and Economic Opportunity," in Overseas Development Council, *Agenda 1975*, chap. 9. New York: Praeger.

Haq, Mahbub ul, 1971. "Employment in the 1970's: A New Perspective." *International Development Review* 13, no. 4. Reprinted in Charles K. Wilber (ed.), *The Political Economy of Development and Underdevelopment*, pp. 266-72. New York: Random House, 1973.

Harbison, Frederick, 1973. *Human Resources as the Wealth of Nations.* New York: Oxford University Press.

Harrison, Bennett, 1972. "Education and Underemployment in the Urban Ghetto." *American Economic Review*, December, pp. 796-812.

Heady, Christopher, 1976. "Alternative Theories of Wages in Less Developed Countries: An Empirical Test." Economic Growth Center, Yale University, Discussion Paper no. 254, October.

Hirschman, Albert O. and Michael Rothschild, 1973. "The Changing Tolerance for Income Inequality in the Course of Economic Development." *Quarterly Journal of Economics*, November, pp. 544-66.

ILO (International Labour Office), 1970. *Towards Full Employment: A Programme for Colombia.* Geneva.

　　1971. *Matching Employment Opportunities and Expectations: A Programme of Action for Ceylon.* Geneva.

　　1974. *Sharing in Development in the Philippines.* Geneva.

Iqbal, Farrukh, 1977. "Growth, Income Distribution, and Poverty in Pakistan: The Experience of the Sixties." Unpublished paper. Yale University, May.

Jain, S., 1975. *Size Distribution of Income: A Compilation of Data.* Washington, D.C.: World Bank.

Jallade, Jean-Pierre, 1974. *Public Expenditures on Education and Income Distribution in Colombia.* Baltimore: Johns Hopkins University Press, World Bank Staff Occasional Papers no. 18.

Jayawardena, L., 1974. "Sri Lanka," in Hollis B. Chenery et al. (eds.), *Redistribution with Growth*, pp. 273-9. New York: Oxford University Press.

Johnson, George, 1970. "The Demand for Labor by Educational Category." *Southern Economic Journal*, October, pp. 190-204.

Johnson, George and E. Whitelaw, 1972. "Urban-Rural Income Transfers in Kenya: An Estimated Remittances Function." *Economic Development and Cultural Change.*

Jorgenson, Dale, 1961. "Development of the Dual Economy." *Economic Journal*, March, pp. 309-34.

Karunatilake, N., 1975. "Changes in Income distribution in Sri Lanka," in *Income Distribution, Employment, and Economic Development in Southeast and East Asia*, pp. 701-41. Papers and proceedings of the seminar sponsored jointly by the Japan Economic Research Center and the Council for Asian Manpower Studies, July.

Knight, John B., 1976. "Explaining Income Distribution in Less Developed Countries: A Framework and an Agenda." *Bulletin of the Oxford Institute of Economics and Statistics*, August.

Kondor, Yaakov, 1975. "Value Judgments Implied by the Use of Various Measures of Income Inequality." *Review of Income and Wealth*, pp. 309-21.

Kravis, Irving B., 1960. "International Differences in the Distribution of Income." *Review of Economics and Statistics*, November, pp. 408-16.

Kravis, Irving B. et al., 1975. *A System of International Comparisons of Gross Product and Purchasing Power.* Baltimore: Johns Hopkins University Press.

Krueger, Anne O., 1978. *Foreign Trade Regimes and Economic Development: Liberalization Attempts and Consequences.* Cambridge, Mass.: National Bureau of Economic Research.

Kugler, Bernardo, 1977. "Pobreza y la Estructura del Empleo en el Sector Urbano de Colombia." Trabajo presentado a la Conferencia sobre Distribución, Pobreza y Desarrollo, Universidad de Los Andes, Bogotá, June.

Kuo, W., 1975. "Income Distribution by Size in Taiwan Area: Changes and Causes," in *Income Distribution, Employment, and Economic Development in Southeast and East Asia*, pp. 80-153. Papers and proceedings of the seminar sponsored jointly by the Japan Economic Research Center and the Council for Asia Manpower Studies, July.

Kuznets, Simon, 1955. "Economic Growth and Income Inequality." *American Economic Review*, March, pp. 1-28.

1963. "Quantitative Aspects of the Economic Growth of Nations: VIII, Distribution of Income by Size." *Economic Development and Cultural Change*, January, pt. 2, pp. 1-80.

1966. *Modern Economic Growth.* New Haven: Yale University Press.

1976. "Demographic Aspects of the Size Distribution of Income." *Economic Development and Cultural Change*, October, pp. 1-94.

Lal, Deepak, 1973. *New Economic Policies for India.* London: Fabian Society.

1976. "Distribution and Development: A Review Article." *World Development* 4, no. 9:725-38.

Langoni, Carlos, 1972. "Distribuicao da Renda e Desenvolvimento Economico do Brasil." *Estudos Economicos*, October, pp. 5-88.

1975. "Income Distribution and Economic Development: The Brazilian Case." Paper presented at the World Econometric Society Congress, Toronto.

Lardy, Nicholas R., 1978. *Economic Growth and Distribution in China.* Cambridge: Cambridge University Press.

Lewis, W. Arthur, 1954. "Economic Development with Unlimited Supplies of Labor." *Manchester School* 20 (May):139-91.

Little, I. M. D., 1976. "Book Reviews." *Journal of Development Economics* 3:99-105.

Little, I. M. D. and J. A., Mirrlees, 1969. *Manual of Industrial Project Analysis in Developing Countries. Vol. 2, Social Cost Benefit Analysis.* Paris: Organization for Economic Cooperation and Development.

Little, I. M. D., Tibor Scitovsky, and Maurice Scott, 1970. *Industry and Trade in Developing Countries.* Paris: Organization for Economic Cooperation and Development.

Loehr, William, 1978. "Economic Growth, Distribution and Incomes of the Poor." University of Denver, mimeo, September.

Lydall, Harold B., 1968. *The Structure of Earnings.* Oxford: Oxford University Press, Clarendon Press.

——— 1977. "Income Distribution during the Process of Development." International Labour Office, World Employment Programme Research Working Paper no. 52, February.

McGreevey, William, 1976. "Issues in Measuring Development Progress." Paper prepared for the Asia Society, Inc., and the Agency for International Development, mimeo, October.

Malan, P. and J. Wells, 1973. "Langoni e a Distribuicao de Renda no Brasil." *Pesquisa e Planejamento Economico,* December, pp. 1103-24.

Mangahas, Mahar, 1975. "Income Inequality in the Philippines: A Decomposition Analysis," in *Income Distribution, Employment, and Economic Development in Southeast and East Asia,* pp. 286-344. Papers and proceedings of the seminar sponsored jointly by the Japan Economic Research Center and the Council for Asian Manpower Studies, July.

Marga Research Institute, 1974. *Welfare and Growth in Sri Lanka.* Colombo: Marga Publications.

Mazumdar, Dipak and Masood Ahmed, 1977. "Labor Market Segmentation and the Determination of Earnings: A Case Study." World Bank, mimeo, November.

Meesook, O. A., 1975. "Income Inequality in Thailand, 1962/63 and 1968/69," in *Income Distribution, Employment and Economic Development in Southeast and East Asia,* pp. 345-88. Papers and proceedings of the seminar sponsored jointly by the Japan Economic Research Center and the Council for Asian Manpower Studies, July.

Mehran, F., 1974. "Decomposition of the Gini Index: A Statistical Analysis of Income Inequality." International Labour Office, mimeo.

Meier, Gerald, 1976. *Leading Issues in Economic Development.* New York: Oxford University Press.

Mellor, John W., 1976. *The New Economics of Growth: A Strategy for India and the Developing World.* Ithaca, N.Y.: Cornell University Press.

Mericle, K. S., 1976. "Corporatist Control of the Working Class: The Case of Post-1964 Authoritarian Brazil," in J. M. Malloy (ed.), *Authoritarianism and Corporatism in Latin America*. Pittsburgh: University of Pittsburgh Press.

Merrick, Thomas, 1976. "Employment and Earnings in the Informal Sector in Brazil: The Case of Belo Horizonte." *Journal of Developing Areas*, April, pp. 337-53.

Mijares, T. A. and L. C. Belarmino, 1973. "Some Notes on the Sources of Income Disparities among Philippine Families." *Journal of Philippine Statistics*, September, pp. 15-22.

Mincer, Jacob, 1974. *Schooling, Experience and Earnings*. New York: Columbia University Press.

Minhas, B. S., 1970. "Rural Poverty, Land Redistribution and Development Strategy: Facts and Policy." *Indian Economic Review*, April, pp. 97-126.

Morawetz, David, 1977. *Twenty-five Years of Economic Development, 1950 to 1975*. Baltimore: Johns Hopkins University Press.

Morley, S. A. and J. G. Williamson, 1974. "Demand, Distribution, and Employment: The Case of Brazil." *Economic Development and Cultural Change*, October, pp. 407-27.

——— 1975. "Growth, Wage Policy and Inequality: Brazil during the Sixties." University of Wisconsin, Madison, Social Systems Research Institute Workshop Series Paper no. 7519, July.

Muller, Ronald, 1973. "The Multinational Corporation and the Underdevelopment of the Third World," in Charles K. Wilber (ed.), *The Political Economy of Development and Underdevelopment*, pp. 124-51. New York: Random House.

Musgrove, Philip, 1977. "Household Size and Composition, Employment, and Poverty in Urban Latin America." Paper presented at the Conference on Poverty and Development in Latin America, Yale University, April.

——— 1978a. *Consumer Behavior in Latin America*. Washington, D.C.: Brookings Institution.

——— 1978b. "The Oil Price Increase and the Alleviation of Poverty: Income Distribution in Caracas, Venezuela, in 1966 and 1975." Brookings Institution, mimeo.

Musgrove, Philip and Robert Ferber, 1976. "Finding the Poor: On the Identification of Poverty Households in Urban Latin America." Brookings Institution and the University of Illinois, mimeo. To be published in *Review of Income and Wealth*.

Naseem, S. M., 1973. "Mass Poverty in Pakistan: Some Preliminary Findings." *Pakistan Development Review* 12, no. 4 (Winter): 317-60.

OFIPLAN (National Planning Office of Costa Rica), 1977. *Urban Assessment of San José, Costa Rica: Focus on Poverty*. Report to U.S. Agency for International Development, September 21.

Ojha, P. D., 1970. "A Configuration of Indian Poverty." *Reserve Bank of India Bulletin*, January, pp. 16-27.

Ojha, P. D. and V. V. Bhatt, 1974. "Pattern of Income Distribution in

268 *Bibliography*

India: 1953–55 to 1963–65," in T. N. Srinivasan and P. K. Bardhan (eds.), *Poverty and Income Distribution in India*, pp. 163–6. Calcutta: Statistical Publishing Society.

Orshansky, Mollie, 1965. "Counting the Poor." *Social Security Bulletin* 28, no. 1 (January):3–29.

Oshima, Harry, 1962. "The International Comparison of Size Distribution of Family Incomes with Special Reference to Asia." *Review of Economics and Statistics* November, pp. 439–45.

Osterman, Paul, 1975. "An Empirical Study of Labor Market Segmentation." *Industrial and Labor Relations Review*, July, pp. 508–23.

Overseas Development Council, 1979. *Agenda 1979: The United States and World Development.* New York: Praeger.

Pant, Pitambar, 1962. "Perspectives of Development, India, 1960–61 to 1975–76: Implications of Planning for a Minimum Level of Living." Reprinted in T. N. Srinivasan and P. K. Bardhan (eds.), *Poverty and Income Distribution in India*, pp. 9–38. Calcutta: Statistical Publishing Society, 1974.

Papanek, Gustav, 1975. "Growth, Income Distribution, and Politics in Less Developed Countries," in Yohanan Ramiti (ed.), *Economic Growth in Developing Countries*, pp. 75–96. New York: Praeger.

Paukert, F., 1973. "Income Distribution at Different Levels of Development: A Survey of Evidence." *International Labor Review*, August–September, pp. 97–125.

Perkins, Dwight, 1979. "Income Distribution (in Korea)." Department of Economics, Harvard University, mimeo.

Perlman, Richard, 1976. *The Economics of Poverty.* New York: McGraw-Hill.

Psacharopoulos, George, 1978. "Inequalities in Education and Employment: A Review of Key Issues with Emphasis on LDC's." International Institute for Educational Planning, Working Document no. IIEP/S49/8A, Paris, October.

Puerto Rico (Estado Libre Asociado de Puerto Rico, Departamento de Trabajo, Negociado de Estadísticas del Trabajo), 1960. *Ingresos y Gastos de las Familias 1953.* San Juan.

Puerto Rico (Estado Libre Asociado de Puerto Rico, Departamento de Trabajo, Negociado de Estadísticas del Trabajo), 1970. *Ingresos y Gastos de las Familias 1963.* San Juan.

Pyatt, Graham, 1976. "On the Interpretation and Disaggregation of the Gini Coefficient." *Economic Journal*, June, pp. 243–55.

Pyatt, Graham and Erik Thorbecke, 1976. *Planning Techniques for a Better Future.* Geneva: International Labour Office.

Ranadive, K. R., 1973. "Distribution of Income–Trends since Planning." Paper presented to ISI Seminar on Income Distribution, February.

Ranis, Gustav, 1971. "Output and Employment in the 1970's: Conflict or Complements," in Ronald B. Ridker and Harold Lubell (eds.), *Employment and Unemployment Problems of Neareast and South Asia*, pp. 59–76. New Delhi: Vikas Publications.

1974. "Taiwan," in Hollis B. Chenery et al. (eds.), *Redistribution with Growth*, pp. 285–90. New York: Oxford University Press.

1978. "Equity with Growth in Taiwan: How Special is the 'Special Case'?" *World Development* 6, no. 3:397–409.

Rao, V. M., 1969. "Two Decompositions of Concentration Ratios." *Journal of the Royal Statistical Society*, pp. 418–25.

Rao, V. V. Bhanoji and M. K. Ramakrishnan, 1977. *Economic Growth, Structural Changes and Income Inequality, Singapore, 1966–1975.* University of Singapore, mimeo. Shorter version in *Malayan Economic Review*, October 1976.

Rasaputram, W., 1972. "Changes in the Pattern of Income Inequality in Ceylon (1953-63)." *Marga* 1, no. 4:60–91 (Hansa Publishers, Colombo).

Rawls, John, 1971. *A Theory of Justice.* Cambridge, Mass.: Harvard University Press.

1973. "Distributive Justice," in E. S. Phelps (ed.), *Economic Justice*, pp. 319–62. London: Penguin.

Reich, Michael, 1971. "The Economics of Racism," in David M. Gordon (ed.), *Problems in Political Economy: An Urban Perspective*, pp. 107–13. Lexington, Mass.: Heath.

Reutlinger, Shlomo and Marcelo Selowsky, 1976. *Malnutrition and Poverty.* Baltimore: Johns Hopkins University Press.

Reynolds, Lloyd G., 1969. "Relative Earnings and Manpower Allocation in Developing Economies." *Pakistan Development Review* 9, no. 1 (Spring).

1975*a*. *Agriculture in Development Theory.* New Haven: Yale University Press.

1975*b*. "China as a Less Developed Economy." *American Economic Review*, June, pp. 418–28.

1978. *Labor Economics and Labor Relations.* 7th ed. Englewood Cliffs, N.J.: Prentice-Hall.

Robinson, Sherman, 1976. "A Note on the U Hypothesis Relating Income Inequality and Economic Development." *American Economic Review*, June, pp. 437–40.

Robinson, Sherman and Kemal Dervis, 1977. "Income Distribution and Socioeconomic Mobility: A Framework for Analysis and Planning." *Journal of Development Studies* 13, no. 4 (July):347–64.

Rosenzweig, Mark, 1977. "Neoclassical Theory and the Optimizing Peasant: An Econometric Analysis of Market Family Labor Supply in a Developing Country." Economic Growth Center, Yale University, Discussion Paper no. 271.

Rothschild, Michael and Joseph E. Stiglitz, 1973. "Some Further Results on the Measurement of Inequality." *Journal of Economic Theory*, 6:188–204.

Sahota, G. S., 1978. "Theories of Personal Income Distribution: A Survey." *Journal of Economic Literature*, March, pp. 1–55.

Schultz, T. Paul, 1979. *Population.* Reading, Mass.: Addison-Wesley.

Schultz, T. W., 1960. "Capital Formation by Education." *Journal of Political Economy*, December, pp. 571–83.

Seers, D., 1969. "The Meaning of Development." *International Development Review*, December. Reprinted in Charles K. Wilber (ed.), *The Political Economy of Development and Underdevelopment*, pp. 6–14. New York: Random House, 1973.

  1974. "Cuba," in Hollis B. Chenery et al. (eds.), *Redistribution with Growth*, pp. 262–8. New York: Oxford University Press.

Selowsky, Marcelo, 1976. "The Distributive Effect of Government Expenditure." World Bank, mimeo.

Sen, A. K., 1970. *Collective Choice and Social Welfare*. San Francisco: Holden-Day.

  1973. *On Economic Inequality*. New York: Norton.

  1976a. "Poverty: An Ordinal Approach to Measurement." *Econometrica*, March, pp. 219–31.

  1976b. "Real National Income." *Review of Economic Studies*.

  1978. "Three Notes on the Concept of Poverty." International Labour Office, World Employment Programme Research Working Paper no. 65, January.

Sheshinski, E., 1972. "Relation between a Social Welfare Function and the Gini Index of Inequality." *Journal of Economic Theory* 4: 98–100.

Singer, P. I., 1971. *Forca de Trabalho e Emprego No Brasil, 1920–1969*. São Paulo: Centro Brasileiro de Analise e Planejamento.

  1977. "Emprego, Producao e Reproducao da Forca de Trabalho." Paper presented at the Conference on Distribution, Poverty, and Development, Bogotá, June.

Skolka, Jiri and Michel Garzuel, 1978. "Income Distribution by Size, Employment, and the Structure of the Economy: A Case Study for the Republic of Korea." International Labour Office, World Employment Programme Research Working Paper no. 66, January.

Smith, Adam, 1776. *Wealth of Nations*. Edinburgh.

Smith, Robert, 1979. "Compensating Wage Differentials and Public Policy: A Review." *Industrial and Labor Relations Review*, April, pp. 339–52.

Snodgrass, D. R., 1966. *Ceylon: An Export Economy in Transition*. Homewood, Ill.: Irwin.

Social Science Research Council. *Social Indicators Newsletter* (periodical).

Souza, Paulo R. and Víctor E. Tokman, 1977. "Distribución del Ingreso, Pobreza y Empleo en Areas Urbanas." Trabajo presentado a la Conferencia sobre Distribución, Pobreza y Desarrollo, Universidad de Los Andes, Bogotá, June.

Srinivasan, T. N., 1978. "Development, Poverty and Basic Human Needs: Some Issues." World Bank, mimeo.

  N.d. "Poverty: Some Measurement Problems." World Bank, mimeo.

Statistical Handbook of the Philippines. Manila, annual.

Statistical Pocket Book of Ceylon. Colombo, annual.

Statistical Pocket Book of Sri Lanka. Colombo, annual.

Stern, N. H., 1972. "Optimum Development in a Dual Economy." *Review of Economic Studies,* April, pp. 171–84.

Stiglitz, J. E., 1974. "Alternative Theories of Wage Determination and Unemployment in LDCs: The Labour Turnover Model." *Quarterly Journal of Economics,* May, pp. 194–227.

——— 1976. "The Efficiency Wage Hypothesis, Surplus Labour, and the Distribution of Income in LDCs." *Oxford Economic Papers,* July, pp. 185–207.

Swamy, Subramanian, 1967. "Structural Changes and the Distribution of Income by Size: The Case of India." *Review of Income and Wealth,* June, pp. 155–74.

Szal, Richard J., 1977. "Poverty: Measurement and Analysis." International Labour Office, World Employment Programme Research Working Paper no. 60, October.

Szal, Richard J. and Sherman Robinson, 1977. "Measuring Income Inequality," in Charles R. Frank, Jr., and Richard C. Webb (eds.), *Income Distribution and Growth in the Less-Developed Countries,* pp. 491–533. Washington, D.C.: Brookings Institution.

Theil, H., 1967. *Economics and Information Theory.* Amsterdam: North Holland.

——— 1972. *Statistical Decomposition Analysis.* Amsterdam: North Holland.

Turnham, David, 1971. *The Employment Problem in Less Developed Countries.* Paris: Organization for Economic Cooperation and Development.

UNCTAD, 1976. *Handbook of International Trade and Development Statistics.* New York: United Nations.

United Nations, 1976. *Towards a System of Social and Demographic Statistics.* Publication No. E.74.XVIII.8.

Uribe, Pedro, 1976. "Estructura de la Desigualdad del Ingreso en América Latina." *Demografía y Economía* 10, no. 1:68–92.

Urrutia, M., 1968. "El Desempleo Disfrazado en Bogotá," in Centro de Estudios sobre Desarrollo Económico, Universidad de Los Andes (ed.), *Empleo y Desempleo en Colombia.* Bogotá.

Vaidyanathan, A., 1974. "Some Aspects of Inequalities in Living Standards in Rural India," in T. N. Srinivasan and P. K. Bardhan (eds.), *Poverty and Income Distribution in India,* pp. 215–41. Calcutta: Statistical Publishing Society.

Van Ginneken, Wouter, 1975. "Análisis de Descomposición del Indice de Theil Aplicado a la Distribución del Ingreso Familiar en México." *Demografía y Economía* 9, no. 1:93–112.

Wachter, Michael, 1974. "Primary and Secondary Labor Markets: A Critique of the Dual Approach." *Brookings Papers on Economic Activity 3: 1974,* pp. 637–80.

Webb, Richard, 1976. "On the Statistical Mapping of Urban Poverty and Employment." World Bank Staff Working Paper no. 227, January.

Weisskoff, Richard, 1970. "Income Distribution and Economic Growth in Puerto Rico, Argentina and Mexico." *Review of Income and Wealth,* December, pp. 303-32.

Welch, Finis, 1970. "Education in Production." *Journal of Political Economy,* January/February, pp. 35-59.

Wells, J., 1974. "Distribution of Earnings, Growth and the Structure of Demand in Brazil during the 1960s." *World Development* 2: 9-24.

Williamson, Jeffrey, 1965. "Regional Inequality and the Process of National Development: A Description of the Patterns." *Economic Development and Cultural Change,* pt. 2, July, pp. 3-84.

Wogart, J. P., 1974. "Contrasting Employment Patterns in Brazil: 1940-1970." Department of Economics and Institute of Inter-American Studies, University of Miami, mimeo.

World Bank, 1975. *The Assault on World Poverty.* Baltimore: Johns Hopkins University Press.

1977. *World Tables.* Washington, D.C.: World Bank.

Index

additional worker effect, 139, 252
Adelman, Irma, 10, 21, 64, 67,
    69, 70, 71-3, 164, 248, 249,
    253
age, 116-20, 124, 127, 144-62,
    178, 253
agriculture and rural development,
    75-7, 95-6, 122, 161-3, 179,
    185, 186, 196, 201, 213,
    214, 219, 222, 225, 228,
    230, 233, 235, 242, 252
Ahluwalia, Montek, 21, 24-5, 64,
    70, 74-6, 85-6, 87, 95, 138,
    147, 164-6, 174-7, 246, 248,
    249, 254
Ahluwalia–Chenery index, 24-5,
    174-7
Ahmed, M., 130, 133, 206, 252
AID (U.S. Agency for Interna-
    tional Development), 1, 2, 8,
    25, 138, 144, 245
Alamgir, Mohiuddin, 88, 173, 177
Altimir, Oscar, 103, 104, 114,
    117-120, 121, 177, 246, 249
analysis of variance (ANOVA),
    64, 71, 135
  decomposition using, 105-6,
    107-123
Anand, Sudhir, 148, 177, 251
ANOVA, see analysis of variance
Argentina, 7, 66, 84, 85, 88, 94,
    115, 145, 163, 170, 171,
    239, 240
Arias, O.S., 255
Atkinson, A.B., 35, 38, 106-7,
    175, 245, 250, 252

Atkinson index, 22, 24
  decomposition of, 106-7,
    107-123
Australia, 7, 66
Averch, H., 220, 256
Ayub, M., 91, 101, 112, 114, 115,
    249, 250
axiomatic judgments, 11, 21-3,
    27, 36-40, 108

Bacha, Edmar L., 143
Bangladesh, 88, 94, 168, 170,
    173, 177, 239, 240
Barbados, 6, 62, 66
Bardhan, P.K., 57, 90, 138, 143,
    150, 159, 173, 206-10, 252,
    255, 256
Barraclough, Solon, 163
barriers to mobility, 131-2, 136,
    179
basic needs, 8
Becker, Gary S., 251
Belarmino, L.C., 92, 173, 222
Berg, Elliot, 251
Berry, R.A., 94, 254
Bhagwati, Jagdish, 97
Bhatt, V.V., 205
Bhattacharya, N., 206
Bhatty, I.Z., 177, 205
Birdsall, Nancy, 161
Blaug, M., 251
Blitzer, C.R., 10
Bolivia, 5, 65, 254
Botswana, 3
Boulier, Bryan, 161
Bowles, Samuel, 249

Bowman, Mary Jean, 26, 252
Brazil, 2, 6, 12, 56, 65, 86, 89,
     94, 97, 114, 115, 116, 138,
     145, 151, 155, 160, 163,
     170, 171, 174, 175, 177,
     181, 185, 210-18, 222, 239,
     241, 242, 243, 252, 254, 256
Bronfenbrenner, Martin, 245
Bruton, Henry, 97
Burma, 5, 65, 146

Cain, Glen, 252
Calvo, Ml. Felipe, 193
Canada, 60
Carnoy, Martin, 249
Céspedes, V.H., 89, 173, 186,
     188, 189, 193
Ceylon, *see* Sri Lanka
Chad, 2, 5, 65, 114, 147
Champernowne, D.G., 38, 109,
     249
Cheetham, R., 220, 256
Chenery, Hollis, 24-5, 64, 76-7,
     174-7, 248
Chile, 2, 6, 66, 114, 115, 119,
     128, 145, 162, 163
China, 95, 114
Chiswick, Barry, 73-4
Chiswick, Carmel, 28, 103, 104,
     105, 109, 114, 116, 249
Choo, Hakchung, 249
Clark, P., 10
Cline, William, 21, 69, 84, 86,
     162, 164, 249, 253
Colombia, 2, 6, 62, 65, 86, 97,
     98, 112, 114, 115, 117, 128,
     134, 145, 163, 168, 174,
     175, 249, 250, 251, 252,
     253, 254
consumption versus income,
     141-2
Costa Rica, 2, 6, 12, 65, 86, 89,
     94, 115, 118, 145, 170, 172,
     174, 181, 185-94, 219, 239,
     240, 241, 242, 243
Cuba, 95

Da Costa, E.P.W., 150, 160

Dahomey, 2, 5, 65, 147
Dalton, H., 38
Daltonian condition, 38
Dandekar, V.M., 138
Das, T., 250
decomposition of income growth,
     42
decomposition of income
     inequality, 98-124
  choice of procedure, 107-11
  empirical findings, 111-24
  methodologies for, 101-11
    ANOVA, 105-6
    Atkinson, 106-7
    Gini, 101-3
    Theil, 103-5
  types of problems, 99-110
    by economic sector, 99-100,
       114-15, 123-4
    by functional income source,
       99, 111-14, 123-4
    by income determinants,
       100-1, 115-22, 123-4
Denmark, 7, 60, 62, 66, 78, 81
Dervis, Kemal, 141
development strategies, 94-6,
     181-244
Dieguez, Hector L., 173
Doeringer, Peter, 131, 162
Domike, Arthur L., 163
Dominican Republic, 2, 145
D'Silva, Emmanuel H., 245
dualism, 11, 30, 183-4, 219-20,
     228
  welfare economics of, 33-58

earnings functions, 11, 12,
     100-1, 110-11, 121, 124,
     125-37, 178, 251
ECLA (Economic Commission
     for Latin America), 89, 188
economic growth
     and inequality, 67-71, 77-98,
       122-213, 181-244
     and poverty, 162-180,
       181-244
Ecuador, 2, 6, 65, 145, 163, 253

education, 13, 16, 75-7, 95, 97,
    105-6, 116-20, 122, 124,
    127, 130, 133-6, 144-62,
    167, 178, 185, 191, 194,
    196, 199-200, 212, 213,
    216-18, 236-7, 253
Edwards, Richard, 133
Egypt, 2
El Salvador, 2, 6, 60, 62, 65, 86,
    89, 94, 145, 174, 175, 239
employment status, 116-20, 127,
    144-62, 191, 194, 214, 223
employment structures, changes
    in, 13, 181-244

factor inequality weights, 102,
    113-14
family size and poverty, 144-62,
    253
Fei, John C.H., 10, 22, 31, 36,
    38, 63, 70, 101-2, 111-13,
    115, 116, 173, 213, 232,
    234, 249, 250, 257
Felix, David, 90
Ferber, Robert, 138
Fields, Gary S., 21, 38, 57, 101,
    105, 112, 114, 115, 117,
    134, 135, 173, 212, 249,
    250, 251, 256
Fiji, 6, 65
Finland, 7, 66
Fishlow, Albert, 56, 89, 97, 104,
    114, 116, 138, 148, 177,
    216, 217, 218, 249, 254
Flanagan, Robert, 131
Fleisher, Belton, 252
Foxley, Alejandro, 164
fractile measures of inequality, 22
France, 7, 66
Freedman, Marcia, 130, 133
Friedman, Milton, 141
Fuchs, Victor, 29
functional distribution of income,
    10, 14, 16-17, 126, 225, 230
Furtado, C., 216

Gabon, 2, 6, 65, 147

Galenson, Walter, 166-70, 233,
    234, 237, 253, 257
Garzuel, Michel, 249
Ghana, 168
Gini coefficient
    change over time, 85, 87-94,
        181-244
    decomposition of, 101-3,
        107-123
    definition of, 22
    international evidence on, 65-70
    in social welfare judgments, 18,
        34, 55-6
Gollás, Manuel, 90, 173
Gordon, David, 132, 133
government economic activity, 72
Grant, James P., 257
Greece, 7, 66
Green, Reginald H., 95
Gregory, Peter, 251
Griffin, K., 167-70
Guatemala, 2, 62, 162, 163
Guyana, 2, 145

Haiti, 254
Harbison, Frederick, 248, 251
Harrison, Bennett, 252
Hawkins, E., 220, 256
head count of poverty, 26, 57,
    139, 141, 177-8, 189, 198,
    207-10, 211
    see also poverty, absolute
Heady, Christopher, 251
health indicators, 13
Hirschman, Albert O., 39, 246
Honduras, 2, 145
human capital investment, 72-74.
    see also education
human capital theory, 73, 127-9,
    178, 251

ILO, *see* United Nations Interna-
    tional Labour Office
immiserization of the poor, 55,
    164-6, 222, 253
impoverishment, *see* immiseriza-
    tion of the poor

income distribution
  absolute income approach, 23-5,
    29-32, 35, 125-80, 239
  absolute poverty approach,
    25-8, 29-32, 35, 125-80,
    239
  absolute vs. relative measures,
    13-58, 182, 206-10, 212,
    239-40
  dispersion of, 15
  functional vs. size distribution,
    11, 14, 16-17
  vs. income inequality, 14-16
  relative inequality approach,
    21-3, 24-32, 59-124, 239
  relative poverty approach, 28-9,
    29-32
  see also inequality; poverty,
    absolute; poverty, relative
income growth measures
  problems with GNP, 8
  problems with within-decile
    measures, 184
  problems with within-sector
    measures, 183
income recipient unit, choice of,
    139-40
income shortfall, 26, 57, 139,
    141, 177-8, 211-13, 254
India, 2, 5, 12, 31, 56, 57, 60, 61,
    62, 65, 86, 90, 94, 138, 140,
    143, 146, 150, 154, 155,
    159, 162, 170, 173, 174,
    175, 177, 181, 185, 204-10,
    239, 240, 241, 242, 243,
    252, 253, 255
industrial development, 96,
    190-1, 212, 214-17, 219,
    222-4, 230, 232, 236-7, 242
industry, 134-5, 178, 186, 191,
    194, 201-14, 222, 228, 233.
  see also industrial development;
    sector
inequality
  axiomatic judgments in, 11,
    21-3, 36-40, 108
  in Brazil, 212
  changes over time, 77-98, 122-3
  changing tolerance for, 39
  in Costa Rica, 188-9
  cross-sectional evidence, 59-77,
    122
  decomposition of, 98-122,
    123-4
  and development, 61-71, 77-98,
    122-213, 181-244
  disagreement among relative
    measures, 53
  and economic structure, 71-7
  and growth, summary table,
    88-93
  in India, 204-6
  interregional, 17
  of labor incomes, 12, 17, 100-1,
    111-15, 124
  personal vs. sectoral characteris-
    tics, 124
  in the Philippines, 220-1
  rural-urban, 17
  in social welfare judgments,
    18-23, 29-32, 33-58
  in Sri Lanka, 197-8
  in Taiwan, 229-31
  in world, 5-7, 65-70
  see also decomposition of
    income inequality; income
    distribution
International Union for the
    Scientific Study of
    Population, 252
inverted-U pattern, 54, 61, 71,
    78-98, 122-3, 248
Iqbal, Farrukh, 149
Iran, 86, 146
Iraq, 6, 65, 146
Israel, 7, 60, 66
Italy, 7, 60, 62, 66
Ivory Coast, 2, 6, 65, 147

Jain, S., 15, 64, 188, 197
Jallade, Jean-Pierre, 249
Jamaica, 2, 6, 65, 145
Japan, 7, 60, 66, 220
Jayawardena, L., 93, 203
Johnson, George, 128, 139
Jorgenson, Dale, 36

Karunatilake, N., 93, 173, 196, 197, 198, 199, 200
Kenya, 2, 62, 249
Knight, John B., 248
Kondor, Yaakov, 38, 70
Korea, South, 2, 5, 65, 86, 146, 175, 249
Kravis, Irving, B., 60, 248, 252, 253
Krueger, Anne O., 97, 252
Kuo, W., 10, 63, 93, 101-2, 112, 115, 117, 149, 173, 231, 232, 235, 249, 250, 257
Kuznets, Simon, 21, 31, 34, 54, 55, 60, 61, 62, 63, 64, 70, 78-84, 85, 86, 115, 139, 161, 248, 252
Kuznets ratio, 22

labor income, inequality of, 12, 17, 100-1, 111-15, 124
labor market segmentation, 12, 129-37, 179
labor movement, 72
Lal, Deepak, 248, 253, 255, 257
land and poverty, 154, 161-3
Langoni, Carlos, 56, 89, 97, 105, 114, 116, 217-18, 249, 252
Lardy, Nicholas, R., 95
Lebanon, 6, 65, 146
Lewis, W. Arthur, 36
Lima, 121
Little, I.M.D., 25, 96, 253
Loehr, William, 254
log-variance, 22
  see also analysis of variance
Lorenz criterion, 21-2, 34, 37-8
Lorenz curve, 15, 16, 21, 28, 31, 34, 37-8
  in Costa Rica, 187-9
  in developed vs. less developed countries, 61, 63
  in India, 204
  in modern-sector enlargement growth, 49, 52-3
  in modern-sector enrichment growth, 49-51
  in the Philippines, 220

  in Sri Lanka, 197-8
  in Taiwan, 229-30
  in traditional-sector enrichment growth 42-50
Lydall, Harold, 64, 74, 248

McGreevey, William, 139
Madagascar, 2, 5, 65, 147
Malan, P., 216, 218
Malawi, 2, 6
Malaya, 65
Malaysia, 128, 130, 146, 152, 155, 156, 160, 168, 220, 251, 252
Mangahas, Mahar, 101, 103, 114, 115, 249
Marga Research Institute, 255
maximin principle, *see* Rawlsian criterion
Mazumdar, Dipak, 130, 133, 252
Meesook, O.A., 149, 173
Mehran, F., 101, 114, 249
Mellor, John W., 255
Mericle, K.S., 217
Merrick, Thomas, 252
Mexico, 6, 62, 66, 84, 85, 86, 90, 94, 96, 114, 117, 118, 145, 170, 173, 174, 175, 239, 240
microeconomic vs. macroeconomic approach to development, 1-12
migrant status and poverty, 151
Mijares, T.A., 91, 173, 222
Mincer, Jacob, 127, 251
Minhas, B.S., 162, 206, 207-10
Mirrlees, J.A., 35
mobility, 131-2, 136, 141, 179
modern-sector enlargement effects, 42, 45, 189, 194, 201, 232, 237, 243
modern-sector enlargement growth
  and Ahluwalia-Chenery index, 176-7
  changing Gini coefficient in, 247-8

modern-sector enlargement (*cont.*)
   and decile income growth rates,
      184
   defined, 30–1
   welfare economics, 29–33, 52–6
   within-sector inequality in, 54
modern-sector enrichment effects,
   42, 43, 45, 243
modern-sector enrichment growth
   defined, 30–1
   welfare economics of, 51–2
Morawetz, David, 245, 254, 257
Morris, Cynthia Taft, 21–64, 67,
   69, 70, 71–3, 164, 248, 253
Morley, S.A., 222, 256
Morocco, 5, 65
Muller, Ronald, 164
Musgrove, Philip, 138, 161,
   253, 254

Naseem, S.M., 173
Netherlands, 7, 60, 62, 66, 78,
   80
new directions in development
   assistance, 8
Nigeria, 5, 65, 147
Northern Rhodesia, 62
Norway, 7, 66, 78, 81
nutrition, 13, 25, 138, 167, 196,
   220, 245, 252, 254

occupation, 116–21, 127, 144–62,
   190, 194, 201–2, 212, 214,
   226–7, 232–4, 253
Ojha, P.D., 75, 205, 207, 208
Orshansky, Mollie, 138
Oshima, Harry, 60
Osterman, Paul, 252
Overseas Development Council,
   245

Pakistan, 2, 5, 65, 91, 94, 114,
   115, 146, 149, 153, 155,
   158, 160, 170, 172, 239, 250
Panama, 2, 6, 66, 86, 114, 115,
   119, 145, 174, 175
Pant, Pitamber, 252
Papanek, Gustav, 253

Pareto criterion, 27, 34
Parikh, A., 250
Paukert, F., 7, 21, 64, 66, 67, 68,
   69
Perkins, Dwight, 249
Perlman, Richard, 26
Peru, 2, 6, 65, 86, 115, 119, 128,
   145, 175, 253, 254
Petrecolla, Alberto, 173
Philippines, 2, 6, 12, 65, 86, 91,
   94, 115, 146, 168, 170, 172,
   174, 175, 180, 181, 185,
   218–28, 239, 240, 241, 242,
   243, 256
physical quality of life indicators,
   13
Piñera, Sebastian, 103, 104, 114,
   117–20, 249
Piore, Michael, 131
population growth, 45, 75, 95,
   122, 164, 185, 200, 214, 256
potential for economic development, 72
poverty, absolute
   in Brazil, 211–13
   in Costa Rica, 189
   definition of, 25, 137–43, 182
   and development, 162–80,
      181–244
   and growth, summary table,
      171–3
   head count, *see* head count of
      poverty
   income shortfall, 26, 57, 139,
      141, 177–8, 211–13, 254
   in India, 207–10
   in the Philippines, 222–23
   poverty gap, 26, 211
      see also income shortfall
   in social welfare judgments, 19,
      29–32
   in Sri Lanka, 198
   in Taiwan, 229–31
   in world, 1–4, 144–7
poverty, relative, 19, 21, 28–9,
   29–32
poverty gap, 26, 211
   see also income shortfall